COUNTRY EDITOR'S BOY

OTHER BOOKS BY HAL BORLAND

The Outdoors

An American Year
The Enduring Pattern
Beyond Your Doorstep
Sundial of the Seasons
Countryman: A Summary of Belief
Our Natural World (Editor)
Hill Country Harvest
Homeland: A Report from the Country

People and Places

This Hill, This Valley
High, Wide and Lonesome
The Dog Who Came to Stay

Fiction

The Seventh Winter
The Amulet
When the Legends Die
King of Squaw Mountain

Folklore

Rocky Mountain Tipi Tales
The Youngest Shepherd

Poetry

America Is Americans

COUNTRY EDITOR'S BOY

Hal Borland

J. B. LIPPINCOTT COMPANY
PHILADELPHIA AND NEW YORK

For Barbara

It was for ripeness in and all around us
That winter passed and spring and summer found us.

FOREWORD

This is a story of youth—the transition years of a boy, of a town, of the culture of an area. Because I happened to be the boy, it is autobiography; but because the area was the High Plains of eastern Colorado and the time was those years when the Old West was passing and the New West was emerging, it partakes of social history. The town itself was young, but it too began to grow up in those years. The area—well, people and their towns are young or middle-aged or old, but the land itself is almost beyond ageing, except in the millennial terms of geology. The area itself did not much change, but change was wrought upon it.

It was a time when we still heard echoes and already saw shadows, on moonlit nights when the coyotes yapped on the hilltops and on hot summer afternoons when mirages shimmered, dust-devils spun across the flats, and towering cumulus clouds sailed like galleons across the vast blueness of the sky. Echoes of remembrance of what men once did there, and visions of what they would do tomorrow.

We heard the echoes of prayer chants, war chants, hunting chants of Arapaho and Cheyenne. We saw the hills dark with buffalo, more buffalo than man could count, meat to feed the plains people forever; and we heard the echoing rifle shots of the buffalo killers, who took tongues and hides and left the carcasses for the carrion eaters, the bones for us to find in the eternal grass forty years later. We saw the shadowy herds trailing north, Texas cattle, heard the echoes of their bawling, their hoof-and-horn rattle, the sad chants of their night herders. We saw the railroad builders come, thrusting steel rails westward, rod by rod, heard their grunt-and-heave, their profane brag, their spike hammers ringing, smelled their sweat, watched the black-smoke locomotive and the clanking iron wheels follow them, mile by mile.

We saw, heard, smelled, felt, almost tasted the past.

We saw the homesteaders come, saw them string their barbed wire, plow their shallow furrows, plant their corn, build their dugouts and soddies and new-pine shanties. We saw them come and we saw them go, drouthed out, grasshoppered out, plain discouraged out; and always a few, a steadily growing number of them, hanging on by their teeth and their broken fingernails, bellies full of jack rabbit and cornmeal mush and plain sand-grit. Settling up the country. We heard the first chuff and cough of tractors, saw them ripping up the sod, the buffalo-grass sod that had been there since the last Ice Age, and planting wheat. In the heat of July afternoons we heard the harvesters come with their clatter and rumble and roar, saw their clouds of dust and chaff, watched the golden river of grain flow from high, far fields to the railroad in a stream of trucks that never let the dust settle. We felt the bite on our cheeks, tasted the grit between our teeth, when dust-devils danced across the harvested fields, forerunners of black blizzards of desolation still to come.

We saw, heard, smelled, felt, tasted the new, displacing the old.

We who were young in that time and place were fortunate to know something of that old heritage at the same time that we were growing up into the new. Actually, in that area—and I am sure it must have been true in many other parts of this country too—the nineteenth century did not end with the 1890s. It persisted, and the twentieth century did not really take over until some time between 1915 and 1920; not until after World War I in our area. And it is about those years, that time of change from one century to another, which happened to defy the calendar, that I am writing here.

This book is a companion story to the one I told in *High*,

Wide and Lonesome, and in terms of time it is a sequel. In the earlier book I wrote of a frontier vanishing before the eyes of a boy who lived on a homestead under primitive pioneer conditions. Here I have written of that same boy, now somewhat older and somewhat more civilized, at least amenable to life in a community. And I have written of that boy's father and mother, both somewhat changed by the homestead experience. The boy himself is in the process of basic, inevitable change; not only is he no longer a pioneer, but he is growing up, still in transition from one age to another but reaching toward adulthood. The fact that I was the boy in the earlier book and the youth in this one does not in any way alter the background or the history. It merely makes possible a first-hand account with more truth than if I were writing about someone else. Actually, at this point in life I look back at that boy, that youth, as someone I knew intimately years ago and miles away, but definitely not as the self I now know and am. But I did know him better than I could possibly know anyone else, so it is his story that I have told.

It is always difficult to achieve perspective on the past that we have known, particularly if it has been a time of swift and profound change. I remember things my father said when, in his late fifties, he was asked what it was like to be a pioneer. Father said, "I don't know. I wasn't a pioneer."

"But," the interviewer said, "you were one of the earlier settlers here in eastern Colorado, weren't you?"

"Not particularly early. We came in nineteen ten. There were at least two big waves of homesteaders before we came, but not many of them stayed. The ranchers were here before those homesteaders. The ranchers began to settle here soon after the Civil War."

"Was the land really settled up when you came?"

"No. Our closest neighbor was a sheep camp, a herder and a couple thousand head of sheep. And the camp closed for the winter."

"You came to Flagler in nineteen fifteen?"

9

"That's right. Flagler was a growing town by then. It wasn't settled for several years after the railroad came through in eighteen eighty-seven, but it wasn't a primitive settlement, by any means, in nineteen fifteen."

It is a matter of definition. Father was using dates and years as his criterion. Actually, we were pioneers on the homestead; we built the first house on that land, dug the first well, plowed its sod for the first time. And he was, if not actually a pioneer editor, at least the editor of a weekly newspaper in a town just turning from the old to the new when he arrived. To me, a pioneer is one who helps create a new line of thought or action, and in that sense he was a pioneer editor. He was one of the principal forces for change.

So, as I was saying, this is a story of change. With it I have completed my account of how one small family, and especially the son of that family, experienced the transition in one semi-isolated area from the early, primitive life of the sod-house frontier to the modern age between that son's small boyhood and his manhood. Others have written many accounts of the past half century's intense urbanization, its social and economic turmoil, its technological domination, and its incessant wars, between man and man, man and the elements, man and his own environment. I would not add to that list. But not many of us have been hurtled from the equivalent of the 1850s to the 1920s in a single decade, and still fewer of us have written about that experience.

In *High, Wide and Lonesome* I wrote that "a frontier is never a place; it is a time and a way of life. . . . Frontiers pass, but they endure in their people." Because I still believe that, I have written this book. The memories should endure. Unless we know where we came from, something about the road we traveled as a people, how can we know who we are and where we are going?

H. B.

Salisbury, Conn.
1970

COUNTRY
EDITOR'S
BOY

1

Three things happened that day. Four, counting the rain storm, though rain doesn't just happen on the high, dry plains; rain comes or it doesn't, and men thrive or go broke according to the rain. But a boy gets his first long pants only once, there is a first time you see the mountains, and only a few times in your life do you meet a strange man who says things you will always remember.

We were moving, my mother and I, to join my father in a new, strange town where he had bought a weekly newspaper. Flagler was only a little over a hundred miles south of Brush, but to get there we had to travel more than twice that distance on two sides of a huge triangle, first to Denver on the Burlington train, then back to Flagler on a Rock Island train, with several hours' wait in Denver between trains. And although we had lived in Colorado five years, neither Mother nor I had ever seen Denver.

We were to catch the midmorning train out of Brush. The household goods had been packed and shipped and we had spent the night with friends. At the last minute, just as we were about to board the train, an argument arose about my dog, Fritz. The station agent had said Fritz could travel in the baggage car with only a leash and an express tag, but the trainman in the baggage car insisted that all dogs must be muzzled. Finally the conductor, impatient at the delay, settled it. "Get that dog on board," he ordered. "If he bites you, bite him back. We can't wait all day." So Fritz was taken in the baggage car, we settled ourselves in a coach, and we were off. But I was too worried about Fritz, and too excited, to pay much attention to details of the trip to Denver. When we arrived in the Union Station I wanted to go to the baggage room and see if Fritz was all right, but Mother said no, it would just start the argument all over again. So we checked our valises and went out for our first look at Denver.

We went out into Seventeenth Street, through the big iron grillwork arch that bridged the street and held high its legend, "Welcome." Up Seventeenth Street as far as I could see lay Denver, a maze of clanging trolley cars, clattering horse-drawn drays, crowds of people on the sidewalks. The street was lined with a bazaar of shops, cafés and warehouses. I vaguely remembered Lincoln and Omaha, back in Nebraska, but Denver was nothing like either of them. Denver roared and clanged with a wholly different air, an air of ranches and mines and sawmills and energetic business. It was several years before I saw the new, beautiful, expensive Denver that lay beyond that cheap, rundown, railroad station area of tourist traps and laborers' supplies. That day, the first time I saw it, it was a wonderful, almost incredibly busy place.

We walked slowly up the street, staring at the brightly lighted windows filled with catch-penny wares. We passed dark chili parlors that breathed spicy fragrance and loud laughter, hurrying past them as though they were barrooms. We paused at clothing stores whose windows were crammed with boots and hats and work shirts and Levis. We drew back from a huge dray drawn by a four-horse team of big, dappled Percherons as it came out of a dark alleyway. Mother glared and stiffened as two women, their faces rouged and their clothes exaggeratedly fashionable, passed us, laughing and watching the men along the street. And then we came to a clothing store with a few dress shirts and several pairs of blue serge trousers in a far corner of its cluttered window. We stopped and looked and finally Mother said, "Come on," and we went inside.

An eager, smiling clerk greeted us and Mother said, "I want to look at long trousers for my son, something to match his suit."

What happened after that is still a confused memory. At the time I scarcely knew what was happening. Long pants, my first long pants! In those days, long pants were a sign that a boy was no longer a boy; he was a man. Perhaps not quite a man, if his voice was still changing, as mine was, but no longer really a boy. On the homestead I often had a man's responsibility and I usually wore overalls, long pants of a sort. But after we left the homestead and moved to Brush I was a schoolboy in knickerbockers. I had left Brush in a blue serge knickerbocker suit. Now, though I wanted long pants more than anything else in the world, I wasn't ready for manhood all at once.

There was bargaining, I am sure of that, and there was argument over color and material. But eventually Mother chose a pair that almost matched my jacket. I do remember that she argued the price down from three dollars to two dollars and a half. Then I tried them on, the clerk measured them for length, promised to have them ready in an hour, and we went out into the street again.

We started back to the station, I still in a daze. We were almost there when Mother stopped, caught my arm, and exclaimed, "Look!" Off to the west, in a gap between two tall buildings, was the incredible loom of the mountains twenty miles away. They were huge, bare and rocky. Beyond them rose other mountains, dark and green with trees, countless mountains. We stared at them, fascinated, and we turned down a side street and walked two or three blocks to a place where we could see them better. The sun shone on them, almost glinting, and big, high clouds cast dark shadows that climbed their slopes as we watched. They looked only a few miles away in the clear, thin Colorado air. Seeing them, I knew that some day I would have to go to them, climb them, see what lay beyond. But not now. Now they were a barrier, a rugged obstacle to eyes familiar with the flat immensity of the plains. I was both a plainsman and a boy, the long pants quite forgotten in that breathless moment; I wanted no part of such barriers, no hemming in. I was glad we weren't moving to a town in the mountains. Flagler was a plains town where, Father had written, you could see forty miles in any direction.

We went back to the station and ate the box lunch Mother had brought with us. By then the hour was almost up, so we went back to the clothing store and I put on the new, long, blue serge pants. The clerk made a package of my knicker-bockers and we returned to the station. The pants flapped around my ankles and I felt as conspicuous as though I hadn't any pants at all. Then I remembered my stockings and felt better. Beneath those new trousers I still wore the long black cotton stockings of boyhood. I wore those stockings, literally as well as figuratively, for months, until my voice began to find its stable register, until the boyhood stockings were worn out and could be replaced with adult socks.

Our train was ready and waiting. We got our valises from the checkroom, went aboard, chose seats in a coach. The green plush seats had a look and feel that still means train travel to me, and the whole train had that warm, faintly sweet, musty odor tinged with coal smoke that gave way to the smell of sweat and stale tobacco smoke only when the diesel dis-placed the coal-burning mogul. There was a turmoil of voices, the rattle of baggage trucks, and finally the echoing, "All aboooard!" Doors slammed, iron platforms clanged, and the train began to move. I settled down to watch the passing streets, the factory clutter and tenement confusion of drab, rundown houses, littered back yards, grimy washings on sagging lines, that has marked the urban trackside as long as I can remember. And finally we were out in the open country again, heading southeast, angling back on the second side of that huge triangle.

The train *clack-clacked* on the rails, the telegraph poles flew past, the locomotive hooted at an occasional crossing, the plume of dark smoke streamed past, and when I looked back the mountains had begun to sink into the western horizon. Ahead and on both sides lay the plains, green with mid-June as far as the eye could reach, gently rolling and without a tree in sight. Here and there was a distant, lonely house, a homesteader's soddy with its nearby barn and privy, and from time to time there was a lone windmill with its low, round galvanized tank, a watering place for some ranchman's cattle.

We stopped at a series of small towns, those nearest Denver bright with paint and kempt with care; but the paint diminished and the green of lawns thinned away as we left Denver farther and farther behind. Otherwise the towns were much alike, each with a main street leading down to the railroad station, the street lined with false-front store buildings, hitch racks with a few saddled horses, a few wagon teams, and a clustering of houses that scattered out into vacancy only a few blocks beyond the main street.

Mother was very quiet. She probably was wondering, as I was, if Flagler would be like these towns, or better, or worse. Of the five years since we left Nebraska, the years on the homestead had been the most difficult she had ever known, years that would mark her character all her life. To me they had been fascinating, though they have shaped my life, too. Father almost died of typhoid fever; we lost our horses when they ate death camass, a poisonous weed; we sometimes had nothing to eat but jack rabbits and cornmeal mush. But there was eventual triumph. Father proved up on the homestead, got a deed signed by President Woodrow Wilson. Then we moved to Brush, the Platte valley town where he had worked as a printer to get out of debt. He took a full-time job and we lived there a year while Father and Mother caught their breath, laid aside a few hundred dollars, and I began to catch up on my schooling.

But Brush was never more than a way station, really. Mother knew that, and so did I when I stopped to think about it. Father wanted to be his own boss, have his own newspaper. So this spring he quit his job and went to look at several papers that were for sale. He chose *The Flagler News*, bought it, took possession the first of May. He wrote Mother to pack up and move as soon as school was out. The *News*, he wrote, wasn't much of a paper now and didn't have much of a plant, but Flagler was a coming town and he knew he could make good there. That was six weeks ago. Now we were on the last leg of our move. To Flagler, whatever it was like.

Somewhere around Deer Trail—that town's name still fascinates me; I doubt that there has been a deer there in a hundred years—near Deer Trail I saw a jack rabbit loping across the flats with that crooked, leisurely gait as though its legs didn't quite track. Then I saw the ant hills, a dozen or more of them, two feet across and a foot and a half high. I pointed them out and started to talk about them to Mother. The ants that built such hills fascinated me. I had watched them for hours on the homestead. But Mother hated ants. She shook her head, not wanting to hear me talk about them.

Without warning, a man across the aisle leaned toward us and said, "Pardon me, but I would like to hear about those ants. May I?"

Mother was startled and embarrassed. She looked at him and forced a slight smile. He was a stocky man, middle-aged, in a dark suit and a high, stiff collar. He looked citified except for the deep tan on his face and hands. But he had a friendly look and a reassuring smile. Mother turned to me and said, "Go over and talk to the man about those ants, if you want to." She said the word "ants" as though it was "rattlesnakes."

So I went across the aisle and the man made room on the seat beside him. "Those are harvester ants, the big red prairie ants, aren't they?" he asked.

"Yes, sir," I said. "And they bite like fury."

"So I have read. Have you ever examined a cross-section of their mound, dug into one?"

"Lots of times." And I told him how the main tunnel, starting near the top, branches off into store rooms, some filled with grass seed, some with big white eggs, some with nothing at all in them. I told him about the smaller black ants that usually live there, too. "And once," I said, "I found half a dozen little blue beads on an ant hill. Indian beads."

"Wonderful!" he said. "Maybe there was an Indian buried under that hill. But more likely just a lost moccasin." Then he told me that the black ants are captives, slaves, and how the red ants are divided into castes: fighters, harvesters, nurses, builders, and all that. He explained that the eggs, as I called them, were pupae, immature ants already hatched from the eggs. He told me their Latin name, which I wrote down: *Pogonomyrmex occidentalis*. He knew more about those ants, without ever digging into a mound, than I thought I could ever learn.

He told me he was a biologist, from some college back east, in Illinois. He used the word "entomology" and explained that it meant the study of insects. He had been out in Utah, studying Mormon crickets. He asked how I knew so much about the big red ants, and I told him about the homestead and how I spent a lot of time watching ants and grasshoppers and tumblebugs and prairie dogs and weasels. Finally he said, "You have a good start toward being a naturalist. Is that what you plan to be?"

19

I said I wasn't sure what I was going to be, but my father was a printer who had just bought his own newspaper and was going to be a country editor. Maybe I would be one too.

"Whatever you do," he said, "never stop watching and studying the life around you, plants and animals and birds and insects. They are the ones who really own this world. Man just thinks he does."

I said, "Thank you, sir," and as I said it my voice broke and I felt foolish and embarrassed and wished I had on my knickerbockers. But just then the conductor came through the car shouting, "Limon. Next stop Limon. There'll be a fifteen-minute stop and you can get coffee and sandwiches in the station café."

The train slowed down and nearly everybody got off, and the man who had talked to me offered to treat us to something to eat. But Mother said, "Thank you, my husband is waiting to take us to supper when we get to Flagler." Mother never took favors from strangers, and she wasn't going to waste money for a sandwich in a railroad café, so she and I left the crowd and walked down the long station platform.

At the far end of the platform I looked out across the plains to the south and east and felt more at home than I had since we moved to Brush. Brush was a green town with tree-lined streets, set in the midst of alfalfa and sugar-beet fields, a river valley town where you had to go several miles to see and feel the plains. From the station platform in Limon I could see cactus in bloom, and soapweed clumps, and rolling flatlands all the way to the horizon. Limon was a plains town.

We walked the length of the platform twice, and then I noticed the big dark cloud bank in the east. It was rising fast, black and boiling, though the sun was still shining low in the west. Mother saw it too and said, "I hope it's just rain, not wind and lightning." She hated lightning. She said the thunder made her head ache. Even as we watched there was a flicker of lightning, far off and quick as a snake's darting tongue but dazzling against the darkness of the clouds. "We'd better get back to our seats before the crowd," Mother said, so we got on the train again.

The storm didn't break till we had left Limon. It struck first as wind, fierce gusts that made the train almost shudder. The smoke from the locomotive raced past, swirling and billowing, only a shade darker than the clouds. Then the first big, close flash of lightning split the clouds. I was sitting next to the window and even I winced. The thunder, only a few seconds later, made the train's windows rattle. Mother caught her breath and gritted her teeth. She closed her eyes and clenched her fists. Lightning flashed again and again and the thunder boomed. Then we were in the rain and I could hear its roar above the noise of the train. It didn't splash on the windows; it washed down them in a flood. Looking out, it seemed as though we were running along the bottom of a river. But the lightning began to ease off, as though the rain quenched it, and Mother opened her eyes, drew a deep breath, and whispered, "There!" Then she said, "I expect they need the moisture. Maybe it's a good sign."

The train slowed for another stop, Genoa. It was the smallest town yet, only a grain elevator, a couple of stores, and a few houses. I could barely make them out because the rain was still coming down in a torrent. We went on and Mother said we were almost there, only one more stop, so I got the valises down from the overhead rack. By the time we stopped at Arriba the torrent had begun to ease off into hard, steady rain. Arriba was only a little bigger than Genoa.

Beyond Arriba I could see the plains again, low hills rolling in great swells that looked as I imagined the ocean must look. The buffalo grass was green and fresh looking, washed by the rain, and there were quite a few big fields of wheat, much greener than the grass and much taller. "It looks like good

21

country," Mother said. Then, "I hope your father is there to meet us. I wish I hadn't packed my umbrella."

The locomotive hooted for a crossing, the whistle sounding very loud as it echoed from the low clouds. Then the train began to slow down. The conductor came through the car, saw us, grinned, and shouted, "Flagler, metropolis of Kit Carson County! Flagler." He stopped at our seat and said, "Here, I'll take your bags," and we followed him to the vestibule at the end of the car.

The train wheezed to a stop at a long, low, red station just beyond a big red water tank. The conductor opened the iron floor-door with a clang, swung down our valises, set the metal step on the station platform, and held a hand to Mother. And out of the rainy dusk under the station's broad eaves came my father, a short, stocky man in a dark suit, a stiff white collar, and a soft black hat. He took the valises, set them under the eaves out of the rain, then hugged Mother and put out a hand to me. "You got here!" he exclaimed, and he led us into the station.

The train pulled out and the agent came in, with Fritz. Fritz saw me, came leaping and whining and thrust his head into my arms, then saw Father and barked and dashed about the waiting room, trailing his leash. The agent laughed and Father said, "George, I want you to meet my wife. And my son." As he said it, Father looked at me and his wide mouth opened in surprise. He had seen my long pants. But he didn't say a word about them.

Then another man came in, a farmer-looking man in overalls, lean and gaunt, and Father said, "Sarah, this is Ora Groves, the drayman. He's going to take us up to the hotel."

Mr. Groves said, "Glad to meet you. Kind of muddy underfoot so I brought the carriage." He spoke with a trace of Missouri drawl. He picked up the two valises and went out again, and the agent said to Father, "Well, I guess you've got everything. Your woman, your boy, your luggage, and your dog. Got the bill of lading for your furniture today, so it looks like you're really going to stay."

"The rest of my life," Father said. "All the rest of my life."

2

It was only a few blocks to the hotel, which was on Main Street, but we went around several corners to get there and I could see, even in the deep dusk, that Flagler was different from all those other small towns. Main Street didn't lead to the railway station; it didn't even come all the way down to the tracks. The rain was still falling, and the street was so muddy the horses' hoofs made sloppy, sucking noises. But I saw that there were cement sidewalks, store buildings on both sides, and houses, most of them with lighted windows, stretching away beyond. Main Street was dark except for the hotel and the café across the street from it. The hotel was a square two-story building whose second floor extended out over a broad porch across the front. On each side of the central entrance was a big window with a table inside on which was an oil lamp with a frosted globe big as a basketball. The light from those two lamps glowed on the porch and reached out into the street.

Mr. Groves drew up at the curb, and Father handed Mother down and hurried her up the steps onto the porch. A little man with brown chin whiskers came out to greet them, and I heard Father say, "This is Henry Blancken. He's going to take care of us till we get settled." I was getting the valises out of the back of the carriage, which actually was a buckboard with a flat top, trying to hold on to Fritz's leash and hoping I wouldn't get my new pants wet and muddy. Suddenly there was a jerk on the leash, a yelp, a snarl, and I was in the middle of a dogfight. A big, black, slick-haired dog had come out of nowhere, challenged Fritz, and Fritz wasn't taking anything from anybody. They leaped and snapped and yelped and I was tangled in the leash and tripping over the valises. I shouted, Mother cried, "Oh, for goodness' sake!" and Mr. Blancken laughed. Then Mr. Groves was on the sidewalk with me, right in the middle of it. He slapped Fritz across the muzzle, booted the black dog in the ribs, said, "Get out of here, Nig!" And like that, it was all over. Nig ran and Mr. Groves, as though nothing had happened, picked up the two valises, set them on the porch, and drove away.

Fritz was still bristling, but I got him up onto the porch and calmed him down. Everybody was talking at once. Mr. Blancken, who had a slight German accent, said, "Come on in. My wife kept supper warm for you, but first you want to wash your face. Come, I show you your room." He led us into the lobby and up the open stairway to an upper hall lit by oil sconce-lamps. Ours was the corner room on the right, facing the street. He turned up the oil lamp on the varnished oak table at the front window and said to Mother, "My best room."

Mother looked around and said, "It's a very nice room."

I was in the doorway, Fritz at my side. Mr. Blancken looked at us and said, "The dog can stay for now, just so he don't get on the beds. My wife give me fits for that. We'll find a place for him later. What's his name?"

"Fritz," I said.

"No! Fritz, that is my brother's name." He was still chuckling as he left us.

The room's two windows had white lace curtains and green roller shades, and on the floor was a big linoleum rug with red roses on a tan background. There were two chairs, one a rocker, two iron beds, and a varnished oak commode. On the commode's white marble top were a big china wash bowl and a matching water pitcher, white with sprigs of red roses. In the cupboard beneath were a big enameled slop pail and two chamber pots sprigged with roses to match the pitcher and bowl. The heads and feet of the beds were of white iron rods in elaborate scrolls and each corner post had a bright brass knob. The beds were covered with bright patchwork quilts.

Mother took off her hat and coat, looked around again, and said, "This must be the most expensive room in the hotel."

"It is," Father said.

"How much did it cost?"

"Not a cent."

"Will Borland," Mother exclaimed, "I've never sponged on anybody and I don't intend to start now!"

"We're not sponging," Father said quietly. "I just don't have to lay out cash for it. Henry takes it out in trade."

"You said you wouldn't go into debt, except the mortgage on the paper."

"I'm not going into debt. I'm swapping what I've got for what I need. I'm not laying out cash, which I haven't got, for things I can swap advertising space for. No need to get upset. I'll explain the whole thing later. Let's get washed up and go down and eat."

Mother shook her head, but she poured water from the big pitcher into the bowl. "I just don't want to go further into debt. It's so hard to get out. . . . I feel gritty all over, from the train." She washed her face and hands. Then I washed and poured the water from the bowl into the enameled slop pail.

The dining room was back of the lobby, a big low-ceilinged room lit by two hanging lamps with red shades. At one side was a long table with chairs for at least twenty places. On the other side were half a dozen small tables, each with four chairs. The long table and all but one of the small ones had oilcloth covers patterned like red-and-white checked table-cloths. All had places set with plates upside down, cups bottom up in their saucers, knives and forks beside the plates,

spoons in spoon holders that matched the big cut-glass sugar
bowls. At the back of the room, near the door to the kitchen,
one small table had a white cloth and the plates and cups were
right side up. That was our table.

As we sat down a chubby little woman with a red face and
hair drawn back into a tight knot came in from the kitchen.
She hid her hands under her gray gingham apron. Her blue
eyes were full of shyness. "My wife," Mr. Blancken said,
"the cook." She bobbed a greeting like a polite little girl,
though she must have been at least five years older than
Mother, maybe even forty. "So good to know you," she said.
"I hope you like chicken and dumplings." And she vanished
into the kitchen. She returned almost at once, bringing the
food.

First was a huge bowl of stewed chicken and dumplings,
yellow with fat and steaming hot. Then a bowl of canned peas
in a cream sauce. Then a bowl of snowy mashed potatoes, a
heaped plate of soda biscuits, a fresh pound of butter with an
acorn-and-oak-leaf pattern from the round butter mold. There
were two kinds of jam, strawberry and peach, three kinds of
pickles, sweet, sour and mustard, big wedges of dried apricot
pie with thick golden juice, a wedge of yellow cheese, a pitcher
of thick cream, steaming black coffee. A feast.

We spread our linen napkins and served ourselves. Mr.
Blancken drew back the fourth chair and sat down to talk
while we ate. I had just taken my first forkful when Fritz, on
the floor beside my chair, sat up, sniffed, and whined softly.
Mr. Blancken reached for a biscuit and said, with a wink at
me, "My brother is hungry too."

Mother looked up. "No! Don't feed him at the table!"

Mr. Blancken was astonished. "You got rules, for the dog?"

"He never gets fed from the table," Mother said firmly.

Mr. Blancken put the biscuit back on the plate. Then
he got to his feet, took the leash, which was looped
over the back of my chair, and said, "Nobody goes

hungry here, not even a dog. Come, Fritz, you eat in the kitchen." And they were gone before there could be further argument.

A few minutes later Mr. Blancken came back, smiling again. "There. He gets his supper too. And he can sleep in the shed, where it is warm and dry. All right?" he asked Mother. "That," Mother said, "will be fine." I knew she was trying to apologize for being so sharp. But rules were rules.

We ate, and Mr. Blancken talked about the big things happening in Flagler. Plans were under way for a new school as soon as the bond issue was voted. Several new houses were going up over in the east part of town. There was talk of dividing the county, making Flagler the county seat of this west end. The town band was all ready to give Saturday evening concerts. "I like a good loud band with oom-pah, oom-pah!" Mr. Blancken laughed. "Ed Schlote makes a fine oom-pah on that tuba." And there would be orchestra music next winter. "Only question is who will head it, Anderson or Knies. You know those two," he said to Father. Then to Mother, "They play the fiddle, both of them. Good. But they get along like—like your dog and that black Nig." He chuckled. And, he went on, crops never looked better. Prosperity. Lots of good wheat. Everybody would have money this year, if the rains kept coming. "Like this one. *Your* rain," he said to Mother. "You bring us good luck, I think."

Mrs. Blancken appeared from time to time, to urge second helpings. Mother said it was a wonderful meal but she couldn't eat another bite. I had a second piece of pie, Father had more coffee, and we went back to our room.

Stuffed, tired, and full of the day's events, I lay down on my bed, but Mother told me to get up and take off my shoes and my new long pants. She smoothed out the creases and hung up the pants, and Father said he hardly knew me when we got off the train. Mother told him the story of how we bought them, how much they cost, how she bargained the price down. Then she said, "Now, you were going to tell me about this way you have found to live without money."

Father rolled a Bull Durham cigarette and lighted it before he answered. "Well, you know how farmers come to town and swap butter and eggs for sugar and flour and coffee."

"I ought to," Mother said.

"Yes, you had to do it often enough on the homestead. Well, I haven't got butter and eggs, but I have got advertising space. So I've been swapping that."

"You can't pay paper bills that way. Nor the mortgage."

"There's cash, and there'll be more. I've taken in about twenty-five dollars a week, cash, since I've been here. I've got a little over a hundred dollars in the bank."

"There'll be rent for the house."

Father shook his head. "I made a deal for that, too. Coo-coo takes the rent out—"

"Who?"

"Coo-coo, LeRoy Coo-coo. That's his name. He spells it C-U-C-K-O-W, but he pronounces it Coo-coo. He owns a garage and half a dozen little houses. I rented one of them. It's not much of a house, but there wasn't much choice. And the rent will come out of advertising."

"How much is the rent?"

"Ten dollars a month. Coo-coo runs an ad that costs seven and a half a week, so I'm twenty dollars a month to the good, in cash, with the house rent all paid."

Mother slowly shook her head. "I guess it's all right. But you know how I worry about going into debt. And there's the mortgage."

"We'll make out. I sized things up before I bought. I wrote you about Kit Carson. It's a bigger town and older than Flagler, and it's a good paper. But he wanted too much money, more than I could afford. And Wild Horse didn't amount to a hill of beans, just a wide place in the road. But the minute I got here I liked Flagler. It's up and coming with a live bunch

of business men. I inquired around and most of them promised to support me. The other paper—"

"There's another paper here?"

"Yes, the *Progress*."

"You didn't tell me that."

"Ed Gibson runs it. Nice fellow, but easy-going and an
old-line Republican. Things are changing. The Democrats are
going to win the next election in the county, maybe the state.
I had a talk with the leaders in Burlington—that's the county
seat, forty miles east of here. There's never been a Democratic paper in this end of the county."

"I don't like to see you get into politics."

"You know I've been a Democrat all my life, even back in
Nebraska. I just told them I'd support the party here if they
would support me. I didn't make any deals, but if the Democrats win the next election I'll get my share of the county
printing. They've already given me some legal advertising,
and there'll be more. But regardless of politics, I'm for Flagler and its best interests. I said that, just about that way, in my
first issue. I'm trying to make the *News* a *news*paper, print all
the news I can get, without fear or favor."

"Will, you're not going to print scandal!"

"I said news. No, I don't intend to poke into personal affairs, and I'm not going to print gossip. If a man has a fight
with his wife, I consider that scandal. But if he has a fight
with the whole neighborhood, that's news and I'm going to
print it. Don't you agree?"

"I guess so."

"People like to see their names in the paper, so I am putting their names in, using all the local items I can get. I've
lined up a string of regular correspondents out in the country
who send in items about their neighborhood every week."

"I guess you've been pretty busy."

"This is the first night I haven't gone back to the shop
after supper."

"I couldn't see much when we came in, but Flagler looks

about the size of Sterling." Sterling was the town in Nebraska where I was born, the town we left to come to Colorado five years before.

"About the same size, around five hundred people."

"Sterling couldn't support two papers."

"Flagler is different. It has twice as many stores and business places. It draws trade from a big territory north and south, farmers to the north, ranchmen to the south. A lot of Missourians, good farmers, out north. They grow big wheat crops. And cattlemen and sheepmen out south, with quite a few farmers too. Flagler is starting to boom. There's a lively crowd of young business men here who are giving the old-timers a run for their money. They are the ones I'm counting on to make a go of it. They've never had a really live editor to get behind them and help push."

Mother yawned. I was getting sleepy too. "Well," she said, "I just hope we don't live to regret it. If we could have sold the homestead you could have paid cash and we wouldn't be in debt."

"The deal didn't go through," Father said, "and that's that. With other land all around the homestead selling for eight and ten dollars an acre, I wasn't going to let it go for five. You froze and starved to get that land and I'm not going to give it away now."

"You worked too. We all did. I just hope you're right." Then she asked, "How big is the house you rented? I hope we don't have to get more furniture right away."

Father laughed. "We'll do good to get what furniture we've got in that house. It's only three rooms. Not much bigger than the house on the homestead. But we won't live there forever. Something better will open up one of these days."

"Oh, Will," Mother said, "it doesn't matter where we live, just as long as things go right. I'd live in—in a boxcar, till we get out of debt!"

I must have been half asleep by then because Father's laugh made me sit up and blink. "That's practically what you are

31

going to live in—a boxcar. Coo-coo bought half a dozen old railway cars, the kind they use to house construction crews, and he put new roofs on them and fixed them up a little. That's what those houses are, old railroad cars. But the one I rented was the only vacant house in town, absolutely the only one."

I was yawning and rubbing my eyes. Mother said, "You'd better get ready for bed, son, before your father has to undress you."

She opened a valise and got out our nightclothes and I unbuttoned my shirt. Then I remembered Fritz. I asked where he was.

"Mr. Blancken said he could sleep in the shed," Father said.

"I remember now. I want to go down and see that he's all right."

"I'll go. I want to talk to Henry anyway. He said he wanted me to print some letterheads." He put on his coat and turned to Mother. "I get cash for job printing. Anything that needs material I have to pay cash for, I charge cash. I only swap advertising space. And subscriptions. A farmer from up north, out in the Shiloh neighborhood, came in and wanted to swap two hens for a subscription." He grinned. "I told him all right but not to deliver them till next week, after we get settled."

"I hope," Mother said, "you told him to bring them in alive. I like to dress my own chickens."

"I told him. I'll bet when word gets around we'll have so many chickens we have to build a chicken pen."

"Tell the next person who wants to give you chickens to bring laying hens. Then I'll have my own eggs."

Father went downstairs, and I pulled on my nightshirt and got under the covers. It was still raining. I could hear the steady drumming on the roof and the wash off the eaves above the side window. Mother pulled down the shades and turned down the lamp, and I was asleep before Father came back.

3

The next day was one of those June days when the whole
High Plains world seems fresh and renewed. The rain had
ended, the sky was clear, and the sun streamed through the
east window when I wakened. Mother and Father were up and
dressed, and Mother was combing her long dark hair. I washed
the sleep out of my eyes and began to dress, but when I
reached for my long pants Mother shook her head, took two
bone hairpins from her mouth, and said, "I got out your blue
knickerbockers. As soon as we have breakfast we are going
over and look at the house, and it's muddy out."

I was ready to argue but didn't have to. Father said, "It's
his first day here. Let him wear the new pants."

"I wanted him to save them for good."

"Just today," Father said, and that settled it.

So I put on the long pants and felt both dressed up and
grown up. It was almost seven o'clock. Mother finished with
her hair, put on her jacket, and we went down to the dining
room.

Three traveling salesmen were at one of the small tables
and half a dozen local men, two of them in overalls, were at
the long table. They looked up, gestured to Father, and he
greeted them by name. We went to the table where we had
eaten the night before. The white cloth was gone; it had the
same red-and-white checked oilcloth as all the others. We were
just folks this morning, not special guests.

Mrs. Blancken came in from the kitchen with a gray granite-ware coffeepot. "Nice day after the rain," she said as she filled our cups. "You sleep good?"

"Fine," Father said, and just then Mr. Blancken appeared with Fritz, who bounced to me, licked my hand, and lay down beside my chair. Mr. Blancken said to Mother, with a twinkle, "Don't feed him from the table! He had his breakfast already." Then Mrs. Blancken was back with stewed apricots, fried eggs, fried potatoes, a platter of bacon and a heaping plate of pancakes. Butter, cream, syrup and jam were already on the table. Mr. Blancken was right. Nobody went hungry at his tables.

When we had eaten, Father got his hat and Mother's rubbers from our room and we went out onto the street. Father pointed out the stores and business offices and said who ran each one, but I didn't get them straight except that the two-story brick building across the street at the next corner to the north was the Farmers State Bank building. "The *News* office." he said, "is under the bank."

"You mean in the basement?" Mother asked.

Father nodded. "The entrance is around the corner. We'll go over there after we've seen the house."

A few doors down the street from the hotel was a gray frame building with big front windows and a sign, "The Flagler Progress." Through the windows I could see racks of type cases and, in the shadowy back, the big newspaper press. "The opposition paper," Father said.

Mother paused to look through a window. "It doesn't look like much of a shop," she said.

"It's a pretty good shop," Father said.

"I'll bet the *News* is better."

"It will be." Father didn't seem to want to talk about it. "Come on, let's get over to the house."

We went on down the street and turned east, passed the livery stable with its big board corral out back, crossed another street with a smoky blacksmith shop on the corner. The blacksmith, already at work, shouted, "Morning, Will," as we passed. The sidewalks had ended. We followed a muddy footpath and Mother turned to me. "I said you should have worn your knickerbockers. It *is* muddy." And Father said, "Better roll up your new pants, son."

Another two blocks and I could see the whole expanse of the plains to the east. Just ahead, though, were four little houses set in a row and about fifty feet apart. They were exactly alike and still looked like boxcars. But they were painted brown and they had low pitched roofs. Each one had a clothes line and a privy out back and between each pair of them was a well and hand pump. The yards around them were as bare as the plains themselves, without a tree or a shrub and with the native buffalo grass worn thin by a lacing of footpaths.

We went to the last house in the row and Father unlocked the front door. We went in. Mother took a deep breath and looked around. We were in the front room, as we always called it, a room about twelve feet square with the door and one window in the front, one window on each side. Beyond it was the middle room, somewhat smaller, and beyond that, at the back, was the kitchen, identical with the front room. The kitchen door led to the back yard and paths to the nearest pump and the privy.

Mother walked through and came back to the front room and ran her finger along a window sill. She shook her head.

"I had a woman in to clean it up," Father said.

"She may have swept the floor, but she didn't do any scrubbing." Mother sighed. "Well, I'm not afraid of soap and water. I just hope it's not full of bedbugs." Then she turned to Father. "We'll put the heat stove here, and our bed over there. Your bed will go in the middle room, son. The chiffonier will have to go in there too, and maybe the wardrobe. We'll eat in the kitchen, where it's handy. It's bigger than the homestead house, but not much. We'll make out."

35

We went back to Main Street. The stores were beginning to open, and men in shirt sleeves came to the doorways to call greetings and be introduced to Mother. All of them spoke of the rain, thankful for it. Then we came to the corner with the brick bank and there, on the side street, was a wide stairway leading down to the basement. It had a railing of iron pipe, and a sign on the railing said, "The Flagler News." There was a big window facing the open stairway and through it I could see a rack of type cases.

Mother hesitated at the top of the stairway, stared at the weatherbeaten sign, then slowly went on down. Father unlocked the door, and as we went in I sniffed the familiar odors of a print shop—paper, ink, press rollers, lye water, benzene, the subtle odors of printing presses and type itself.

It was a big low-ceilinged room with a short L at the doorway. The only light came through the big window at the stairway and two little ones, like cellar windows, high on the far wall. Opposite the door was an old flat-top desk with a clutter of newspapers, letters, copy paper, scribbled notes, a telephone and an old green Oliver typewriter. Beside the big window was the rack of type cases I had seen as we went down the steps. In the middle of the big room was the composing stone, a thick marble slab about three feet wide and six feet long set on a cabinet of shallow drawers and with a rack of leads, slugs and wooden "furniture" above it. On the stone were several steel chases, frames in which type is locked to be put on the presses. On back in the half-light were two job presses, one big, one small. In one corner was a Fairbanks-Morse gasoline engine, its exhaust pipe thrust through a hole in the wall, and overhead was a line of shafting with pulleys to provide belt power to the presses. In another corner was a paper cutter with an open paper cabinet beside it. Across the far end, under the little cellar windows, was a long wooden table. At one side stood the proof press, a shallow metal trough in which galleys of type could be placed and inked, with a padded drum a foot in diameter that rolled over the inked type and impressed it on a strip of paper.

That was Father's print shop, his newspaper plant and office. Mother looked at him, just looked, and he said, "This is it. All of it." He reached for his bag of Bull Durham and began to roll a cigarette. His fingers were shaking. "A shirttail full of type, two job presses, a stone and a paper cutter." He lit the cigarette, inhaled, blew out a long stream of smoke. "Not much to look at, is it?"

"No." Mother sank into the chair at the desk. For a moment I thought she was going to cry. Then her jaw tightened and she said, "Well, we're here, and we'll make the best of it."

Father took a deep breath. "I print the paper one page at a time on the big Gordon. I put in the gasoline engine last week. Until then I had to pedal the presses, but you can't get along that way. I had to order some new type, display as well as body type. The job work has started to come, and so has the advertising. Bill Hall—he runs the big general store—wanted half the front page for an ad every other week, but I'm not that hard up yet. I let him have half the back page."

"How many subscribers are there?" Mother asked.

"Almost three hundred, and growing. I got twenty new subscribers in the last two weeks. But half the old ones aren't paid up. I've been sending out bills and they're beginning to pay up." Then he added, "The *Progress* list is under five hundred."

"It's dark down here," Mother said.

Father took down a big gasoline lamp from its hook on the ceiling, pumped up the pressure, held a match to the mantles till they began to glow, and hung it back on its hook. The light made the room look bigger, and dingier.

"I'll scrub the walls," Mother said. "Then we'll paint them white. Where's a broom?"

"I'll sweep out when I get to it."

"I'll sweep out right now! I'm going to do *something!*"

Father got the broom. He probably knew she had to work off her disappointment and frustration. But as he handed it to her he said, "You've got on your good dress."

She didn't answer. She began sweeping, furiously, raised a cloud of dust almost at once. Father began to cough and she stopped to blow her nose and wipe her eyes. "It's even worse than I thought!" she exclaimed. She stood the broom in a corner. "Come on, son. You're going to get out of those good pants and help too. Will, get a pail of water and some rags and a bar of soap. You can start on the big window while I'm gone."

She and I went to the hotel and changed into work clothes. When we got back to the office a grizzled little man with a slit mouth and light blue eyes was talking to Father. He glanced at us and went on talking. "Seems pretty steep, just for a few lines of print at the top of a sheet of paper."

"It takes just as long to print those few lines as a whole page," Father said.

"How about two hundred and fifty sheets? That would be half as much as five hundred, wouldn't it?"

"No. That would be a dollar less. It takes just as long to make ready for a short run as a long one."

"I'd think, you being new here and wanting to get a start, you might make me a price."

"I made you a fair price, Mr. Wheeler. It's the same price for everyone."

The man shook his head. "I'll have to think it over. Money don't grow on trees, as you'll find out." And he left.

Father turned to Mother. "I didn't get to wash the window."

"Who is he?"

"One of the old-timers. He runs a store down the street. So tight, they say, he squeaks when he walks. He didn't really want any letterheads. He just wanted to try me out, see what

I'd say. If I'd come down a dollar he'd have wanted me to come down two. Now, shall I start on that window?"

"Leave it for now. Till I get through sweeping." She had brought a dish towel which she tied over her hair. And when she finished sweeping, all three of us went to work scrubbing the walls.

We swept and scrubbed till noon, and after dinner at the hotel we went back and scrubbed till midafternoon. Then Mother said we'd done all that could be done with soap and water. Father went to the hardware store and came back with paint and brushes. We started in the entrance L, where the walls were dry, and by suppertime had the L gleaming white. After supper we went back and worked by lamplight. By nine o'clock we had painted two walls of the big room and were dog-tired. Father said to call it a day, that he and I could finish the walls the next morning and the ceiling would have to wait till next week.

"I've got to get the type distributed and start on next week's paper. After all, I am getting out a weekly newspaper." He turned to me. "And you're going to help."

Mother was choosing rags and putting them into the empty pail with scouring powder and soap. "Not tomorrow, he isn't," she said. "He can help finish painting the walls tomorrow morning, but I may need him in the afternoon. That house is as bad as this place was. We may have to paint it too."

"All right," Father said to me. "You start working here next week. You can work in the office mornings, and if your mother doesn't need you you can have the afternoons to do whatever you want to. All except press day. Then I'll need you all day."

"I'll be working here too," Mother said.

"No need of that," Father said. "But he's going to learn the printer's trade. I don't care what else you do when you get through school, son, you'll always have a trade to fall back on. You can always get a job and make a living."

"As soon as I get acquainted," Mother said, "I'll use the phone and write locals. And I'll keep the books."

Father didn't seem to be listening. He was sitting on the high stool at the rack of type cases, looking out at the big room and the grotesque shadows of those few pieces of equipment, his few meager tools of editorship. "One of these days," he said, "I'm going to have a linotype in here. And a Miehle press. I know just the press I want and I know where I can get it, when the time comes." He was talking half to himself. "One of these days this will be the best paper in the county, and the only paper in town. The time will come when Ed Gibson will *ask* me to buy him out."

He sat quiet for a long moment, a slight smile on his tired face. "We're going to have electricity here, probably a municipal plant. That's one thing I'm going after. And we'll have our own water, municipal water. And with water, we will have trees, and lawns, and flowers. This is going to be a beautiful town. And it's going to grow. I'm going to help it grow. And the *News* will grow with it."

Then he seemed to bring himself back. He got down from the stool and said to Mother, "I couldn't write you about the shop, Sarah, not the way it really is. Every time I tried, it seemed so little, so—well, such a bad bargain. But it isn't just the shop, what's down here in this hole in the ground. It's what I can put into it, what I'm going to make out of this paper. And I couldn't say that the way I wanted to in a letter. But now you can see, can't you?"

Mother nodded, but there seemed a reservation in her.

"It isn't just a couple of old job presses and a few cases of battered-up type," he said. "It's what I can *do* with it!"

"Yes," Mother said. "Yes." She stood up. "I'm tired. So are you. Let's get some sleep." She looked around the office. So did Father. "We made a start," she said.

"It looks a lot different," he said, "than it did this morning."

She handed me the pail with the rags and soap.

Father reached for the big lamp to turn it off, and I opened the door and started up the stairs. Everything went dark inside and all I could see was the stars overhead. Then they were coming up the stairs behind me, arm in arm.

4

Father and I finished painting the office walls the next morning, and when Mother decided at noon that she didn't need me after all I went back to the office with Father. He said I could start learning the printer's trade the way he did, by washing the little job press so he could print an order of envelopes. So I washed the rollers and the ink disc with benzene-soaked rags, one of the dirtiest jobs in a print shop. I washed it twice, once to my satisfaction and again to please Father. Then he said, "Wash your hands and you can take the afternoon off." I had to wash my hands twice, too. Then, Fritz at my heels, I set out to see the town.

A boy doesn't explore a new town the way a grownup does. He absorbs it as he goes along, the way he makes friends. He doesn't have to be introduced. He meets boys, one way and another, and sorts them out without really thinking about it. I started down Main Street, and there in front of Dr. Williams' drug store was the big black dog that had jumped Fritz the evening we arrived. Fritz growled and the black dog growled and bristled. And just then a boy came out of the drug store, saw what was about to happen, and shouted, "Nig!" The black dog turned, the boy caught him by the collar, then looked at me and grinned. "Maybe we'd better let them fight it out and get it over with," he said.

"All right," I said, "but my dog is half wolf."

"Mine's half lion!" He let go of Nig's collar and the two

dogs sniffed, growled, walked around each other, and decided they didn't want to fight. Maybe they told each other bragging lies too. Nig came and smelled of my hand and Fritz smelled of the other boy's overalls, and they both wagged their tails.

"I've got to go down to the depot," the other boy said. "Want to come along?"

He seemed to know who I was. Word gets around in a small town. And before we got to the depot I knew that he was Little Doc Williams, the doctor's younger son. His name was Justin, but nearly everybody called him Little Doc because he was tall and thin like his father and said he was going to be a doctor too. He was about my age but was a year ahead of me in school because I hadn't made up all the schooling I missed on the homestead.

At the depot the agent greeted us both by name and gave Little Doc a small express package marked "Drugs." We listened to the *clack-clack* of the telegraph instruments and went into the freight room and weighed ourselves just because the scales were there. We went out onto the station platform and looked south. There wasn't a house in sight, just the rolling flats as far as you could see. Little Doc said, "You can't see from here, but about five miles off there are the bluffs along the river. There isn't any water in the river but there's a couple of Indian caves in the bluff. We'll go dig them out, some time."

We went up the tracks, walking the rails, to the big red water tank where the locomotives stopped for water. Two towering cottonwoods, watered by the drip from the tank, shaded a small pump house that throbbed softly as its steam engine drove the pump. A big red-faced man in overalls, Mr. Davison, who was in charge of the pumping station, sat on the bench outside, chewing a toothpick. He said hello and watched as we stood under the tank and caught the icy drip in our open mouths. Then we went back up the street to the drug store.

"You got a bike?" Little Doc asked. I said mine wouldn't

be there till our furniture came, so he borrowed his older brother's bicycle for me. His brother's name was Marion and he worked in the drug store. Most people called him Emp because his initials were M. P. Little Doc on his bike and I on Emp's rode up one street and down another, across and back and all around. I suppose he was showing me the town. Our two dogs followed us, and now and then another dog tried to cut in and our dogs chased him and had as much fun as we did.

We passed the oldest house in town, a soddy on Main Street just a block north of the brick bank. We went over to the two old school buildings, on side streets and several blocks apart. We rode up to the north end of Main Street, where they planned to build the new high school when they ended the argument over whether to build one or not. From there we went down to Seal's slew, a big swale in the northwest corner of town where snow melt and spring rain collected in a pond several acres in extent. Little Doc showed me the boat he and Spider Miner had built the year before. It leaked but he said that didn't matter because the slew was only knee deep in the deepest part. We shoved it into the water and poled out fifty yards or so before it sank. We left it there and waded back to dry land and emptied our shoes and wrung out our socks and sat in the sun while they dried.

I asked what kind of fish were in the slew, and Little Doc said there weren't any fish. "Just frogs. I dissected a couple of frogs last year. You ever dissect a frog? Fascinating skeletal system! But the slew dries up by the end of July and the frogs go away. There's ducks in the spring, but they don't stay either. Some of them go down to Verhoff's Dam. The dam's on the way to the Indian caves. You swim?"

"Not very good." Actually, all I could do was dog-paddle.

"We'll stop at the dam on the way to the caves."

We rode back downtown and over to the grain elevator and the stockyards, but nothing was happening at either place.

44

So Little Doc said, "Let's see what Spider's doing." We rode
back to the north end of town to a house so new its boards
were still yellow. Back of the house was a garden plot, fenced
to keep the rabbits out, where a tall, skinny boy was half-
heartedly weeding. "Aren't you through *yet?*" Little Doc asked.

Spider straightened up with a haughty, superior air. "Watch
thy manners, Pilgrim. Let not thy tongue play asp!" Then he
grinned, a grin that spread his broad mouth even wider and
wrinkled his light blue eyes almost shut. "What you been
doing?"

"Inspecting. When his bike gets here," Little Doc said,
nodding at me, "we're going down to the dam and the Indian
caves."

"Ah! I shall join the party. We shall dig up old Last of the
Mohicans. Or his brother, Next-to-Last. . . . I got a flat
tire."

"Again? Can't you stay out of the cactus? Oh, all right,
I've got half a tube of Never-Leak you can have."

Mrs. Miner, a plump, very blonde woman, came to the
back door. "Stanley," she called. "when you finish weeding
bring the boys in for cookies and milk. But finish the weeding
first."

Spider groaned. "Get down on your patella," Little Doc
ordered, "and get to work. We'll help, but we won't do it all."

"Oh, what you said!" Spider jeered. But Little Doc shoved
him to his knees, and the three of us, crawling down the rows,
finished the weeding in ten minutes. Then we went into the
kitchen and Mrs. Miner gave us cold milk and ginger cookies
fresh from the oven. Spider's sisters were there. Marjorie, a
year older than Spider, was ironing. Very blonde, very pretty,
and very shy, she said hello to Little Doc, smiled at me, and
didn't say another word. Virginia, a pig-tailed ten-year-old,
chattered like a magpie. They, like everyone else in town apparently, knew who I was, when we arrived, where we came
from, and where we were going to live. Mrs. Miner asked,

45

"Are you getting settled? Hope your mother likes Flagler. Your father is such a nice, friendly man, I know I'll like her." The Miners were from Minnesota. They had come to Colorado a few years before because Spider's older brother had asthma. The climate had almost cured him and he now was helping his father, who was a carpenter. They were related to B. M. Bower, who wrote a series of books about a cowboy named Chip and a ranch called the Flying U. I had read several of those books and couldn't believe it when they said the B in B. M. Bower stood for Bertha. I didn't see how a woman could have written those books.

We finished the milk and most of the cookies, and Little Doc said he had to get home and do the barn chores. Spider came along, riding double on Little Doc's bike. The Williamses' house was a big two-story place with a barn and buggy shed out back. Dr. Williams had an automobile, but he kept a team and buggy to make his calls when the car wouldn't start or the snow was too deep. And like quite a lot of people in town, he had a cow. We put fresh hay in the mangers and chopped grain in the feed boxes and we bragged about our horsemanship. I didn't have to brag much, really. On the homestead and in Brush I had done a lot of riding on all kinds of horses. But I did let them feel the bones I had broken when horses fell on me or bucked me off. Little Doc, acting very professional, felt the knots and said they were real breaks, and Spider was properly impressed. The worst he ever had was a broken collarbone when he fell off an old milk cow.

We took Spider home, went back downtown, and I returned to the print shop. Father had finished the envelopes and was distributing the type from the newspaper. "You're just in time," he said, "to wash the press again." That time I washed it clean enough to suit him the first time. While I was washing my hands he asked, "Well, where did you go? What did you do?"

"We just poked around."

"You and who else?"

"Little Doc."

"So you met Justin Williams, and he showed you the town."

"We just poked around."

Father asked no more questions. He probably knew that while he, like any grownup, had to make a conscious effort to meet people and ask questions about the new town, that wasn't a boy's way. Flagler was new and different, but even if he had insisted I couldn't have put the difference into words that day. To myself, of course, I compared it with Brush. Brush, in the well-watered Platte valley and much older than Flagler, was a town of trees and grass. Flagler still had a raw look, a few trees and only an occasional lawn. It was a dry-land town still taking root. Buffalo grass grew in every vacant lot, and where it had been trodden away there were Russian thistles and resin weeds and even clumps of cactus. Every house had its own well, and the older houses had windmills out near the barns. Only those places with windmills to provide water for irrigation had gardens. And only near the center of town, close to Main Street, were the houses close together. From there they scattered out, most of them with barns and small pastures with a cow or two and at least one saddle horse. Half the side-street houses had pens where chickens clucked and cackled. Only one or two of the side streets had sidewalks. All but about half a dozen houses had outside privies.

Flagler's main street was a block west of the depot and didn't reach all the way to the railroad tracks. The street that went straight to the depot was a back street with only a livery stable, a blacksmith shop, and lumber yard on it. And instead of straddling the tracks, with a good part of town on one side and a poor part on the other, Flagler was all on the north side with no below-the-tracks area. It seemed to stand apart, almost to disown the railroad.

Later I learned its history. It had been an independent town from the beginning, even before the railroad came through in 1887, only twenty-eight years before we went there. At that time a man named Robinson had a store and post

47

office three miles to the east. His store served the cattle ranches throughout that whole area, and he called his post office Bowserville, for his favorite dog. When they built the railroad Mr. Robinson wanted them to put a station and lay out a townsite at Bowserville. Instead, they put the station and townsite three miles away and named it Malowe, for the railroad's attorney, one M. A. Lowe. For several years Malowe was only a side track, a water tank, and a dismounted boxcar that served as combined railroad station and living quarters for the man assigned the dual job of station agent and engineer at the pump for the water tank. Trains didn't stop at Bowserville, though it was right beside the tracks, and they wouldn't even toss off mail pouches there. So Robinson finally gave in and moved his store and post office to Malowe. But he still called the post office Bowserville.

A few other settlers came, including W. H. Lavington, who set up a competing store in a tent while he was putting up a frame store building. The settlers didn't like the name Malowe because they didn't like railroad lawyers, and they thought Bowserville was a ridiculous name. But they had to pick a name the railroad would accept, so finally, partly as a joke, I imagine, they picked the biggest railroad name in sight, Flagler. Henry M. Flagler, one-time partner of John D. Rockefeller millionaire and railroad magnate, may have passed the town once on his way to Denver, but he certainly never stopped in Flagler—or Malowe, or Bowserville. Anyway, they picked his name, the railroad and the post office department accepted it, and that was the end of both Bowserville and Malowe.

All the western railroads received extravagant land grants when they were built, and to cash in on this land they promoted settlement. Settlers came, some to buy railroad land, others to homestead government land. The big ranches dwindled, already hard hit by the bitter winter of 1886–87 and now increasingly choked by the plowmen and their barbed wire fences. Periodic drouth starved out some of the settlers, as did plagues of grasshoppers. Financial crises back east spread hard times to the plains. The Panic of 1907 hit that area late but hard. Settlers sold out for a song and went back east "to live on the wife's folks," as the saying went. Men with a little cash and a lot of hope bought abandoned land for as little as fifty cents an acre. W. H. Lavington was said to have taken several tracts for unpaid grocery bills and to have swapped a gold watch for a half section just outside of town.

Recovery was slow, but about 1910 there was a new wave of settlers. The financial crisis passed. So did the drouth cycle. By 1915 there had been several good crops, and war times had raised the price of wheat close to two dollars a bushel. More and more midwestern farmers had moved in to plow the grassland, plant wheat, and make enough on their first crop to pay for the land. Most of them stayed. Flagler had begun to boom. When we arrived it had a population of between 500 and 600 people and was the trading center for a farming area that extended thirty or forty miles to the north and a ranch area that reached halfway to the Arkansas river a hundred miles to the south.

Characteristic of the boom were the real estate men. Three had offices on Main Street and two others had offices at home. Representative of the changes taking place were three lumber yards; two hardware and implement dealers; three general stores where you could buy anything from a silk shirt to a flitch of bacon, from lariat rope to patent leather shoes; two cream stations where farmers sold dairy produce—and where, since the man who ran one of them was a musician, you could order anything from a flute to a piano, from a tuba to a violin; two garages, a livery stable, a blacksmith shop, a tinsmith's shop, two cafés, a pool hall, and two barber shops. One barber shop had a bathtub in the back room where, for a dime, you could take a bath complete with soap and a towel. You could also take a bath down at the railroad pumping station, in a huge tin tub with hot water from the steam engine's boiler. There a bath cost only a nickel, with the towel but without soap.

There were two doctors in town, but no dentist and no lawyer. There was a second bank, though you might have to look twice to see it in its modest white frame building across the street from the big brick Farmers State Bank. The Flagler State Bank was usually called the Lavington bank. It was managed and largely owned by the man who started as a store-keeper in a tent, and some said you had to mortgage your life to get a loan there; but nobody denied that it was one of the soundest banks in the state.

And there were two newspapers, the prosperous-looking *Progress* on Main Street, and the struggling little *News* in its dark basement.

I sensed some of these things, but by no means all, that afternoon, I suppose. But mostly I was aware that Flagler was a new and different town, still raw, still relatively new, still with peeling buffalo horns and bleached skulls in the grass at the edge of town. Men who had hunted those buffalo lived there, and men who came up the trail with the big herds from Texas. The past was right there on the flats, so near you could still hear its echoes on quiet nights if you listened. The old trails were not all grass-grown. But change was under way. A new generation, my father's generation, who already dreamed of tomorrow, was beginning to take charge. Change was in the air. Father had sensed it, counted on it.

All I really knew, that afternoon, was that this was going to be home, where I would learn a trade, go to school, grow up as boys inevitably do. It was new, but it had enough links with the past that had already shaped me so that I would feel at home there.

Father asked no more questions. He distributed the last few handfuls of type, washed up, and we went to the hotel. Mother was there, tired but triumphant. The kitchen wouldn't have to be painted. Once she got the dirt scrubbed off, the paint wasn't too bad, she said.

We went downstairs to supper, and Father said, "Clarence

Smith told me today that this is going to be the best wheat year this country ever had. Out north, he said, the wheat may go thirty bushels to the acre."

"Mr. Smith," Mother said, "is a real estate man, isn't he?"

"Yes." Then Father amended the report somewhat. "Not all the wheat will go that heavy, but he thinks the average will be close to twenty. Just think of it, twenty bushels of two-dollar wheat to the acre! On land those farmers bought for fifteen dollars an acre just a few years ago! That's prosperity. That's what makes a boom."

"Farmers," Mother said, "don't advertise, do they?"

"The merchants who sell to the farmers do. They have to go after the farmers' business. Mark my word, when this bumper crop is harvested, this town will really hum."

"What if it hails?" Mother asked.

"Well—" Father hesitated. He didn't want to think about hail. Nobody did. Hail could wipe you out in the passing of a cloud. "Well, there hasn't been any hail yet. And in another two weeks they'll be harvesting."

Mother said nothing more. She seemed to be full of her own thoughts. The men across the room, at the long table, were talking crops, loud in their optimism. I saw that Father was listening to them. I listened too, and I could see Father smile deep inside, a glow as though there was a warm, golden dream in there. Finally I heard one man declare, "There won't be enough boxcars to haul it away. They'll be piling wheat in the streets!" Then the inner smile lit up Father's whole face. He turned to Mother, about to say something. But she was still deep in her skeptical, hardheaded thoughts. He glanced at me, took a deep breath, slowly let it out, and reached for another piece of meat. His eyes were shining, but he kept the dream to himself.

5

Father was too hopeful about railroad freight schedules. The furniture didn't arrive for another week and there was plenty of time to scrub the whole house and paint the front room, the only one, Mother decided once the grime had been removed from the walls, that really had to have fresh paint. Then, with curtains up, carpets down, and furniture in place, we began to settle in, as settled as we ever would be in that house. It was a place to eat and sleep, which was all that mattered. Most of our daylight hours were spent at the office.

I spent that summer learning the printer's trade.

I have to say that firmly and flatly because that is the way I remember it. One way. Actually I remember two boys and two summers, and it is almost impossible to think of them as the same boy and the same summer, though I know they were. One of those remembered boys was an apprentice, a printer's devil, practically indentured, who spent all his waking hours in that dark print shop, learning the printer's craft the way my father learned it. But the other boy in my memory had afternoons off and even whole days of freedom, to come and go as he pleased, to do whatever he wished, follow his whims and be almost as free as the sunshine and the wind.

Both memories are true and absolute, and their duality—actually it is multiplicity—is a part of boyhood and youth. Young emotions are intense, and a boy has a remarkable capacity for total absorption. He can in one day live not only two but sometimes half a dozen lives. I know that I lived two sharply defined and complete lives that summer; and I know that I cannot write of both simultaneously. The best I can do is write of them one at a time.

First, then, the apprentice, the printer's devil.

That term, "printer's devil," comes from the drudging tasks that are the apprentice's lot in a print shop, most of which involve printer's ink. He washes forms of inky type, washes inky presses, cleans and refills the ink fountains on those presses, washes the inky rollers that ink the type, gathers and burns the inky waste paper. At every turn he encounters printer's ink, thick, sticky and usually black. He may scrub his skin raw, but that black ink persists, in every pore and around every nail. He looks like an imp of hell, a devil indelibly marked.

My first job each morning was to sweep out the office. I might satisfy Father with a lick-and-promise job, but when Mother arrived about nine o'clock, after she had done her housework, she looked around and said, "Get the broom, son. Sweep out the corners." So I swept. I carried out the waste paper and burned it in the alley. I ran errands. I folded papers. And I washed the type and presses. Father was as demanding about the way I washed type and presses as Mother was about the way I swept.

I worked for weeks and months at such drudgery. This statement, of course, is rank exaggeration, but I am dealing now with memory, not fact, and in memory I relived my father's apprenticeship. He worked for two years as a printer's devil before he was allowed to start learning the basic skills of the trade. So if my time sense is somewhat askew, that is why. For me those two years were compressed into a few weeks. By the end of that summer I had the basic skills, and over the next few years I became a competent journeyman printer. Eventually I became a linotype operator and repairman. I learned my trade, as my father had planned. But I am remembering now the beginnings, and, as I said, the time sense is all askew.

I worked for weeks and months at the drudging tasks, then, until the morning when Father said, "I guess you can start learning the case." He chose a piece of copy, handed me a printer's stick, and told me to get up on the stool at the type case and start setting type. "You know how to hold a stick and justify a line," he said. "The rest is just a matter of practice and memory."

A printer's stick is a short, shallow, metal tray that the compositor holds in his left hand. He assembles the type in it, letter by letter, line by line, until he has "a stickful," about a dozen lines. Then he transfers that type to a long steel tray called a galley and starts over with an empty stick. That part, the actual assembly of the type, the letters, is easy. Your fingers soon learn the necessary motions. But to become a real compositor you have to "learn the case," as a typist learns the keyboard of a typewriter. Your hand must learn where to reach for each letter.

The type is in shallow wooden trays, or cases, partitioned into separate boxes for the individual letters. There are two cases, one for the small letters, the other for the capitals. The two cases are set on a rack, the one with the small letters immediately in front of the typesetter, the one with the capitals just beyond and at an angle, uptilted. From those two cases come the names "lower case" for the small letters and "upper case" for the capitals. The upper case, with the capital letters, is easy to learn because the boxes for the letters are arranged alphabetically, left to right and top to bottom. But the lower case, with the small letters, has boxes of various sizes arranged by frequency of use. The bigger boxes, closest to hand, contain the most-used letters, e, t, a, i, s, n, h and r. The rest of the letters, as well as punctuation marks and blanks for spaces between the words, are arranged around those big boxes.

I had watched Father set type many times. It seemed ridiculously easy. He never seemed to hurry. He would glance at the copy, read a line, and there would be a steady *click-click-click* as he set the letters in the stick. The lines seemed to fill automatically and properly spaced. He could set type and carry on a conversation at the same time.

That first morning it took me half an hour to set my first stickful, a dozen lines. I hunted all over the case for the letters, fumbled, dropped them, got them in wrong side up. Father, at work at the stone, finally asked, "Having trouble, son?"

"A little," I admitted.

"Maybe this will help." He got a soft pencil and marked the letters on the partitions of their boxes. "I've known apprentices to get fired for marking the boxes," he said. "But you didn't do it. I did. . . . There. See if that doesn't make it easier."

It did. I set the next stickful in twenty minutes. By noon I had set almost half a galley, about six stickfuls. Before we went to dinner Father told me to pull a proof and he would read it as soon as we got back. I felt rather proud of myself until he read it and handed it to me, without a word. He had found at least one error in every line. I couldn't believe it. I looked at him, and he said, with a smile, "A little dirty. But you'll do better next time. Make your corrections. Then I want you to wash up the little job press."

I got the galley, wet the type with a sponge—water makes type stick together, easier to handle—and started making my corrections. But I had the problem of reading type to see where to make the changes. Type is all backward, the reverse of the printed letters, and if you try to read it right side up the lines are backward too, right to left. So a printer reads type upside down, from left to right but from the bottom up, line by line. The trick of this is learning to recognize the letters upside down and backward. Reading type was another skill I had to learn, and it, too, could be learned only with practice.

When I finally had made my corrections and pulled another proof Father glanced at it and said, "That's pretty good. I didn't mark the logs. We'll let them go for now."

"Logs?" I asked.

"Logotypes, compound letters. I marked them on the case, but I guess you didn't see them. There's an eff-el, an eff-eye, a double-eff-el and a double-eff-eye, each on a single type. They're in the boxes up there at the top of the lower case." He picked up an "ffl" logotype and showed it to me. "They save time in composition and they look better in print. You'll learn them, in time."

I did, but it took weeks. Finally Father's patience with me snapped. He culled a pile of fillers clipped from other newspapers, chose two, and handed them to me. "Set these," he ordered, and I knew by his tone of voice that something was up. I began to set the first one, about flies and fly screens. I had set almost a stickful of type from it before I saw Father watching me with an almost malicious gleam. Then I saw all those "flies" in the copy, every one of them calling for the "fl" logotype. I made the corrections before I emptied the stick, and watched every line from there on. And the second piece was about offices and officials, full of "ffi's." By the time I had finished with those two pieces of copy I knew where the logotype boxes were, and I never forgot. I still remember— they are right up *there!*

So I learned to set type, which then was basic to the printer's trade. It was a skill that then dated back about 450 years, to Johann Gutenberg and his first movable type, the beginning of modern printing. It was a dying craft even when I learned it, already giving way to the machine; and today more complex machines and even computers have taken over. The skill of setting type by hand is now a lost art except for a few special purposes. But I learned it, and in the learning I also learned about grammar, syllabification, punctuation and spelling, probably more than I ever learned in school. Father never finished the eighth grade in school, but he was a remarkably good speller, knew all the basic rules of grammar, was meticulous about punctuation, and was a firm disciplinarian about word division and punctuation. He was one of the few people I ever knew who actually studied the dictionary. An avid and critical reader, he had an uncanny sense of words and a large vocabulary. Yet in his occasional editorials he wrote simple, forceful English that was pared to the bone. He got a basic education at the type case, broadened it with books and magazines, and was both articulate and informed. He gave me the rudiments of strength and clarity as a writer.

Mother never learned to set type. She suggested it, but Father said no. He must have known she had neither the patience nor the temperament for it. Instead, she learned to use the typewriter and typed the local news she gathered by telephone. In odd moments I too learned to use that old green Oliver which to Father was simply "The Mill." He also learned to use it, but to the end of its life a few years later he fought with it, hammered it, cursed it, detested it. The only reason he used it was that his own handwriting was almost illegible, even to him.

The Oliver was a strange typewriter. From the front it looked something like a grinning dog with upthrust ears and, grotesquely, three rows of white teeth. The ears were the twin banks of type bars, one bank on each side. The three rows of teeth were the three rows of keys. It had only three rows instead of the conventional typewriter's four because it was a "dual-shift" machine. When you used one shift key it printed capitals. When you used the other shift key it printed numerals and punctuation marks. In use, it sounded like a miniature threshing machine. I never saw an Oliver with a ribbon that wasn't red and blue, though there must have been red-and-black ribbons and perhaps all-black ribbons too. Half the copy I set was typed in blue, the other half in red. Mother used the blue part till it wore dim, then shifted to the red part and wore it out before she put on a new ribbon. After all, new ribbons cost 35 cents each.

When I had learned the case well enough to be of some help, Father taught me to feed press. Today such work is done automatically. There were automatic-feed presses even then, but not in small-town newspaper offices. Again, I learned the old craft, which required that every sheet be put into the press by hand, imprinted, then taken out. This was called press feeding. It wasn't a complicated job, but it called for coordination, timing and rhythm. A good, fast press feeder was likely to find a job open in any busy print shop.

Both of Father's presses were platen presses, machines with big iron jaws that opened and closed with a simple mechanism of cogs and lever arms. A form of type was locked on the back jaw of the press where the soft rollers, gathering ink from the ink fountain at the top, came down and inked the type for each impression. The front jaw, or platen, had movable guides to hold the paper in position as it was inserted, sheet by sheet. When the jaws closed, the sheet was printed. When they opened, the printed sheet was taken out and a fresh sheet inserted. All you had to do, once the type was set and the form locked in the press, was start the press, put the sheets in one at a time with your right hand, take each sheet out a moment later with your left hand, pile them on the shelf immediately in front of you, and do this over and over. A good press feeder could do this unbelievably fast. Thirty impressions a minute were not unusual. I have known my father to print a thousand letterheads in half an hour and seem to loaf while he was doing it.

He started me on billheads for the office. He set the type, locked it in the chase, put the chase on the press, set the guide on the platen, and printed a few sheets. Then he turned the job over to me. "Just remember two things. Don't try to hurry —you've got plenty of time. And don't get your fingers caught.

If a sheet looks crooked when you put it in, let it go. Don't *ever* reach in after it. Paper's cheap, but you can't buy new fingers."

I took his place, leaning against the ledge for the finished sheets. I moistened the fingers of my right hand, set the first sheet in place, and let in the clutch. The press closed, opened, and I took out the printed sheet with my left hand. But I forgot to put in a fresh sheet. I reached desperately for the throw-off lever, which would prevent an impression, and missed it in my haste.

"All right," Father said, letting out the clutch and slowing the press. "You missed. Get some benzene on a rag and wash the platen. Then try again."

I washed the platen, washed my hands, and started over. That time I printed three sheets before I missed, and that time I reached the throw-off lever. I was hurrying, unsure of myself.

Father shut off the motor and hooked up the treadle on the press. "Try kicking it. You can make it go as slow as you want until you get the hang of it. Now watch."

I stepped aside. He started the press very slowly, pushing the treadle with his right foot, and he moved his hands so deliberately that I couldn't fail to see every motion. His right hand was sliding a fresh sheet into place even as his left hand removed the one just printed. "Rhythm," he said. "That's all there is to it. Making your hands work together even though they are doing different things. Now you take it again. But not too slow. That spoils the rhythm."

I began to get it. The rhythm came, a rhythm dictated by the press itself. And the amazing thing was that once I had the rhythm it was easier to feed press fast than slow. The hands fell into the rhythm almost automatically.

Many years later I went into a small-town print shop to buy manuscript paper, and the owner was hand-feeding letterheads on a job press much like those my father had. I watched for a few minutes and, on impulse, asked, "Do you mind if I see if I still remember how to feed press?"

He stepped aside and I took his place. I missed three sheets out of the first ten. Then I caught the rhythm and fed close to a hundred sheets without a miss. That was enough. I stepped back, and the printer asked, "How long has it been since you fed press?"

"Thirty years or more."

He nodded and smiled. "The hands don't forget."

So I learned to set type and feed press, in those years of my apprenticeship—years, I say, though I know it was really only that one summer. I worked and learned, and raised my basic pay from one dollar a week to two dollars and a half. I advanced from the status of printer's devil to that of a real apprentice. I was on my way to learning the trade.

And along the way I learned many other things, for Father was an expert printer. He had special skills at handling color and making layouts. Before he was married he worked for a year or two as an itinerant printer all over eastern Nebraska and western Iowa, and the year I was five he was a traveling salesman and job printing advisor for a printing supply house in Omaha. From him I learned to lay out advertisements as well as special job printing. I learned to coordinate type faces, to appreciate the value of white space, to mix colors, to be cautious with color and thus gain emphasis.

Because that little shop in Flagler had a limited amount of display type, I learned to make extra letters for the big wood-type display font by gluing linoleum to wooden cut bases and carving out the letters with a sharp pocket knife. I learned how to cast new ink rollers with a mixture of glycerine and molasses. I learned the formula for tabbing glue. I learned how to overlay and underlay and mask to get special effects on the job press.

I wondered where Father learned all these things. He

laughed. "When you've knocked around as many shops as I have, you pick up lots of tricks and shortcuts. There are some mighty good printers in country shops, as well as some awful dubs. But some of the best printers I ever knew were tramp printers."

Tramp printers, as he called them, were a breed even then beginning to vanish. They were itinerants, men with itchy feet, and a good many of them were addicted to the bottle. They drifted from place to place, usually riding the freight trains like ordinary hoboes. But, as Father said, some of them were first-class printers—just as long as they were sober. Too often, however, they would work only long enough to buy new clothes and a bottle of liquor. Then they would go on a binge, sober up enough to climb into a freight car, and be on their way again.

From time to time one of them would appear at the *News* office, usually when he was thrown off a train by a hardhearted brakeman or conductor. Few itinerant printers would have stopped in Flagler otherwise. He would come shuffling down the steps, hesitant, dirty if not ragged, unshaven and often bleary-eyed. He would pause at the doorway, stiffen his shoulders, fight off the hangdog look, and come inside. If Mother was at the desk she would give him one cold look—she seemed to sense a tramp printer's identity even before he opened his mouth—and say, "If you're looking for a handout you can look somewhere else." That usually turned the man on his heel and got rid of him. But now and then it backfired.

One afternoon a seedy-looking man in old dusty clothes and with several days' beard came in, and she gave him the cold look and the curt dismissal. But this man stood his ground, smiled at her, then looked around for Father. Father saw him, called out, "Hello, John!" and came to the front of the office to shake hands. He introduced the man to Mother, who still watched him with cold suspicion, and the seedy-looking visitor gave Father an order for twenty-five dollars' worth of printing. He was, Father explained after he had left, a sheep rancher from thirty miles south of town, and he and his herders had just trailed a flock of fifteen hundred lambs to town to ship to Kansas City, a consignment that probably would net him around twelve thousand dollars.

But now and then a tramp printer appeared when Mother wasn't in the office. He would come in, look around, see Father at the stone or the job press, and ask, "Need a printer?" Father would stop what he was doing, talk for a few minutes, point out that his was a one-man shop, and suggest that there might be work in Limon or Burlington. And always he gave the man either money or a credit slip for a meal and a bath and shave, then tried to hurry him out before Mother returned.

The day came, inevitably, when Mother came back just as the seedy printer was pocketing the money and thanking Father. She stood bristling while the man, sensing trouble, hurried out. Then she turned to Father. "So, you gave him a handout." There was both anger and bitterness in her voice.

"Yes, I gave him the price of a meal."

"If you're so free with your money—" Mother hesitated, seeing the set of Father's jaw. He seldom crossed her, but when he did he couldn't be budged. Now he reached into his pocket, drew out a half dollar, and held it out to her. She refused to take it, turned away, and went to the desk, flushed and bristling. He followed her, tossed the coin onto the desk in front of her, and went back to work at the stone.

"That's not what I meant!" Mother exclaimed.

Father didn't answer.

"He's just another booze-fighting tramp printer!"

Father looked at her and asked, his voice low but tense, "How do you know what he is? You didn't even talk to him."

"I could tell just by looking at him!"

Father shook his head. He worked quietly for a few minutes, then asked, "Remember where it says in the Bible, 'Cast thy bread upon the waters'?"

"What do you mean by that?"

"I mean that some day my own son may be hungry and out of a job. I hope that if he goes into a print shop and asks for work and there isn't any work for him, the boss will give *him* the price of a meal. That's what I mean."

"Oh." Mother bit her lip, fighting back the angry words. She probably had just paid the interest on the loan at the bank and knew how little money there was in that tin box in the vault. She may have been wishing she could afford a new dress, or that Father could buy a new suit. I know there wasn't any extra money that summer for new clothes, sometimes barely enough to buy groceries. She fought down the angry words, blinked back the tears, and began to type, furiously banging the old Oliver's keys. Slowly she worked out her anger.

Half an hour later Father went to the desk, picked up the half dollar still lying there, and handed it to her. "I wish you'd get some round steak for supper," he said quietly. "We haven't had a good piece of steak in quite a while. Steak and gravy and fried potatoes would taste awfully good."

He went back to work, and a few minutes later Mother put on her coat and left. We had fried steak and milk gravy and fried potatoes for supper, and not another word was said about tramp printers.

The summer passed and I served out my apprenticeship. I learned the basic skills of the printer's trade, which I would polish and improve over the next few years until I became a competent journeyman by the time I had finished high school. It was a long summer, the way I remember it, ten hours a day, six days a week, the same hours that Father worked. What hours were left for that other boy, that other self who had afternoons off and even whole days of freedom? I can't say, exactly. That other self lived another life, and this chapter is about the printer's devil, the young apprentice who started the summer getting one dollar a week, and not even worth that, and ended the summer getting three dollars a week and worth twice that, Father said proudly. Mother heard him say it, and she said, "Maybe so, Will. But if you remember, you were only making ten dollars a week when we were married." Father smiled and said, "That was more than sixteen years ago. Times change." Then he turned to me. "Son, you could hold an apprentice job in almost any print shop now. Another year and you'll be worth fifteen dollars a week, maybe more than that in a city shop."

That was one of the proudest days I could remember.

6

Meanwhile—life is full of meanwhiles; that's what makes it so difficult to tell the whole truth—I was discovering myself and that new world around me. As I found the twin arrowheads, and the snakes, and the strange rocks on Kit Carson Hill.

It was the last Friday in June. The paper was printed for that week and I had the whole day off. Mother asked what I was going to do and I said I didn't know, maybe go down to the river and hunt arrowheads. She made two bread-and-butter sandwiches for me and said, "Just be home in time for supper." I put the sandwiches in a paper sack, tucked it inside my shirt, told Fritz I didn't even want him along, and set out on my bike on the road east, the road to Seibert. I didn't know why, but I knew I had to go alone and find whatever it was I was looking for.

It was almost eight o'clock. The sun was nearly four hours high, but the night's coolness, typical of the High Plains, still hung in the air, especially in the hollows. It was a graded country road but it followed the contours of the land, and when I coasted down a slope into a hollow it was like easing into a cool stream. But the hilltops were already warming up and I knew that by noon it would be a brassy-hot day. The sky was a vast blue bowl that sat on the horizon without a tree or a mountain to dent its rim.

On the high ground the meadow larks were singing. They probably had stuffed themselves with chilled beetles and grasshoppers and now they perched on fence posts and whistled loudly. Their breasts were gleaming yellow and the V's on their chests were coal black. As they sang they lifted their heads, opened their long beaks, and seemed to stand on tiptoe, putting their very hearts into it. By afternoon they wouldn't make a sound. They would hunt the shade, even the shade of a fence post, and stand with wings half spread, beaks agape. Then, just before sundown, when the cool returned, they would sing again.

In the road and at the roadside the horned larks were feeding on weed seeds or taking dust baths. They rose in front of me, half a dozen at a time, twittering as they spiraled upward, a good many of them young, of that year's broods, without the yellow throat-patches of adults. They were past their peak of song by then. Earlier they had sung beautifully as they spiraled high, a sweet, warbly song that seemed to spill out of the very sky.

The plains were just beginning to show the bronze of ripening buffalo grass, later than usual because of the wet spring that had made such a good wheat crop. Another few weeks and they would be tawny. But the roadside had its bright green fringe, Russian thistles not yet gone to seed, resin weed with its gummy green foliage and inconspicuous yellow flowers, and, in the sandy places, prickly poppies and sand verbenas. The verbenas sprawled along the ground and lifted fragrant white clumps of blossom as big as baseballs. We called the prickly poppies fried-egg flowers because with their overlapping white petals and big polleny-yellow centers they looked very much like fried eggs. They were true poppies, though their light silvery-green foliage and stems were thickly set with prickles as long and sharp as those on bull thistles.

I stopped to look at a clump of verbenas and smell their almost too-sweet fragrance, and was surprised to see how many bees and ants were already busy there. Still stiff with the night chill, the ants walked like arthritic old men and the bees had to sit in the sun and flex their wings before they could fly away with a load of pollen. There were half a dozen kinds of bees, from tiny black ones to brown-and-gold ones as big as honeybees. I wondered where they lived and where they stored their honey. Probably, I decided, underground like bumblebees, maybe in ground-squirrel holes. Some day, I thought, I would try to follow them and find a honey hoard. I tried several times, that summer and the next, but I never found a High Plains bee's nest.

I rode on, singing inside. The world was a good place to be, and it was all mine that morning. Or I was the world's. It didn't matter which. It wasn't a matter of ownership; it was a matter of being, of belonging. I belonged right where I was.

Two miles from town I passed a wheat field, a quarter section, half a mile square, where the sod had been plowed the previous autumn and seeded to winter wheat. It stood almost three feet tall, gleaming in the morning sun, gently rippling like a golden sea as a few breaths of breeze crept over it. The bearded heads were four inches long and heavy with fat kernels, the bumper crop everyone in town was talking about. Another week and the harvesters would move in, begin to reap the precious grain. Not only here and in a similar field half a mile down the road, but north of Flagler where dozens of such fields rippled in the sun.

I rode slowly past the wheat, marveling, wondering what Flagler would look like with harvested wheat overflowing the elevator bins and piled in vacant lots like huge ant hills of golden grain. Then I went on, toward the river. Wheat was a money crop, tamed, domesticated; and that day I was wild and free, an untamed wanderer without a nickel in his pocket or a care on his mind.

The river was five miles east of town. It was called the Republican river, but it wasn't a river at all. It was just a broad valley with a gravelly run winding through and no flowing water except at the height of the spring melt or after a summer cloudburst. It was supposed to have a stream of underground water, and the occasional long, narrow, willow-lined water holes in the dry river bed seemed to prove it. The only flowing water was at Crystal Springs, in the hills north of the road just before one came to the river valley. It was one of the few springs in the whole area, sweet water that bubbled from a rocky ledge and fed a small pond whose overflow became a narrow creek that wound down into the big valley and in turn fed one of the river's bigger water holes. A wagon trail angled across the flats from the main road to the spring.

Little Doc Williams had told me about Crystal Springs. He and Spider Miner and I were going out there some day and catch bullfrogs. But we hadn't got around to it, and this morning when I came to the wagon trail I knew I had to go there alone. I started to ride down the trail but soon knew that I would have to leave my bike and go on afoot. That hilltop was one of the few places around where cactus throve, an old sheep range that had been overgrazed a few years before and taken over by grizzly-bear and prickly-pear cactus. The past few wet years had begun to restore the grass, but the cactus persisted. Most of it was grizzly-bear, as we called it, with grayish-green pads and covered with white-tipped spines that glistened frostily in the morning sun. The few clumps of prickly-pear were greener, less thorny, and had bigger fruit. All the cactus had bloomed early, with the wet spring, and the fruits, big as a man's thumb, were beginning to show touches of red ripeness. A few more weeks and those fruits would be apple-red and juicy, those of the prickly-pear reddest and juiciest by far, but all of them so full of ivory-hard seeds that they were hardly worth eating.

There was too much cactus for bicycle tires. Those thorns could penetrate even a heavy work shoe. So I left my bike beside the trail and walked, watching for snakes. Where there was cactus there usually were rattlers, and on a morning like this they probably would be sunning themselves in the trail's warm dust. By afternoon they would be out in the grass and in the shade of the cactus clumps. Sure enough, as I rounded a sharp turn in the trail I saw a huge silvery snake writhing and rippling just ahead of me. I leaped back. But when I looked again the snake floated right up out of the trail and into a clump of cactus. It caught on the thorns for a moment, then ripped loose and was blown away, no snake at all but the cast skin of a snake five feet long and big around as my arm. I caught my breath, but my heart still thumped. It was a warning. Snakes were molting, and molting rattlers sometimes strike without warning. I walked on warily.

Half a mile from the road I came to the crest of a slight rise and saw the whole rolling panorama of the river valley: high rounded hills, deep valleys, and the shadowed line of still higher hills beyond the river. Just to the right of due east and beyond the river was Kit Carson Hill, highest of all.

I went down the slope to the brink of the sandstone ledge. It was a sheer drop of about fifteen feet, and below it a little valley widened into a hollow several hundred yards long where a pond of clear, sweet water rippled and glistened in the sunlight. The far side of the pond was fringed with willow brush and cattails, with a few scraggly cottonwoods lifting their green heads above the brush. The near side was mostly grass and reeds. At the foot of the ledge, just beneath me, where the spring bubbled and whispered and fed its constant flow of water into the pond, was a thicket of poison ivy, its glossy leaves deceptively inviting. It was the only poison ivy in the whole area and probably was planted there by the droppings of birds from better-watered places far away.

I sat on the grass at the brink of the ledge and watched a dozen killdeers on a sand bar just off the near shore. They bobbed, ran about, fed on small insects, peeped; and now and then one would leap into the air, crying *kill-dee, kill-deee-dee-dee*, circle the pond on graceful wings, and return to the sand bar. Beyond them, at the far side of the pond, half a dozen ducks came out of the reeds, mallard drakes with gleaming green heads and canvasback drakes with heads exactly the color of a sorrel horse. They swam about, upending grotesquely from time to time to feed on something at the shallow bottom. The females apparently were hiding back in the reeds, with their ducklings.

At the lower end of the pond were several grebes—we called them hell-divers or mud hens. I thought there were four, but there may have been more. They were diving, and a hell-diver can swim a long way under water, and every time I tried to count them one would disappear and another would bob up somewhere else. High overhead a big hawk was circling, just floating without a wingbeat. I watched it, expecting it to come rocketing down and catch a duck. But it just floated there, in a great circle. But even as I watched the hawk, something swept in, seemed to brush the treetops, and climbed again with a blackbird in its talons. It was a prairie falcon. I knew it by its sharp wings and the light color underneath, almost white except for black patches at the base of the wings. I hadn't even seen the blackbird in the cottonwood.

I sat there half an hour, maybe even an hour—time had no meaning—watching, feeling the warmth of the sun, smelling the water and the reeds, which had such a different smell from that of cactus and buffalo grass. Then two big green-bodied dragon flies came and hovered not two feet in front of me, seeming to look at me with those huge dark eyes. A dragon fly can make you feel very foolish, just hovering and looking at you, maybe because they have been around so much longer than man has. In the fossil beds at Florissant, Colorado, they have found dragon flies at least 250 million years old. Those two hovered and stared at me, and I stared back a little while, then gave up, got to my feet, and followed the path down around the ledge to the pond. It was a cowpath probably made by the buffalo long before the cattle came, a very old path, worn right into the soft rock.

I went down through the reeds, and big frogs leaped into the water with wet *clunks* and the ducks swam back among the reeds on the far side. I wasn't wanted there, wasn't needed. I was an intruder. I was about to turn back when a strange quivering shook the grass and I saw a big dark-brown water snake. It moved a little way, stopped, seemed to shiver its whole length, then moved on again. Then I saw its head. A big green frog's leg dangled from its mouth, still twitching, and its throat was swollen to twice its normal size. It shivered again, a kind of gulping convulsion, and the frog's leg disappeared and the lump in its throat moved a few inches. I remembered the day on the homestead when I saw a big bull snake swallowing a half-grown prairie dog. It gulped the same way, a convulsion that ran all the way to its tail, and the prairie dog's tail disappeared.

The water snake saw me and turned and glided into the pond, making hardly a ripple. And I thought how dragon flies eat flies and gnats, frogs eat dragon flies, snakes eat frogs. I wondered what eats snakes. Hawks, maybe, though I never saw that happen.

I had seen enough. I went back up the path and back along the trail to where I had left my bike. As I leaned over to pick it up I saw an arrowhead, a perfect red chert point an inch and a half long. I admired it and put it into my pocket, and as I wheeled my bike back to the road I wondered if it had been a Cheyenne or an Arapaho who had shot that arrow, what he shot with it, where he came from, where he went. I wondered if he had sat on the ledge above the spring and been stared at by a dragon fly.

It was past midmorning and warming up. The meadow larks had stopped singing. I rode on east and came to the crest of the long hill that flanked the river. The valley made a big curve there below me and ran almost due north before turning northeast again, toward the northwest corner of Kansas where the river became a flowing stream, a real river. I coasted down the long hill, trailing a cloud of dust, and crossed the gravelly dry wash on the narrow concrete slab that gave solid footing for cars and wagons. There was no bridge, just that concrete slab, over which the periodic flood waters could wash harmlessly. Beyond, the road wound around the slope of Kit Carson Hill and up through a gap to the flats again, on the far side of the river.

I was going to climb Kit Carson Hill, but first I explored the dry watercourse. Stones have their own fascination, especially stream-bed stones. Every stone was once a part of something bigger, something that time has worn down to a hard, round kernel, smoothed and polished by the years. Most of the stones there were about the size of hen's eggs, with a few as big as a man's fist and an occasional one big as a man's head. All were rounded, water-worn and shaped by each other. And they were of all colors, reds, yellows, whites, grays, browns, like a vast tray of gigantic beads waiting to be drilled and strung.

I walked upstream, then down, marveling. And searching. I was looking for something I knew I wouldn't find—a stone hammer, a stone axe, a spear point. Among so many stones, there just might be something a man had shaped to his own use. But if there ever had been one there it would have been worn and ground beyond all recognition by time and travel, all human marks wiped away. It was like looking for Indian pony tracks in the grass, and I knew it. But I kept looking, for somehow I was a part of that dry watercourse, a part that partook by being there, by walking on those stones.

Then I had looked long enough. The sun had passed the meridian, the nooning. I took my bike and went up the road that wound out of the valley, up the flank of Kit Carson Hill. I knew I had come, not to see Crystal Springs or the river bed, but the hill itself. Legend said, or hearsay, that Kit Carson had used that hilltop for a lookout. What he looked for, I don't know. Buffalo, perhaps, or Indians, or maybe just the horizon. Kit Carson, to me at least, was a man who might have looked at the horizon, or the clouds, or the stars, as the Indians looked at them, as a part of the universe to be known and valued for themselves. Anyway, that was the story, and if one were the kind of skeptic who said that Carson's Colorado home was at La Junta, near Bent's old fort, a hundred miles south of Flagler, or that he was more mountain man than plainsman, that made no difference. This was Kit Carson's hill, tradition said, and sometimes tradition is more real than fact.

I rode until the hill became too steep, then pushed my bike until I was just below the crest. There I left the bike and quit the road. It was a stiff climb, up a steep slope carpeted with buffalo grass and with a scattering of soapweed clumps. Then I reached the top, a rounded knoll perhaps fifty yards across, where the grass was thin and the soil gravelly. And on the very crest of the knoll was a rough square, about ten feet on a side, outlined with chunks of reddish sandstone each about a foot square. It wasn't a foundation or the remains of one, and it was not a tumbled wall. Just those rough sandstone blocks, half buried in the grass, in an irregular square. They had been there a long time. To this day I do not know who put them there, or when, or why. But in that square was a flower garden, fifteen or twenty low-growing, dusty-green plants with clusters of brick-red, five-petaled blossoms. They were flowers we knew as wild geraniums or cowboy's delight. Eventually I learned that the botanical name is *Malvastrum coccineum*, that it is a member of the mallow family and distant cousin of the hollyhock. The plant seldom grows more than six inches high and the flowers are only about an inch across. But there they were, those wild geraniums, as I then knew them, in full bloom. And they were the only ones on that whole hilltop.

I stared at the square outlined by those stones and at the brick-red blossoms, wondering, marveling. Then I turned and looked out and away. In every direction I could see the horizon.

Below me was the river valley, broad and deep. Beyond, to the west, was the smudge that was Flagler, recognizable only by the upthrust of the grain elevator; and far beyond that western horizon were the mountains. To the north the valley disappeared beyond its flanking hills, angling northeast again; and beyond those hills and flats to the north, a hundred miles away, lay the valley of the Platte. To the east were the gently rolling uplands that slowly fell away, bronzing green flats that sloped gently into Kansas and all across Kansas to the Missouri. To the south were the flats again, reaching beyond the horizon and all the way to the valley of the Arkansas. On that southern horizon lay a dark cloud mass, the only cloud in the sky.

I was on top of the world. It reached away in all directions, out and away.

I was hungry. I sat down beside the rectangle of stones and began to eat my sandwiches. The only sound was the soft *shhhhhh* of the breeze in the grass around me. Then a hawk, perhaps the one I had seen circling over Crystal Springs, began to scream, a faint, faraway, *kaa-kaa-kaa*, and I looked up and saw it high overhead, a gnat-size dot against the sky.

My eyes were dazzled, for the sun was only an hour past midday. I lay back on the grass and closed my eyes, but the dazzle persisted, lightning against my eyelids. I covered my eyes with one arm and gradually the lightning faded. I felt the warm earth beneath my shoulder blades. I was one with the earth, like the grass. I had been there forever, since grass grew, since the ocean went away, since the stones in the dry river bed were ledges on the distant mountains. I drifted off to sleep.

Thunder wakened me, violent, crashing thunder. I sat up, bewildered, not knowing where I was. The sky was dark, the air hot and tense. A flash of lightning ripped the clouds off to the southwest, and an instant later another thunder crash shook the earth beneath me. The southern horizon had vanished. In its place was a gray curtain that seemed to hang from the boiling, greenish-gray cloud mass that towered to the very zenith. The band of cloud I had seen before I slept had built up to one of those violent High Plains thunderstorms that are like the very wrath of the gods.

I watched in awe, wincing each time another crashing peal of thunder jolted the hills. The wind freshened into gusts, now damp and cool. The gray curtain advanced swiftly, blotted out the second line of hills, and I heard a faint, distant roar. I was going to get wet. I got to my feet, debated whether to stay there on the hilltop and take it or to head for home. Then I realized that a cloudburst up the valley would send a flash flood boiling down the river bed. Unless I got across before it came I would be marooned, unable to get home until the flood went down, maybe overnight.

I hurried down the hillside toward my bike, barely able to keep my feet on the steep slope. Halfway down I tripped and fell, and got to my knees and saw that I had fallen over an old buffalo skull half buried in the sod. My foot had tripped on the peeling black horn and torn the skull from its bed. It lay there, one gaping eye socket seeming to stare at me. And in the uprooted sod was something that looked like a dark clot of blood. I scuffed it with my toe. It was an arrowhead, red chert and intact, a companion of the one I had found beside the trail to Crystal Springs. I picked it up, compared the two. They were mates, line for line, almost flake for flake; they must have been made by the same hand, from the same stone, perhaps were shot from the same bow.

A spatter of cold rain splashed my face. I heard a roar from up the valley. Thrusting the two arrowheads into my pocket, I ran on down the hill. The rain came in a sheet before I reached my bike, but I got on, pedaled furiously, and raced down the road toward the concrete slab. Half blinded by the downpour, I almost missed the slab. Then I was on it, the first lap of water already spilling over it. The water sprayed

from my wheels, but I kept going, reached the far side, struck
the muddy road beyond, and lost control completely. Down I
went, flat in the mud. And got up, the roar of rushing water
close behind me, and pushed my bike on up the slope another
fifty yards. Then I looked back and saw the wall of water three
feet high and still rising, as it boiled over the concrete crossing
and went rolling on downstream.

I plodded up the hill, pushing my bike. The rain roared, but
even louder was the roar of the flash flood I had just escaped.
The road was sloshing mud, creeks rushing down its edges. I
was soaked to the skin. Then the chill came, icy chill, and the
first burst of hail. The stones, about the size of marbles,
bruised and stung. They whitened the air for a few minutes,
then let up, then came again. Three waves of hail, and the
rain in between was almost as cold and bruising as the hail,
for it came with gusts of wind that almost took me off my
feet.

And finally I was at the hilltop and the hail had passed.
The rain still beat down, but the gusting wind had eased.
Hail lay in white drifts in the buffalo grass, washed like foam
in the roadside streams of runoff. Up on the flats again, I tried
to ride my bike, but the road was slick with mud. After two
falls I gave up and walked, my shoes sloshing at every step.

I walked a weary mile, and the storm eased, the rain slackened. Lightning still flashed, but distant now, off to the northeast, and the thunder was a distant rumbling growl. The sky
began to clear on the southwestern horizon. A faint mist
hung over the flats, fog rising from the hail still there in the
grass. Then the sun burst through and the whole world was
dazzling, fresh washed and gleaming clean.

The road was still too muddy to ride. I trudged on, warm
again after the cold drenching. I came to a place where the
road was barely damp and rode for almost a mile, exulting.
Then I came to mud again, and rifts of hail in the grass. And
just ahead was the first roadside wheat field. What had been a

wheat field that morning, rather. Now it was a hail-beaten scene of devastation. That golden sea of grain was gone, the stalks downed and beaten into the soil. As far as I could see, there wasn't an acre of wheat still standing. What hadn't been hailed into the ground had been knocked down by the wind and beaten into the mud by the driving rain.

I went on, and saw a meadow lark at the roadside, bedraggled and dead, stoned to death by the hail. I saw another. Then I saw a horned lark trying desperately to fly with a broken wing. I tried to catch it, put it out of its misery, but it got away in the roadside weeds. I passed the second wheat field, not quite as completely devastated as the first one but so wind-blown and rain-beaten that it was scarcely worth harvesting.

After I passed the second wheat field I came to drier road and was able to ride again, and the closer to town I got, the less rain they had had. My bike was kicking up dust the last mile into town.

It was almost six o'clock when I got home. Mother was cooking supper. She looked at me and said, "Aren't you a mess! You must have got caught in the storm."

"I was," I said.

"We got an awful thunderstorm, just awful. But not much rain, just a sprinkle. It got so cold I thought we were going to get hail."

"They had hail, out east of town," I said.

"They did?" She sighed. "Well, get washed up and change your clothes. Supper's almost ready and you can't come to the table looking like that. I don't know what's keeping your father, but he should be here any minute."

I washed, put on a clean shirt and clean overalls, and we waited. It was half past six before Father came home, walking like a very tired man, his shoulders sagging. He came in, saw me, and said, "I'm glad to see you here. I hear they got a bad storm out along the river."

I said yes, it rained awfully hard, and there was a lot of hail. I wasn't telling about how I crossed the river just ahead of the flash flood.

He kissed Mother and went to hang up his coat and hat. When he came back he said, "I guess they got hailed out up north. Clarence Smith just told me he heard the storm swung out across the wheat country up there and practically wiped them out."

He didn't say anything about the harvest or the bumper crop that was going to overflow the elevator and put money into everybody's pocket. But it was all right there in his eyes, the pain and hurt and disappointment. He had so wanted Flagler to boom and prosper, and it wasn't going to boom that year.

Mother saw it too. She said, "Supper's on the table. Let's eat. If they got hailed out, they'll have to do what they've done before. They'll make out, somehow. So will we."

7

The heartbreaking thing about hail is that it wipes you out in the passing of a cloud. It is worse than drouth or grasshoppers, the other scourges of the High Plains, because it waits till you've built big hopes and dreams, then wipes them out in one devastating stroke.

Drouth doesn't raise your hopes, really. You plant your wheat in late summer, watch it sprout and stool out before snow comes. It winters over and starts to grow again, like the grass, in the warmth of early spring. But the spring rains peter out and drouth sets in. Week after week the wheat stands there, slowly turning yellow, never making growth, never heading. Then it withers and is gone, and you say, "Next year."

Or if it's grasshoppers, they usually come early, before the wheat is fully headed, before the kernels have begun to fill, and they cut it down stalk by stalk, day by day, not all at once. You keep hoping that maybe tomorrow the grasshoppers will die or move on and you will get half a crop, or a third of a crop, or at least enough to pay for your seed. But they stay and your hopes die slowly as the grasshoppers keep gnawing away. And one day there isn't any wheat left, and again you say, "Next year."

But hail waits till the wheat is tall and golden with ripeness, the heads full and the kernels fat, the wealth right there, only a week or two away from harvest. You can almost hear the dollars clinking in your pocket. Then that greenish cloud comes and the air turns cold as November and the lightning rips the sky apart. Between lightning flashes it is as dark as dusk. It starts to rain, slashing rain, and you stand in the doorway and watch the dark rain turn to a white curtain coming across the fields. You hear it coming and you know nothing in God's world can stop it. It comes across the wheat fields with a deafening roar and across the farmyard and on across the fields beyond. And when it has passed you go out and walk across the yard, the ice crunching underfoot, hail sometimes the size of peas, sometimes big as hen's eggs. You see but don't notice the chickens stoned to death. You see the broken windows and the splintered shingles on the roof, and you don't notice them either. You are looking at the devastated fields, the beaten, ragged wheat fields now covered with hail, devastation that came and passed, ruin complete, in ten minutes. Half an hour ago you had a half section of wheat, 320 acres, maybe twelve or thirteen thousand dollars' worth of wheat, ready to harvest and haul to town. Now you haven't got a penny and you owe the bank twenty-five hundred dollars, plus interest, due the first day of October. Now you are broke and in debt. You have half a dozen cows and a team of horses and maybe two dozen chickens still alive, and you've got your wagon and plow and seeder. You've got a leaky roof and broken windows. And a wife who says, "I don't see why we keep on farming when things like this happen. I so hoped this year—" And she begins to cry. You are filled with weariness, bone tired, and there's a nauseating gripe in your belly, a wrenching at your heart. You can already taste the mush and beans you'll have to live on next winter. But you'll try again. You know that. You'll go to the bank and try to get another loan to pay for seed wheat, pledging your land because there's nothing else left to pledge, not one blessed thing.

That's hail. That's what hail does to a man. That's what it did to a good many of the farmers up in the North Country. Not all of them. Some would salvage half a crop, a few hadn't been hurt at all, and some of those who were wiped out had hail insurance, maybe ten or fifteen dollars an acre, enough to pay for seed and a few sacks of flour and beans to eat. But at most there wouldn't be more than half the total crop everyone had been counting on, even counting the scattered fields of wheat west of town that hadn't even been touched by the storm.

Harvest was begun the next week, but even when it was in full swing there was no steady stream of trucks to town with wheat for the elevators. It came, truckload after truckload, but with plenty of room between trucks for the dust to settle.

At first people didn't want to talk about it, as though it were a bad dream from which they would wake up to a golden tomorrow. But by the time most of the new wheat had been harvested, the worst of the shock had been absorbed. A few could even joke about it. W. E. Hall, who owned the big general store, said he had to send back a whole order of men's trousers for alterations. "I had them made up special, with outsize buckskin pockets for all those silver dollars. Now I've sent them back to have the pockets changed to plain muslin and half size, for nickels and dimes."

There was some money, of course, but even those who had good harvests weren't spending it lavishly. A few weeks earlier the farmers had been buying canned goods by the case, peaches, corn, beans, tomatoes. Now even those with money bought things a few cans at a time, and the bulk of their buying was of dry beans, flour, cornmeal and salt pork.

Several storekeepers stopped advertising in the *News*. They had stocked up for a boom that went bust and now, they said, they had to pull in their belts. They couldn't afford to advertise. Father tried to tell them they couldn't afford not to advertise at a time like this. "Cut prices, sell your overstock, at cost if necessary, and get your money back. Be ready for next year."

"I've got my stock for next year," one storekeeper said with a wry smile. "I'll just keep it till I can sell at a profit. No use to advertise when nobody's buying."

"But people will buy," Father insisted, "if you make it look like a bargain and advertise, tell them about it."

"Buy with what?"

"Money," Father said. "There's money around. I saw quite a few truckloads of wheat coming in to town, and nobody gave it away. There isn't as much money as we expected, but there's money around. Those who have it, though, are going to hold onto it unless they see a bargain."

The storekeeper shook his head. "I can't afford to cut prices. And advertising's just a waste of money now."

"That's up to you," Father said. "But if I had ten or twenty thousand dollars tied up in stock I couldn't sell at a profit, I'd sacrifice the profit and get my money out, maybe put some of it out on loan at ten or twelve percent."

It was no use. The man cancelled his advertising and left.

The only merchant who listened was W. E. Hall, who owned the biggest store in town, the one upstairs over the *News* office. He listened to Father a few minutes, then said, "You don't have to persuade me, Will. All I want to know is whether you're ready yet to let me have that front-page ad."

Father didn't know quite what to say.

"I agree with you, right down the line," Mr. Hall went on. "I'm going to cut prices and move merchandise, and I want to tell folks about it in big type on the front page."

Father still hesitated. Like a good many of the wheat farmers, he had a mortgage coming due. And he didn't even have hail insurance to provide eatin' money, as they called it. "I'll have to think about that, Bill," he said. "My front page is for news."

"Look," Mr. Hall said, "my ad will be news. Folks will want to get the paper just to see what Bill Hall is going to do next. Everybody will want to subscribe."

"Not if you run the same ad in the *Progress*," Father said.

"I'm talking about an ad in the *News*," Mr. Hall said. "If we can get together I may decide I don't need to advertise anywhere else. What are you going to charge me for the bottom half of your front page?"

"For how long?"

"Every week for six months, to start. Till after Christmas. Then we'll take another look and see if it's worth going on."

Father was making quick mental calculations. "All right, I'll let you have that front-page position for just twice what the half page on the back is costing you."

Mr. Hall shook his head. "Too much, Will. I can't pay that and cut prices the way I want to. I've got to break even to stay in business. Tell you what I'll do. I'll pay half again what I'm paying for that ad on the back page now."

Father considered for a long moment, then said, "All right, it's a deal." He held out his hand and they shook hands on it.

Later, discussing it with Mother, Father said, "It will just about make up for the ads I've lost. Not quite, but almost. And unless I miss my guess, the ones who quit will be back before long. They can't hold out with Bill Hall making a big noise on the front page of the *News* every week."

But Father was wrong. The advertisers who quit didn't come back soon. Some of them didn't advertise again until just before Christmas; even then they took only token space, six-inch, two-column ads. But the circulation of the *News* did go up, as Mr. Hall had predicted. In his ads he listed a few specials every week, in big, bold type that nobody could miss. People came to town on Saturdays, to watch the crowds at the store if not to buy. In those days there were few automobiles, and it didn't cost a penny to come to town in a horse-drawn wagon or buggy.

Every week some of those people came down to the *News* office and said they would subscribe to the paper if Father would take eggs or butter or maybe a chicken or two in trade. Father was willing; but after the first couple of weeks Mother made a point of being at the office Saturday afternoons and handling all such trades. She seemed to know instinctively who made good butter, who would have fresh eggs; and she always did know a young, tender hen from a tough old biddy. She dealt and dickered, came to know most of the farmers and farm wives from up in the North Country. She kept the young hens, Father and I built a coop out of old packing cases and got a roll of chicken wire for a pen, and she soon had more chickens and eggs than we could use. So she began dealing off the tough old hens and the excess butter and eggs to Mr. Hall. He had an eye for attractive women, and he may have started taking that excess off her hands just to humor her, but he soon found that he had met his match as a bargainer. Father wouldn't haggle with anybody over nickels and dimes. "Waste a dollar's worth of time arguing over ten cents!" he snorted. But Mother would haggle over nickels and pennies, and so would Bill Hall. Sometimes their arguments seemed more important than the money, but Mother usually won.

Bill Hall had a kind of genius. It is hard to say whether the wheat crop failure brought it out in him or whether he was ready to bloom by then in any case. The advertising got results, but only because he had that touch of genius as a merchant, a combination of showmanship and business instinct.

He was a small, wiry, blond man who wore nose-glasses and looked more like a clerk in a business office than a merchant. But he was full of energy and bubbling with ideas. He had been in business in Flagler only a few years when we arrived and had just built up his store from a little dry-goods shop with a grocery counter into one of the best-stocked general stores in that end of Colorado. Like Father, he had borrowed from the bank to stock up for the expected boom. He couldn't sit back and wait for a good crop next year. He wasn't a man to sit back and wait, anyway.

The front of his store was stocked with women's wear, everything from silk stockings to hats, petticoats, and ready-made dresses, from yard goods to shoes and notions. A big alcove was given over to men's clothing, work clothes mostly, shirts, socks, shoes, overalls, jackets, underwear. And there were sample books from which a man could order a dress suit, made to measure, for $15, $17.50 or $20.

The whole back of the store was the grocery department, shelved to the ceiling and with counters clear across the store, a good sixty feet. Coffee came in hundred-pound bags and was ground in the big mill with twin red flywheels while you watched and sniffed. Dried beef came by the shank and was sliced, paper-thin, while you waited. Cheese came by the two-foot wheel and was wedged out with the big cheese knife, right there on the counter. There was a glassed case of candies, sold by the pound, and another glass case for cigars and chewing tobacco. Star and Horseshoe chewing tobacco came in slabs a foot long, half an inch thick, and was cut into plugs on a gummy miniature guillotine. Canned fruits and vegetables lined the shelves and were stacked in the basement storage room in cases, wooden cases stacked seven feet high. Dried prunes, apricots and raisins came in wooden boxes and were sold in bulk. Soda crackers came by the barrel and by the ten-pound box. Flour, sugar, dried beans, both the spotted Mexican beans and the white navies, were stored in huge piles of bags in the store room just back of the grocery shelves. And at the end of that back room was the big icebox, for meat and butter. It had to be iced every day, and ice had to be brought in by rail and was expensive. I doubt that more than five or six houses in town had their own iceboxes, and in the country there was no refrigeration at all since there were no ponds from which to cut winter ice and store it. Farmers, and townsmen who had come in from the farms and kept to country ways, ate fresh meat only in the winter. After hard frost in the fall they butchered a hog or two and maybe a young steer and had red meat until the spring thaw. The remainder of the year they ate cured meats, salt pork, bacon, ham, dried beef, bo-

logna, or barnyard poultry, usually chicken. The Hall store
dealt mostly in cured meat, but there always was a hind
quarter of beef for affluent townsmen who wanted an occasional round steak even in summer. Pork was strictly winter
meat. The old cattleman's prejudice against sheep in any form
carried over, even among newcomers; it would be another
fifteen or twenty years before you could buy lamb chops in
Flagler.

But otherwise you could get almost anything in Bill Hall's
store except heavy hardware and hard liquor. If there was
something you wanted and he didn't have, Bill Hall would get
it for you, or do his best. And when he got it he was so triumphant you had to be triumphant too. Instinctive showman
that he was, he shouted it from the housetops—and the front
page of the *News*. He did everything in those ads, as Mother
once said, except tell dirty stories. The most outlandish one
was the perfume ad he ran that fall. He must have bought a
case lot of perfume at a bargain, and he came to Father with
a fantastic idea. He wanted his front-page ad to be per-
fumed with that scent.

At first Father wanted none of it. "No, Bill, no! You know
what folks'll say, don't you?"

Mr. Hall laughed. "All right, so some men will say it smells
like a cat house. If they say that, their wives'll ask, 'How do
you know?' We'll start a lot of talk, believe me! And I'll sell a
lot of perfume. Some of the men who talk big will have to buy
it for their wives to square themselves. And some of the
women will buy it just out of spite. Either way, nobody will
ignore the paper next week, I'll bet on that!"

Father finally agreed, but for extra money to pay for the
extra work involved. In the middle of the Hall ad he printed a
circle about an inch in diameter and the words, "Smell Here."
Mr. Hall brought down several bottles of the perfume, and
when the papers were all ready to take to the post office we
went through and dabbed perfume on every front page with a

wad of absorbent cotton. The papers reeked, the *News* office reeked, the post office reeked. Father and I reeked—Mother would have nothing to do with it. And there was street-corner laughter and back-room laughter for weeks. But Bill Hall sold all of that perfume he had, and probably a good many other women's items, too.

Mr. Hall probably didn't invent the idea, but he was the first merchant I ever knew who welcomed people in his store whether they bought anything or not, deliberately lured them and entertained them, usually with music. The week after he started the front-page ads he somehow revived a town brass band that hadn't given a concert in months, persuaded the members to practice, and the next week started Saturday evening band concerts on the street in front of the store. He advertised the concerts and put chairs in the women's department for old folk and nursing mothers. Farm families came to town and stayed for the concerts, and townsfolk went downtown after supper to listen and gather in and around the store.

When the nights became too chilly for open-air concerts he tried moving the band inside the store. But the blast of sound in there was deafening. He gave up on the band and encouraged a group of the town's younger folk to hold Saturday evening "sings" at the store. There was always at least a quartet of good voices to lead the singing, and all fall the store was crowded on Saturday nights.

Later in the winter Mr. Hall brought in a man and his wife who played piano and drums, friends of friends of his who were trying to make a living playing for dances up near Denver. He brought them to Flagler, gave them living money to play at the store on Saturday evenings, and helped them find dance engagements in the area, for less critical dancers than those near Denver. Their music in the store was a drawing card for a time, but it never had the attraction of either the home-town band or the volunteer singing. The pianist and her drummer husband were not home folks; maybe that was it. Participation was still important to people, in those days. Radio and television hadn't come along to make most of us listeners and spectators. The old tradition of making your own amusement, creating your own entertainment, was still in force. On the frontier you made it or you did without, whether it was music or a batch of bread; and Flagler was still very close to the old frontier.

One day in early October when Mr. Hall brought down the copy for his ad that week, Father glanced at it and said, "Either you had a lot bigger inventory than it looked like you had or you've been reordering pretty heavy."

Mr. Hall smiled. "Does it matter," he asked, "as long as I'm moving merchandise?"

"Not one bit. I'm just curious. I let you have half of my front page for just about half what it's worth, and without that ad—" He hesitated.

Mr. Hall finished the sentence. "Without that ad you'd be scraping bottom, if you were still in business. And I would be fighting to make a dime. All right, it's been a bargain for me, and a life-saver for you. Yes, I've moved a lot of merchandise, about a third more than I did last year. Considering everything, the wheat failure and all, that's pretty good. I haven't made as much money, quite, because I cut my margin to the bone. But I'm still in business and still solvent. I met my notes the first of this month, and I take it you did yours."

"Yes, I did. Not much to spare, but I made it."

"Then we're both winners, aren't we? For a while there it looked like we might both get folded up. . . . Yes, you guessed it. I unloaded all my overstock and now it's just turnover, the way it should be." He started to leave, then hesitated. "You said something about that front-page ad being worth more than I'm paying for it. What are you trying to do? Jump the price on me now?"

"No. No, Bill. We made an agreement, for six months. But

when that agreement runs out it's going to cost you more. That's all I'm saying."

"How much more, so I can start figuring?"

"I'll tell you later, Bill."

"All right, we'll haggle it out when the time comes."

"No, we won't haggle it. Not you and me. If you want to haggle I think I'll turn it over to my wife, let her fight it out with you. Seems to me you two have had plenty of practice, over butter and eggs."

"No you don't! Butter and eggs is one thing, but that ad's something else. Before I got through dickering with her she'd have my shirt. When the time comes, you just tell me what you've got in mind and we'll work something out, you and me."

8

The week after the hailstorm Little Doc said, "We'd better go out and inspect things at Verhoff's Dam. The flood on the river and all, can't tell what's happened to the dam."

"When shall we go?" I asked.

"Can you get off tomorrow?"

"I think so."

"See you in the morning, then. I'll see if Spider wants to go along."

The next day was Friday and I was supposed to have most of the day free, but I asked Father at supper that evening. Before he could answer, Mother asked, "What do you want to do now?" I said Little Doc and Spider and I were going out south, that they wanted to show me the country out that way. Father said, "I don't see why not. Out to Verhoff's Dam, probably, and the breaks along the river. How are you going? On your bikes?"

"Yes."

"What," Mother asked, "is Verhoff's Dam?"

"It's a big earthen dam," Father said, "that a rancher out there put across a draw to catch water to irrigate his alfalfa. He expected to have a lake, but it hasn't worked out that way. All he's ever had, I understand, is a good-sized pond. The only time he has enough water to irrigate is right after a good rain, when he doesn't need to irrigate. . . . After the storm last

week it may be a pretty good-sized pond. I'd like to see it myself, if I had time."

"Just remember," Mother said to me, "you can't swim.
And you're not to try until some day when your father is with
you."

Father was a good swimmer. He and his brothers had
learned as children. The family home was close beside the
mill pond Grandfather Borland had built to power his mill
and blacksmith shop, and the boys swam as naturally as young
otters. Both the dam and the mill pond were gone by the time
I was a boy there in Nebraska, and the Nemaha had shrunken
to a flood-prone, muddy creek with only an occasional hole
deep enough for swimming. A few times, when we went fish-
ing for mud cats, Father tried to teach me to dog-paddle, at
least.

Little Doc and Spider came past for me the next morning.
Little Doc's black Nig was with them, so I let Fritz go along
too. We went down past the elevator and crossed the railroad
tracks on the road south. It was a graded gravel road with
fences on both sides for a couple of miles, then no fences, just
the open country, and the road like a sandy-yellow ribbon that
dwindled to a string and ran straight south as far as we could
see. Just as on my trip to Crystal Springs and Kit Carson Hill,
the morning was cool and bright and alive with meadow larks
and horned larks and sluggish grasshoppers and sweet with the
fragrance of sand verbena. But this time I wasn't a part of it.
I was one of an invading army that whooped and hollered
and yipped and yapped. We were peaceful invaders, but we
had to assert our presence. We didn't want to kill a thing, but
we wanted the world to know we were there. Even the dogs
didn't really want to catch a rabbit. They merely wanted the
world to know they were chasing one. We weren't half a mile
out of town when they jumped the first jack rabbit and went
yelping madly after it. The jack sprinted a couple hundred

yards, then leaped high, looked back, saw that the dogs were giving only token chase, then loped away, almost loafing. The dogs kept going maybe half a mile, using most of their breath yelping, then came back and joined us, panting and thoroughly pleased with themselves. I never knew a more self-satisfied loser than a dog that has been outdistanced by a jack rabbit in the first five minutes. He acts as though the very act of chasing a rabbit was a major accomplishment.

Two miles south of town, just beyond the last roadside fence, was a deserted shanty. Its bare boards were weathered coffee-brown, only a few tatters of tar-paper were left on its shed roof, its two windows hadn't even a sliver of glass, and its batten door sagged half open on one remaining hinge. It stood about a hundred yards off the road in a dooryard still barren of grass and littered with rusty tin cans, broken dishes, rotted harness straps, and small fragments of brown glass bottles that twinkled in the sunlight like smoky topaz.

We poked around in the clutter of discarded junk, unwitting archaeologists looking for clues in the midden heap of a vanished transient. Such deserted shacks were as common on the plains as are old cellar holes in New England, and they had the same half-told story for those who would read: "Someone once lived here, tried to make a home, gave up, went away."

We scuffed about the dooryard. Spider found a rusted pocketknife with half its bone handle and half a blade. Little Doc kept looking for a weapon, a gun. The previous summer he had found a rust-encrusted Smith & Wesson revolver with two empty shells in it at an abandoned homestead shanty. But we found no hint of murder or suicide, not even an old butcher knife. The starveling carcass of what someone once probably called home had been picked clean. We pushed past the sagging door to look inside and found only the remnants of a mattress on a broken iron bedstead, rifled of its stuffing by mice and other rodents, and a battered little iron cookstove, minus lids and doors. On one wall was still tacked a garish calendar picture of a girl in a leather Mother Hubbard with a feather in her hair, a calendar dated 1908.

Outside, the dogs put up a cottontail at the far edge of the yard, and it dashed to the safety of a warren under the shanty. Cottontails always had burrows under those old shacks. The dogs made a frantic clamor and seemed to be trying to tear the place apart as they clawed at the hole and the sill above it. Little Doc stuck his head out one of the paneless windows and shouted, "Sic 'em, Nig! Go get 'em, Fritz!" The dogs made twice as much noise and Spider yelled, "Yip-eeeee!" We all began to laugh and shout, and the dogs barked still louder. Ears ringing, we went back to our bikes, leaving the dogs to follow when they tired of trying to tear the shanty apart.

We rode on south, and soon we could see the bluffs along the far side of the river valley only a few miles ahead. Then we came to a long hill, and as I started to coast down it Little Doc shouted, "Take it easy! We're going to turn off and go to the dam." I braked my bike and let him and Spider go ahead. About halfway down the hill they left the road and took a wagon trail to the right. Unlike the trail to Crystal Springs, this one was across flats carpeted with buffalo grass and not a cactus plant in sight. The trail led over a slight rise and on the far side I could see the dam, the pond behind it, and the whole wide valley.

The dam was just a long mound of earth that had been built across the big draw, a barrier at least a quarter of a mile long and perhaps thirty feet high in the middle. Its top was wide enough for a wagon road. Behind it was the pond, about five acres in extent but looking much smaller in the giant cup of the hills. Its rim was muddy, showing that the water had been almost a foot deeper after the previous week's storm. The mud was pocked with the hoofprints of cattle, for the pond was a watering place for the livestock that grazed that whole area.

We rode our bikes almost down to the muddy margin, and as we stopped two big, dark birds took wing from the shallow water at the far edge of the pond. "Shitepokes!" Spider shouted. "Look at the shitepokes!" They were awkward-looking birds that flew with slow, heavy wingbeats, folded neck and trailing legs. Great blue herons, I eventually learned, and rather rare on the High Plains. But any heron, even the little green which sometimes visited that pond, was a shitepoke to the countryman. I have even heard the sandhill crane called a shitepoke.

Little Doc watched the shitepokes fly away and start a big circle. "If we sit down and wait," he said, "I'll bet they'll come back."

We sat down and the big birds slowly circled back, flew over us, and made another circle. Spider whispered, "If I had my Cannon, I'll bet I could get one!"

"Who wants a shitepoke?" Little Doc asked.

"We could have come in below the dam," Spider said, still in a whisper, "and made an Indian sneak and been right on top of them." He aimed an imaginary gun, made an explosive "Pop!" with his mouth, and announced, "Got him!"

"Ever try to eat a shitepoke?" Little Doc asked him.

"Nah!"

"Then why kill one?"

Spider laughed. "Nobody eats coyote, do they? Or chicken hawk? Nor mountain lion or rattlesnake or prairie dog or—"

"I've eaten prairie dog," I said.

Spider stared at me, mouth open. "Prairie dog!" He stuck out his tongue, retched, and went through the motions of a violent spasm of vomiting.

Little Doc asked, "What did it taste like?"

"About like jack rabbit."

Little Doc nodded. "Prairie dogs are rodents, like rabbits. They eat about the same thing."

Spider had stopped his fake nausea, was watching the herons. They had finished their second circle and came slanting down on the far side of the pond, almost where they had taken off. They stood there, watching us, and Spider stuck out his tongue at them and turned and grinned at us and laughed. The big birds waded into the shallow water and began hunting, probably for frogs.

We sat and watched them, the sun hot on our heads, the grass warm and soft to our bottoms. It was midmorning and the meadow larks had stopped singing. Half a dozen killdeers were darting about, nervous as fleas, on the mucky margin within thirty feet of us. I looked for ducks, but there wasn't one in sight, probably because there wasn't any brush, no undergrowth of any kind.

We were so intent on the shitepokes that none of us saw the dogs. They came down the trail from the road, panting softly, and the first we knew, there they were. I heard a sniffle and felt a cold nose on the back of my neck, and I must have jumped a foot off the ground. Little Doc's Nig leaped at him, almost knocked him flat, and got a resounding slap on his haunches. Then both dogs went on down to the water, waded in, frightened the killdeers and the herons, lapped noisily, waded around until they were sopping wet and dripping black, oozy mud. Then they came out, got as close to us as they could, and shook mud and water in all directions.

Spider got more muddy water than either Little Doc or me. We knew what was coming and flopped over on our bellies and covered our faces. Spider called the dogs every name he could think of, and while he was wiping the dirty water out of his eyes we got up and ran from the dogs, got on our bikes, and headed back for the road. The dogs ran after us, barking madly, and before we reached the road Spider caught up.

We coasted on down the long hill and stopped at the wooden bridge over the shallow gully that was, technically, the river. The gully wasn't much bigger than the main irrigation ditches in the sugar-beet country near Brush. There wasn't a drop of water in it. I wondered how much water had been there after the storm that almost caught me in the flood at the foot of Kit Carson Hill. Then I saw strands of hay caught in the wooden railing of the bridge, hay that hadn't fallen off a hay rack but had been lodged there by the water.

Just beyond the bridge, to the south, rose the bluffs. They began as a gentle slope but soon rose sharply to an upland several hundred feet above the valley. The steep slope was covered with grass almost to the top, with scattered patches of low sage and dwarf buckbrush, as we called it. The road climbed the slope in hairpins, sweeping curves, and crossed the upland in a shallow gap. We rode our bikes about halfway up the slope, then left them at the roadside and went on afoot, carrying our paper bags of sandwiches.

Little Doc led the way. Now I could see that at the very top of the bluff was a bare cliff, apparently the edge of a sandstone layer that capped the whole upland. Big chunks of the rock had been broken loose by rain and frost and had rolled part way down the slope. We passed several half as big as an automobile. All of them had been there a long time, for the grass and brush were rooted all around them. As we neared the top there was more rubble, tumbled from the bare cliff, which was about six feet high. There were a number of hollows in the face of the cliff. Once when we paused for breath Little Doc gestured toward those directly ahead of us. "Indian caves," he said. "Skeletons in them."

We were puffing from the climb when we reached the biggest cave, the one with a mound of yellow, sandy soil at its mouth. The entrance was only about three feet high, and I could see that the cave ran back only four or five feet. Its roof seemed to be solid rock, the sandstone cap rock. We sat down in front of the cave and looked back the way we had come. The road wound down the slope in a big sweep, doubled back on itself, then crossed the bridge and straightened out. From there it ran as straight as a ruler due north to Flagler, which we could barely make out on the horizon, a mere smudge with one upthrust that had to be the grain elevator.

The sun was almost overhead. I was hungry. I took a sandwich from the paper sack I had stuffed inside my shirt for the climb. Doc and Spider got sandwiches from their lunch bags too and we ate, sitting in front of the cave, facing the valley and with the whole world spread out in front of us to the north and the west. There were no physical boundaries, not even the shadowy hint of a mountain on the western horizon. We were too far away to see the mountains. The bluff was behind us, but I knew that if we stood on top of it, all we would see was the stretch of the flats to the south, plains that stretched down across New Mexico and the Texas panhandle and all the way into Mexico.

Spider said, "Up here, it looks big as the ocean."

"You ever seen the ocean?" Little Doc asked.

"Not yet. But I'm going to. I'm going to sail all over the world. In a windjammer like those that go around Cape Horn, yo-ho, yo-ho!"

"I thought you were going to Alaska and be a trapper."

"I am. I'm going to shoot lions in the jungle of Africa, too. To be an author and write books, you've got to have a lot of experiences."

"Are you going to be an author?" I asked.

"Sure. A lot more fun than being a doctor or a lawyer. How long have you got to go to college to be a doctor, Doc?"

"Six years. And then two years as an intern."

"An author don't even have to go to college! He just goes out and has adventures and writes about them."

"You're going to be a doctor?" I asked Little Doc.

He didn't answer. He reached over and caught my wrist, felt for and found my pulse, and stared at the ground, intent as a robin watching a worm, for a long minute. Then he dropped my hand and said, "You're alive. What are you going to do if you ever grow up?"

"I don't know," I said. "I'm going to be a printer. I know that. I can make a living as a printer. I may decide to be a chemical engineer. Or maybe a professional baseball player."

"Walter Johnson Borland, huh?" Spider said.

"Maybe," I said. "Or Grover Cleveland Alexander Borland —just call me Alex."

We played baseball, all three of us, with a pickup team of boys around town. Little Doc and Spider played shortstop and second base and were the backbone of our infield. I was the pitcher because I had a fair fast ball, a good roundhouse curve, and pretty good control. The previous weekend we had played a game with a boys' team in Arriba and won 21 to 3. They had got only five hits off me and I was feeling pretty big for my britches. I had played baseball, football and basketball with grade-school teams in Brush and seemed to have the natural coordination that is essential to any athlete.

Spider was flipping bits of bread from his sandwich to the dogs, who had been lying in the shade of a clump of buckbrush until he tempted them with something to eat. He flipped another bit of bread into the air and both dogs leaped for it. Nig grabbed it and Fritz turned on him, knocked him off balance, and leaped at him. Snapping and snarling, they rolled about in the brush until Little Doc threw a handful of sand at them. They both sneezed, got to their feet, and looked hopefully at Spider. He flipped another chunk of bread at them.

"Cut it out," Little Doc ordered.

"I'm performing an experiment," Spider said. "Here we are in a sled, fleeing across the Russian steppes. The wolves are closing in. I want to see how long I can keep the wolves from eating us."

"You and your experiments!" Little Doc lunged at Spider. "I'll throw *you* to the wolves!" He grabbed Spider's sandwich, broke it in two, and tossed half of it to each dog.

"Varlet!" Spider shouted. "I shall have your life for that!"

But he didn't make a move. He watched Nig gulp down his half of the sandwich, then said, "You kill him, Nig, and I'll bury him in one of the tombs." Nig paid no attention. Spider turned and crawled into the cave on all fours and began digging with his hands. He dug for a minute or two, glanced over his shoulder and saw Little Doc and me watching, yelped, "Woof woof!" and dug madly at the sand with both hands, flinging it out between his legs, dog fashion, and all over us. We covered our faces with our hands and rolled aside, then sat up and watched. Spider kept on digging and a moment later shouted, "Hey! I found something! I found a skeleton!"

Little Doc grinned at me.

"No, it ain't a skeleton!" Spider shouted. "It's a—it's—" He backed out of the cave dragging a short-handled spade. He sat up and waved it over his head. "It's a prehistoric tommy-hawk!"

"Give it here," Little Doc ordered.

"It's mine! I found it!"

"I hid it, you damn fool. You saw me hide it there the last time we were out here."

Spider gave it to him. "Yes, Master Robinson Crusoe, I cannot tell a lie. I saw you hide it. Don't beat poor old man Friday! Please don't beat him!"

"Come on," Little Doc said. "Let's find another cave to dig out. One with real bones in it."

He chose a shallow cave fifty yards farther along the cliff and began digging it out. The sandy soil in it was loose, and as we took turns with the spade we could see that the roof and walls of the cave had once been almost smooth. We dug in three feet or so, had it almost as big as the cave where the spade had been, when I saw bright red flecks in the sand Spider was scooping out and scattering down the hillside. "Wait a minute!" I ordered. "I see something!" And I searched in the fresh sand, found four red beads, the kind of glass beads common on old Indian moccasins and headbands. Then I saw two blue ones. I showed them to Spider and Little Doc, and we all searched the fresh sand. We found about a dozen beads, most of them red, a few blue, two of them white. After that we dug more slowly, watching every spadeful, examining it by handfuls before we threw the sand down the hillside.

In the next hour we found another two dozen beads. But nothing to go with them, not a trace of thread or thong or a shred of leather. I was using the spade and was about to give up when I struck something hard. I dug in with my hands, felt what seemed must be a bone, and carefully uncovered it. It was a bone, about a foot long, a knob at each end. It was hard and dirty yellow in color. I handed it out to Little Doc and went on digging for the rest of the skeleton. I dug for ten minutes and couldn't find another bone, not one.

Spider took my place. Spider was going to find the skull, grinning teeth, empty eye sockets and all. But Spider couldn't find a bone either. Little Doc took a look, shook his head, and said it was no use. "The wolves have been here, or maybe the coyotes. They took the rest of the skeleton. All but this humerus."

"This what?" Spider asked.

"Humerus. The upper bone of the arm."

"Very funny," Spider said. "Very funny. But you don't know your arm from your leg. This is a leg bone. I haven't been a gravedigger forty-four years for nothing. I know a man's leg when I see one!"

"If you are talking about a femur," Little Doc said, "you are crazy as a cross-eyed coyote. Shall I give you a lesson in anatomy? Very well. The head of the femur, where it fits into its pelvic socket, is altogether different from that of the humerus, which fits the scapula. Shoulder blade to the layman. This, my dear, dumb, stupid, ignorant fellow, is a humerus. Very likely a prehistoric Indian humerus."

Spider turned to me. "Shall we stake him out, spread-eagle, and let the hawks eat out his guts, or shall we take him to yon savage colony and sell him as a slave?"

"Let's take him to the nearest village and swap him for a box of shotgun shells and go hunting jack rabbits."

"Yip-eeeee!" Spider yelled. "Let's go!" The dogs barked and ran after Spider as he started down the steep slope, leaping like a pronghorn antelope and somehow maintaining his balance as he jumped over rocks and bushes, unable to stop.

Little Doc and I followed, after Little Doc had put the spade back in the original cave and thrown a few handfuls of sand over it. He carried the bone, the day's treasure. We made our way down the slope, zigzagging from bush to bush and rock to rock, and found Spider waiting for us beside the bikes at the road.

It was midafternoon. The sun was just passing its hottest point. We coasted down the winding road to the bridge, going fast enough to blow a breeze through our hair and balloon our shirts. The dry air evaporated our sweat so fast I felt almost chilly. Then we were climbing the long, gradual slope beyond the river and it was hot again, blazing hot with the sun coming back at us off the yellow gravel road and not a whisper of air stirring. We rode, and got off and walked, and rode again, and pushed; and we were at the top of the long hill and Flagler was only three miles away. Mirages danced in the road ahead of us, and when we stopped on one hilltop and caught our breath I looked west and saw a big, gleaming lake only half a mile away, a lake that sparkled and lapped the grassy shore and was cool and sweet. I pointed it out to Spider, and he said, "That's the Pacific Ocean. I didn't want to mention it because our doctor friend, here, would say I was crazy as a cross-eyed coyote again."

The mirages were with us all the way to town, wherever we looked, ahead or to the west. Some people say they have seen mirages there on the flats of eastern Colorado that had palm trees and sail boats as well as water. I never did. All I ever saw was water.

We got to town and stopped at the drug store. Little Doc's father was there, a thin man with dark hair that was getting sparse and with dark eyes behind steel-rimmed spectacles that always seemed to be crooked on his nose. His name was Harry, but I never heard anyone call him that. He was Doctor Williams, and few people shortened it to Doc. The other doctor in town was almost always Doc Neff, and I never did know his first name, only his initials, which were O. S.

Dr. Williams was at the drug store. We went in and he said, "So the archaeologists are back. Make any big discoveries?"

"We found some beads," Little Doc said, hiding the bone behind him and holding out the scant handful of glass beads.

Dr. Williams glanced at them and nodded. "Trade beads. Worth about twenty-five cents a pound. What else? What are you hiding?"

"A humerus," Little Doc said, triumphant, and he showed him the bone.

Dr. Williams frowned, took the bone, looked at it for a moment, then smiled.

"It *is* a humerus, isn't it?" Little Doc asked.

"Yes, I guess you could call it a humerus. If a calf had arms, this would be the bone of its upper forearm."

"A calf?" Little Doc asked, incredulous.

"That's right, a calf. You found it in one of those caves?"

"Yes."

"And this was the only bone you found?"

"Yes."

"Probably left there by a coyote fifteen or twenty years ago. That's about how old it is. Indians didn't go around burying one arm or one leg. They tried to bury their corpses whole. Find one Indian bone and you find a whole basketful. But keep digging. You may find an Indian yet. . . . How about a soda? It's a hot afternoon."

And we all went over to the soda fountain.

9

School was scheduled to start the day after Labor Day. We boys knew it but, as usual, we didn't think that Labor Day came so soon after the Fourth of July. By the middle of August we thought we were only halfway through summer. Then, bang, September was right in front of us, and school again.

It struck us the Saturday afternoon that we played the boys' baseball team from out in the Shiloh district, in the North Country. We had won five games in a row and had begun to think we were unbeatable. Then those country boys came to town and beat us 5 to 2, on five hits, three walks, eight stolen bases, and four errors, or some such humiliating box score totals. After the game Leon Lavington, who had been graduated from the university in Boulder only the previous June, came over to us and said, "If it wasn't so late in the season I'd take a week off and show you kids how to play baseball. You should have licked the pants off of that team of Jake Wolverton's. They beat you on fundamentals." Jake Wolverton was a farmer who once had played professionally in the Three-Eye League, back in Iowa. Until that day we didn't know he was coaching the boys from Shiloh. Jake thought it was a wonderful joke, beating us Flagler boys that way. We wanted another game with them, and we wanted Leon to coach us. But Leon said, "It's too late. School starts in another two weeks, and then it'll be football season. If you want to play football, let me know."

But we weren't listening. We were an angry, beaten baseball team, and we had just been reminded that we were going back to school virtually day after tomorrow. We growled and made up excuses for our defeat and tried not to think about what was ahead, but by Monday we conceded that summer was virtually at an end. It wasn't that we hated school. It always seemed to me that the hate-school tradition was largely an adult fabrication. There are the inevitable truants and delinquents in every society, but the ideal of schooling, all you could get, was ingrained in those of my generation who grew up in a culture just emerging from frontier limitations. Our parents had faith in education and were determined that we should have more than they had. We knew it was our job to get it.

Schooling in Flagler that year was going to be pretty well mixed up, though. The townspeople had voted, by a rather narrow margin, to build a new school. The contract had been let and work was under way on a red brick building at the north end of Main Street, half a mile north of the railroad tracks. But it wouldn't be ready for classes till after Christmas, at the earliest. Meanwhile, there would be the biggest enrollment in the town's history, and classes would have to be held in two old frame school buildings several blocks apart and in the Congregational church. A part of the increase was from new people in town, like us, but most of it was from the country. Flagler had raised its school from ten grades to twelve that year, making it a full-fledged high school, only the second one in the county. The other one was in Burlington, the county seat, forty miles east of Flagler. Partly as a consequence, four one-room rural schools had been closed and were going to send their pupils to Flagler as tuition students.

Besides the problem of finding classroom space, which was solved by using the church, there was the problem of housing. Some of the country pupils came from farms twenty miles or more from town, and there were no school buses in those days. Parents could bring small children to school by horse and buggy from as far as five miles away, and older pupils could come that far on horseback. But families from farther out had only two choices. They could find someone in town willing to provide bed and board for a helpful boy or girl, or they could go in with several other farm families and rent a house for the children to use as a kind of dormitory.

I have heard those who had no first-hand knowledge speak of the first solution as just another version of the "bound-servant" system. In our part of the country it was, rather, a foster-home arrangement by which many a farm boy got his basic education and many a farm girl got both an education and a taste of town life under wise supervision. During the school year almost every family in Flagler that didn't have a houseful of youngsters of its own had a boy or girl from the country who helped make the beds, wash the dishes, shovel snow, feed the chickens, milk the cow, or anything else that needed doing. And all, for the most part, with a minimum of cash exchange. The farm families came to town every couple of weeks, when weather permitted, and brought what they could spare to help "set table" at the homes where their youngsters were living—fresh meat, milk, cream, butter, eggs, and any home vegetables they might have.

The other solution, the dormitory, required first that they find a vacant house, and second that the mothers take turns living in town, cooking the meals, and seeing that the home-work as well as the housework was done. The big problem that year was finding a vacant house in Flagler. One group from out north rented the converted boxcar next to ours. Another group bought a vacant lot and moved two old homestead shan-ties in, hooked them together, covered them with tar-paper, and made a habitable house of them.

But most of the families had to rely on the foster-home system, which persisted, in that area at least, for another fif-teen years, until centralized schools were established and far-ranging buses were as much a part of the school setup as the classrooms. It was a part of the tradition of self-help and neighborly assistance that had marked frontier life ever since settlement began to move west beyond the Alleghenies.

As a newcomer, I had to register and as far as possible lay out my whole high school program. Mother had gone to my eighth grade teacher in Brush and got a full transcript of my record. In Brush I had made up enough of the schooling I missed on the homestead to finish the eighth grade not only at the top of my class but only one year behind my normal age group.

The school principal, head of the whole school system in Flagler, was Professor W. L. Conley, a short, fat, firm, dignified man to whom education was not merely a profession but a calling. In the usual way of small-town schools, he was teacher as well as administrator, disciplinarian as well as counselor, practical as a piece of chalk, routine as a calendar. His wife, a slim, red-haired woman with a tongue like a whip, taught English and Latin. With four other teachers, they were responsible for all twelve grades.

I went to see Professor Conley in his cluttered little office in the old grammar school building. He looked up from his desk, pushed a pile of papers aside, sat back in his squeaky swivel chair, pushed his steel-rimmed glasses up onto his forehead, and asked, "Yes?" I told him my name and he frowned, summoned his mind from wherever it had been, blinked his eyes tightly, and said, "Yes," again, this time in recognition.

I handed him my record from Brush. He stared at it for a moment. "Brush," he said. "Good school. I knew a Mr. Johnson, Fred Johnson, from there. Met him in Greeley." He hesitated. I made no response. I didn't know any Fred Johnson from Brush. Professor Conley said, half to himself, "Or maybe it was from Eaton. No matter." He picked up a pencil. He was the first person I ever knew who couldn't seem to read without a pencil in his hand ticking off the lines. He nodded, glanced up at me. "You seem to be well prepared. I hope you plan to go on to college."

"Yes, sir."

"You will need sixteen credits for college entrance. Four credits a year, four courses. This first year you will take English and geometry and Latin and a science, chemistry or physics. Which do you want to take this year?"

"Professor Conley," I said, "I want to finish high school in three years. So I want to take—"

"What!"

"I missed quite a bit of schooling while we were on the homestead. I made some of it up in Brush and I want to make up the rest of it now."

He frowned at my record, then at me. "I like to have a student take enough time to get everything out of a course. Not just race through." He shook his head slowly. "Suppose you take the regular freshman course and perhaps take a heavier schedule next year."

"Couldn't I—Look, Professor Conley, I hoped I could take six courses this year and six next year, and then have only four courses in my senior year. Wouldn't that work?"

"Six courses is a very heavy schedule." He took his watch from his pocket, glanced at it, and I knew he wanted to cut this short.

"I think I can handle it," I said.

He gave me a quick, hard glance and reached for his chart of class schedules. He made several check marks with his pencil and reached for a memo pad. "Very well." There was an edge on his voice. "You may start with six courses and we will review your work at the end of the first month. I am putting you down for chemistry rather than physics, to leave you a free afternoon period. That's the only way you can get the two electives. And there are only two that don't conflict with your other classes, botany and geology." He smiled at me then, a strangely triumphant smile, and dismissed me with a sigh and a gesture.

I left thinking I had got what I wanted, feeling quite set up. Then I thought of botany and geology on top of chemistry. Three sciences. But I was interested in both botany and geology, we had had an elementary course in botany in the eighth grade in Brush, and I had read several books from the library about geology, including one textbook.

High school classes were held in the old grammar school building and in the church, diagonally across the street from each other. Even now when I think of a Latin phrase I think of the church basement where we declined Latin verbs for Mrs. Conley beside the big coal furnace. When I reach for a botanical name I think of the upstairs corner room of the old grammar school, dingy and cluttered with makeshift scientific equipment—Professor Conley's classroom, where he taught all the science courses. All of them, which included chemistry, botany and geology, exactly half of my schedule. That was why he had that triumphant smile the day I registered. It was sheer coincidence that the geology textbook was the one I had read in Brush. And since this was the first time he had ever taught botany, the whole first semester's work covered ground I had already been over. If I hadn't been only a good average student in chemistry, about which I knew virtually nothing to start with, I might have passed myself off for a time as a genius. Instead, he probably knew that I was simply a lucky smart-aleck.

School soon began to settle into a routine. But I was restless. I wanted to play football. The boys I knew and went around with in Brush played football from the time they were ten years old. Every grade in grammar school had its football team, and there were two high school teams. Boys learned the game early and thoroughly. But in Flagler the only game that counted was basketball, which, of course, was the ideal small-town sport. It could be played with a squad of only seven or eight players, and in those days they used any big room with a moderately high ceiling as a basketball court. As someone said, you could play the game "any place big enough to swing a lariat and high enough so a man on a horse won't get his hat knocked off." In Flagler they used Seal's Hall, a second-floor room over the hardware store that was also used as a lodge hall by the Masons and the Odd Fellows and as a theater for home-talent shows and an auditorium for lyceum lectures and concerts. It was too narrow for a regulation basketball court, and the ceiling was only twelve or fifteen feet high, but it was the biggest hall in town. Some said, and I think it was true, that the bond issue for the new school building was voted in good part because the plans included a gymnasium with a full-size basketball court and a spectators' gallery.

Flagler's basketball team had lost only one game in four years, and that one by a narrow margin to a semi-pro team from Kansas. Every boy in town with any talent for the game was expected to turn out for the team, but membership on the squad was almost like knighthood in King Arthur's day. Freshmen hadn't even as much standing as pages had in Arthur's court. Everybody knew that the three members of last year's team who were still in school would pick the members of the squad and lay down the rules of practice.

A couple of Saturdays Little Doc and Spider and I went jack rabbit hunting, not for the rabbits so much as for the going, to get out, do something active. I brought up the subject of football, but neither of them was interested. So I finally went to talk with Leon Lavington.

Leon was supposed to have been the first white child born in Flagler. He was the older son of W. H. Lavington, the man who started a grocery store in a tent and who now was the head of the Flagler State Bank. He had played baseball and football at the state university. Now he was in charge of the Ford garage, which his father had established only a few years earlier as the first automobile agency in town. Eventually Leon went into state politics, became an unsuccessful candidate for governor, then was elected state treasurer for a term or two. But that was years later. Now he was fresh out of college, married only a few months, restless in an office, and still very much the athlete.

I went to the garage office and found him sitting back of a desk, looking sour and surly. I said hello, and he just sat there staring at me. Then I said, "You said if we wanted to play football you would coach us."

He brightened immediately. "Have you got a team?" he asked.

"No, not yet. But I'd like to play."

"Oh. Well, ten more and you'll have a team, won't you?" He looked at me and began to smile. I didn't know why, but I know now. I was five feet seven inches tall, and I weighed 115 pounds fully dressed.

"Did you ever *play* football?"

"I played halfback on the eighth grade team in Brush. I did the kicking, and some of the passing, too."

"Well, well," he said, not quite laughing at me. Then he went to a closet, got out a football, and said, "Come on." He led the way through the garage to a big vacant lot out back. "Go down for a pass," he ordered, and I trotted off. He threw a high, hard pass that I had to leap for, but I pulled it in and threw the ball back to him. We threw passes back and forth for ten minutes. Then he said, "Give me a punt this time." The coach in Brush had taught me to put every ounce of my 115 pounds into a kick. I did it now and sent the ball a good forty yards, well over Leon's head. "Do that again," he ordered, and I did. A few more punts and I made a thirty-yard drop kick. Leon signaled that was enough, and we went back to his office. He put the ball away and said, half to himself, "Might even lick Hugo." Then he turned to me and said, "I'll see what I can do."

The next day at school several of the boys said, "Leon Lav-

ington's starting a football team. Let's go see what happens."
Beyond that, I can only guess how it was done, but probably
the athletic rivalry with Hugo was used as bait, especially for
the boys who expected to play basketball. Hugo, county seat
of Lincoln County and more than twice the size of Flagler,
had been an athletic rival for years, the rivalry so keen that
basketball games sometimes ended in free-for-alls, and baseball games between town teams always erupted in fist fights.
Hugo was still proud of its cow-town past and liked to pose as
a swaggering, two-gun cowpuncher who shot out the street
lights every Saturday night. Actually, it was a law-abiding,
progressive community that just happened to have a few
leading characters who habitually thumbed their noses at
conventions. Typical was the editor of the Hugo paper, Jerry
Messimer, who had a ribald sense of humor and a colorful vocabulary of invective. When Hugo installed a municipal sewer
system, Jerry ran the full text of James Whitcomb Riley's underground poem, "The Passing of the Backhouse," in a bor-
dered box in the middle of his paper's front page.

However it was done, fifteen of us boys met Leon after
school that afternoon on the vacant half block behind the
Congregational church. Among us were three basketball players, seniors, and four juniors. Leon started right in on fundamentals, how to catch and carry a football, how to fall on a
fumble. And he told us to wear old clothes the next afternoon
and be prepared for getting bruised a bit. The next session got
down to tackling a runner and blocking a tackler. We got
plenty of bruises that day.

By the end of the week, enough boys were on hand to make
up two opposing lines for a scrimmage, but with only one
backfield. That showed that the vacant lot was too small, so
the school board let us lay out a regulation football field where
the athletic field was planned at the new school building. We
marked the lines with lime and we set up goal posts. And we
learned every move in half a dozen simple basic plays.

We practiced every afternoon for almost two weeks. Then Leon told us we were going to Hugo and play a real game the coming Saturday. "Are you ready?" he asked, with a grin, and we yelled like a Cheyenne war party.

I doubted that there ever was a more motley football team than we were when Leon, Professor Conley and W. E. Hall took us to Hugo for that first game. We had no uniforms. We played in old turtleneck jerseys, the kind we wore to school, and in old corduroys or bibless overalls. Our jerseys were any color we happened to have, red or blue or black. For shoulder pads we cut up old felt horse-collar pads. Instead of cleated football shoes, we wore everyday shoes with makeshift cleats tacked to their soles. Two of the boys had felt-lined helmets. The rest of us let our hair grow, chrysanthemum style. No wonder the gathering crowd of Hugoites whooped with laughter when we got out of the three automobiles, all ready to play. The Hugo team, which didn't take the field for another fifteen minutes, at least had football pants and jerseys of a uniform color.

It was a bitter day, the temperature in the low 20s and a gusty, knife-edged wind blowing. But I began to sweat and was on the verge of vomiting before I made the opening kick-off. Then the tension went out of me like a pent-up breath and the game was on. Within five minutes it was clear how the game would go. The Hugo players were big, slow and over-confident. They soon had cold hands and stiff fingers. They could pound out the yardage through our line, which they outweighed at least fifteen pounds to the man, but they couldn't hold onto the ball. They fumbled and we recovered. Joe McBride, our quarterback, soon found that we couldn't get anywhere with line plays, so he switched to end runs, and we made one touchdown in the first quarter, another before the half ended. I kicked one point and we led 13 to 0.

Between halves Leon told us we were playing it exactly right and to keep on playing for fumbles and, when we had the wind at our backs, to kick on third down, keep them back near their own goal line. And that's what we did all the second half. Time after time they marched down the field, five or six yards at a clip, only to fumble, once inside our ten-yard line. After one recovery Joe McBride carried the ball on an end run, broke into the open, and went ninety-odd yards for our third touchdown. Hugo never scored a point.

And despite our clownish clothes, nobody laughed when we left the field. There wasn't a fight, either. There could have been, for there was some bitter talk and some nasty name-calling, but Leon hustled us into the cars and we headed for home, cold and bone weary, but sky-high with the elation of victory.

The next Saturday we played a team from Limon on our own field, a kind of pickup team of high school students and recent graduates. We ran up a score of 34 to 6 in the first half, and they refused to take the game seriously after that. But it was good practice, and we were glad to get it. We had a return game with Hugo on our own field the following Saturday, the first Saturday in November.

Practically everybody in Flagler came out to see that second game with Hugo. It was an unseasonably mild day with practically no wind, and we expected a hard fight. But Hugo still fumbled, especially when we tackled hard, and we recovered. And we had improved our end runs and added two simple forward pass plays. We scored three touchdowns in the first half, four more in the second; and again we kept Hugo from scoring a single point. I scored two touchdowns, one on a pass, and kicked two field goals. I was insufferable for the next week, no doubt. That game got a front-page story in the *News,* and even one in the *Progress.*

But that was the end of our football season. November weather was uncertain, and basketball practice was starting. As far as I went, it was high time I got back to the principal business of school. In botany the classwork was getting near the end of my material from that wild-flower course in the

113

eighth grade, and in geology Professor Conley was beginning to ask questions about other sources than the one textbook I had read. But now and then a few of us who had played football would talk about next year, when we would get started earlier and play a lot more games.

10

Little Doc and Spider had gone out for football at my insistence, but neither of them liked the game. Spider, who was an inch taller and ten pounds lighter than I was, quit the second day. "I don't trust myself," he said. "I have such a terrible temper and such inner hidden strength that I probably would kill someone in my very first game. Cripple someone for life, at the very least." Actually, he was physically frail, and he covered it with bravado. He would go hunting with Little Doc and me and stick it out even if we walked ten miles; but he would be in bed most of the next day, though we didn't know it then.

Little Doc, on the other hand, had the toughness and energy of a terrier. He probably could have made the team as a light-weight back, as I did; but the game just didn't appeal to him. He continued to come out for practice for a week, then said he didn't have time, and he, too, quit. So we three spent little time together until the week after the second Hugo game. That Friday afternoon Little Doc and I were just leaving school and wondering what to do the next day when Spider caught up with us.

"What's the password?" Spider asked in a whisper. "Do we storm the castle moat at dawn, or go out and steal chickens tonight?"

"The password," Little Doc said, "is jack rabbit. We're going hunting tomorrow. Want to go along?"

"I shall lead the way! Follow me! Day or night, follow me! By day, my golden crown of hair will gleam, and by night my lights will light up like a beacon. . . . Tell me, Doc, what are my lights?"

"Your lights, stupid, are your lungs. You and I haven't been getting enough exercise. Our livers are sluggish, no doubt, so we'll work the bile out of our system. The football hero here has been getting too much exercise. He's so healthy he stinks. He's going to get aired out. And he'll carry the game home."

"Fine idea. But I thought he took care of the game last Saturday."

Little Doc ignored the pun. "Meet us at the store at eight o'clock tomorrow morning. And bring the cannon."

It was raw and cold the next morning, overcast and with a damp wind, which was rare on the plains. All three of us wore mackinaw coats when we met at the drug store and set out, with both dogs. Spider had the old .10-gauge shotgun that Little Doc always called the cannon. It was long-barreled and heavy, and it had a terrific kick. If he shot it quickly and didn't brace himself first, it spun Spider halfway round with its recoil. It must have been a goose gun used by some market hunter on one of the lakes in Minnesota, where the Miners came from. Little Doc had a double-barreled .16-gauge that looked like a rifle alongside the cannon. It was a dainty gun, light in weight and beautiful to see and handle. I wished it was mine, but I wouldn't have swapped my own gun for it. My gun was the single-barreled .12-gauge that Father gave me for Christmas when I was eleven years old. On the homestead, I kept meat on the table with that gun. I knew how far it would reach, what pattern it threw, what I could and couldn't do with it. I wouldn't have swapped it for any other gun in the world.

We headed out east of town, but we took to the flats south of the railroad tracks instead of following the road. There wouldn't be any rabbits along the road. The dogs ranged ahead, as always, though we tried to keep them within gunshot range so we would have a chance at any jacks they might put up. But the rabbits were lying low because of the cold wind. We didn't see a thing in the first mile. Then the dogs got a hundred yards ahead and put up a rabbit and went bellowing off to the south, glad of a chance to run, probably, and really get warmed up. We kept on east, not hurrying because there was a chance that the jack the dogs were chasing would make a big circle and come back past us. Sometimes the jacks did that, but not always. I know the books say they always do, but maybe those jacks we knew didn't read the books. I have known one of them to run straightaway for five miles.

We kept on, and the dogs didn't come back for almost half an hour. By then we had reached the draw where the twisted old cottonwood stood beside the mound that was all that was left of the old Bowserville store. It had been a sod building, and when it was deserted the roof either was salvaged or fell in and the sod walls weathered down into a mound like a huge grave. It was all sodded over with buffalo grass, but if you poked around with your toe or scuffed with your heel you were likely to turn up a piece of broken glass or a rusty nail or maybe a shard of broken pottery.

We stopped there and scuffed the sod in the depression that probably was some sort of cellar, and found the neck of a bottle whose glass had turned purplish brown. And several very rusty old cut nails. And half of a strap hinge. The wind sighed in the bare branches of the cottonwood. There was an echoing whistle off to the east, and the midmorning passenger train came roaring along the tracks, only a hundred yards north of us. Spider leaped to the top of the mound and waved his arms frantically, shouting, "Help! Help! Help!" and the fireman waved back and grinned and the whistle shrieked again with that long wail that wavers in pitch as the train speeds away from you, and the wind whipped the thin stream of smoke over us and around us with its half-warm, sooty, sulphury odor.

Then the train was gone and the dogs came panting back from their futile run and Spider came down from the mound and flopped his arms to warm himself. He got down on his knees, scratched at the grass with his hands, and urged, "Here, Fritz! Here, Nig! Dig! Dig 'em out!" Both dogs came, scratched at the sod for a few minutes, willing to play the game. They sniffed, dug a bit more, then quit and walked away. Spider said, "I'm freezing to death. Let's get going!"

So we went on, southeast now, away from the road and the tracks. And in another mile we came to a rise where we could look down and see a low white house and a big gray unpainted barn with corrals and haystacks in a fenced yard. It was the Rumming ranch and it lay in a broad part of the river valley, had a fifteen- or twenty-acre patch of alfalfa still green beyond the barn, and corrals and native hay and pasture lands stretching up and down the valley. There was no sign of anybody around. The Rummings had moved to town for the winter.

Simon Rumming was one of the old-timers, a one-eyed man who wore a sandy goatee and walked with a slightly bowlegged gait that was almost a swagger but not quite. He was only about five feet four, but stocky and undoubtedly rawhide tough. I never saw him without a smile, and I never heard him raise his voice. There were a number of stories about him, but they added up to the probability that he was English born, had come to America as a small boy, had been in Texas in the 1870s, and came up the cattle trails as a cavvy boy with a Texas trail drover. The name "cavvy boy" comes from the Spanish "caballo," meaning horse, and the cavvy boy tended the horse herd on a trail drive. Simon, so the story went, came up the trail several times with herds of longhorns being brought from the mesquite flats of Texas to rail head in

Kansas or Colorado, the last trip as a cowhand. He saw this country, liked it, picked the place in the Republican river valley, and homesteaded it for a ranch headquarters. There, and on adjoining land he later bought from other homesteaders, he had hay, grass and water, everything he needed. He built up a herd. Some said he got most of his herd "with a long noose," meaning that he took unbranded calves off the range and put his own brand on them. This probably was a romantic lie, but old Simon, who had a wry sense of humor, later said, "Somebody had to brand those calves to keep the rustlers from getting 'em." Another story had it that he won his first herd at the poker table by outwitting a Texas ranchman. I forget the details of the game, but at the crucial point Simon took out his glass eye, set it on the table beside his pile of chips, and said, "Watch 'em, boy, watch 'em!" And the disembodied eye, seeming to stare at him, so distracted the ranchman that he bet his herd on three queens when Simon had a full house. I never had the nerve to ask Simon about that story, or even if he had a glass eye. He never wore one while I knew him. The lid just sagged over that empty socket.

We went on down the slope, the dogs ahead of us, and the dogs put up a cottontail and chased it under the barn and made a great fuss. We let them yammer and went around to the lee side of the barn and tried to get warm, out of the wind. I got warm and Little Doc said he was warm enough, but Spider's teeth were chattering. I thought he was play-acting, but Little Doc felt of his forehead and said, "Come on. We're going home. It's too cold out for people to enjoy, and even we aren't having much fun."

For once, Spider had no answer. He went with us, his jaw set and his shoulders hunched against the cold. He was dragging his feet before we got to the top of the hill above the ranch. I offered to carry his gun. At first he refused, angrily. But finally he said, "Very well, varlet, take the cannon." I took it in my free hand and Spider took a long, quivering breath, then said, "Carry on, Sergeant, carry on. We have met the enemy and they are ours."

We fell into single file, me in the lead, Spider in the middle, and Little Doc bringing up the rear. Spider had fallen silent, hands deep in his mackinaw pockets, head down. But I could hear him breathing behind me, shallow, gasping breaths. Once, just beyond the mound at the old Bowserville store site, Little Doc said, "Let's stop and catch our breath." He and I got on the windward side and gave Spider some shelter, and he stood there puffing for several minutes. Then he began to shiver again and said, "Carry on, Sergeant," and we lined out as before.

It began to sleet while we were still half a mile from town, pellets that stung like birdshot in the freshening wind. We ducked our heads and kept going. The grass underfoot was soon so slick that we all began to slide and stumble. Once Spider went to his knees, but he was on his feet again before we could help him. Little Doc wanted to take his arm, but he shook his head and pushed Little Doc away. Ten minutes later we crossed the tracks and walked up the graveled street in the edge of town. The street wasn't half as slick as the sidewalk.

"We're going to the store," Little Doc said, meaning the drug store, and I headed for Main Street. But Spider said, "I'm going home," and turned up the back street. I was still carrying the cannon, but he seemed to have forgotten. Little Doc tried to argue for a moment, but it was no use. Spider shook his head and went on up the back street. We caught up with him, and we went all the way up to the north end of town, now walking abreast. When we were within a block of his house Spider stopped and took his gun from me, put it on his shoulder, and was about to start on when a spasm of coughing wracked him. He fought it, but he was red in the face before he could stop. Then he had to stand there, with Little Doc practically holding him up, for several minutes before he took a shallow breath and straightened up, lifted his shoulders, and went on, trying to be jaunty. We went with him as far as the front gate, where he turned and said, "Thank you, gentlemen, I shall be seeing you anon, whenever that is." By then his face was pasty white. He set his jaw, bit his white lower lip, and went up the path to the front porch. He stumbled on the steps, almost fell, caught himself, and after a moment crossed the porch and went in the front door without looking back.

Little Doc and I went back downtown. "He's pretty sick," I said.

Little Doc nodded. "He wasn't fooling. Boy, it's lucky we started back when we did!"

"What do you think it is? Asthma?"

"I don't know. But I'm going to tell my father to go up and see him. I'll bet he'll know what it is."

We were almost at the bank corner. I turned to go to the *News* office and Little Doc went on down the street to the drug store, where his father would be if he wasn't out somewhere on a call. Unless it was for a baby case or an accident, he probably wouldn't be out. The farm people didn't call a doctor on Saturday or Sunday if they could possibly wait till Monday.

Fritz and I went down the steps to the office. Fritz was grizzled with sleet. We went in and Father said, "Good! You're back!"

"You didn't think I'd stay out on a day like this, did you?"

"I hoped—" Father ducked and turned away as Fritz, in the middle of the office, shook himself, spattering sleet and dirty water. "I hoped," Father said again, wiping his face with his handkerchief, "you'd have better sense. . . . That dog! Good thing your mother isn't here."

Fritz had gone to the old rag rug in a corner that was his couch at the office, where he lay down and began licking himself clean and dry. It made Mother furious when he shook himself indoors. It was one of the few things they clashed over. He knew he wasn't to get on beds or chairs or to eat out of dishes we ate from. But a law that goes back to Neanderthal times says that dogs can shake themselves indoors. Fritz knew it. Mother never could accept it.

"Where is she?" I asked.

"At the house. And she wants you to go right over and help."

"Help what?"

"Help pack up and move. The Gibbses' things are out and your Mother thinks we can get the beds moved, and the cook-stove, this afternoon, and sleep in a warm house tonight. So you run along. I can't leave. I'm no good at that sort of thing anyway."

I had known for two weeks, rather vaguely, that we might move, but nothing was really settled. And I was too busy with my own affairs to pay much attention to supper-table talk. But I did know there was this five-room house over on the west side of town that was called "the Gibbs house" because it was occupied by the Reverend George P. Gibbs and his wife, who also was an ordained preacher. One of them, or maybe both, had been in charge of the Congregational church in Flagler until a few weeks ago. Then they took a leave of absence and went over in the western part of the state to visit other churches. A few days ago they came back and formally re-signed the Flagler pulpit to accept a call to a church in Creede, Colorado, and they said they were moving to Creede "in the near future."

The Lavington bank owned the house, and two weeks earlier, while the Gibbses were away, Mother somehow got a promise from the bank that she could rent the Gibbs house as soon as it was vacated. And somehow Mother persuaded Mrs. Gibbs, before she and Mr. Gibbs went back on the Friday train to Denver, to pack her belongings and leave orders for her furniture to be shipped to Creede. This morning Mother got hold of Mr. Groves, the drayman, and had him move the Gibbses' furniture and trunks down to the depot to wait for the westbound freight in the middle of next week. Then she went to Mr. Price, the cashier at the bank, informed him that the house was empty, paid a month's rent, and had swept out the whole house before she went back to the *News* office. By eleven this morning she had everything arranged.

When I got to the boxcar house where we had lived for six months, Mother was out back. She had a dish towel tied around her head, cotton flannel work gloves on her hands, and one of Father's out-at-elbows suit coats around her, and she was rattling a broomstick in a section of black tin stovepipe, creating a cloud of soot that streamed away like smoke from a laboring locomotive. She shouted, "Bring out the rest of the stovepipe from the kitchen! And don't spill soot all over the floor!"

In the next hour we took down all the pipe from both stoves, packed the bedding in our two storage trunks, folded the window curtains, and were packing dishes in two big boxes when Mr. Groves arrived with the dray. Mother supervised while he and I loaded the cookstove, the two beds, the trunks of bedding, the boxes of dishes, and a big hot kettle that Mother said was our supper.

The sleet had turned to fine snow, but Mr. Groves had an old canvas tarp to put over the load and keep the mattresses dry. He helped Mother up onto the seat, climbed up beside her, I got on the back, and off we went, across town. The road was slick, the horses slithered, and I heard Mr. Groves shout to Mother, "I don't see why you always do things to the weather! Remember the night you got here?"

"I certainly do," Mother shouted back. "You got the best rain you'd had in months!"

Mr. Groves laughed. "Well, I suppose you could say this is the best snowstorm we've had in months, too."

We pulled up at the Gibbs house and began unloading. When we had everything inside Mr. Groves asked, "Can I help set up the stoves and the beds?"

"We can do that," Mother said. "I'd a lot rather you went back and brought the rest of the furniture before the storm really settles down. By tomorrow it may be too bad to try to move anything."

"How about your chickens?"

"They're all right. I fed and watered them. We can't move them anyway till we get a pen built over here."

Mr. Groves went back for the rest of the furniture, and Mother and I set up the cookstove in the kitchen and I went out to the woodshed for kindling. There was a fresh ton of coal out there. "I ordered it this morning," Mother said. She hadn't forgotten a thing. I got a fire going and Mother put a pail of water to heat, and we got washed up and set up the bedsteads in the two bedrooms, put the springs and mattresses on them, while the fire began to take the chill off the house. By then Mr. Groves was back with the rest of the furniture, which we put in the front room to sort out later. Before he left, Mr. Groves helped me set up the heating stove in the front room, and with the two fires going the house really began to warm up. By five o'clock, when it was so dark we had to light the oil lamps, the place was warmer than the boxcar house ever had been.

Mother had the beds made and the table set when Father came home at six o'clock. He came in and looked around and said, "I don't know whose house I wandered into, but I sure like it here." He kissed Mother and put his coat and hat on a chair in the front room and came back into the kitchen. Mother had washed her face, brushed her hair, and put on a fresh clean apron. Fritz was lying on his old rug in a warm place beside the chimney. The teakettle was singing softly on the back of the stove, and a big pot of stewed chicken and dumplings simmered and filled the kitchen with a special savor.

Somehow, along with everything else, Mother had put a hen to stew that morning and brought it along, in that first load of furniture, still warm in the pot. She had made the dumplings and put them in only a few minutes before Father got home.

"I don't know how you do it," Father said, "but you sure make moving look easy."

"There's nothing to it," Mother said, "as long as *you* stay out of the way. You can help with those things in the front room tomorrow, but right now you can wash your hands and sit down at the table."

Not until we were at the table did I remember that I hadn't eaten since breakfast. I was starved. I finished a big first helping and was on a second before I paused long enough to tell them that Spider was sick. Father, whose stomach had been "touchy" ever since he almost died of typhoid fever, and who thought any sickness must be a digestive disorder, said, "Probably something he ate." But Mother said, "Stanley's not robust. That is his name, isn't it, Stanley? He has asthma, and I wouldn't be surprised if he has weak lungs. He shouldn't have gone with you and Justin today."

"It was all right when we left."

"Yes, I guess it was. It didn't turn stormy till right after dinnertime. Was it still snowing when you came home, Will?"

"It had almost stopped. About an inch on the ground. But it's getting a lot colder." Father heaved a deep sigh. "You know something? This is the first time this winter that my feet have been warm at home. That shack we were living in—" He shook his head. "Maybe I ought to send a letter of thanks to that congregation over in Creede."

"If you want to," Mother said. "But you can thank me, too. Three other people were waiting to see Mr. Price about renting this house when I came out of his office this morning."

The snow stopped during the night, but the temperature dropped to zero and a bitter wind was blowing by the next morning. Father and I went over to the old place to feed and water the chickens, and we didn't see another person outdoors. We went right back to the new house and spent the rest of the day happily indoors, getting the carpets down and the furniture arranged the way Mother wanted it.

It wasn't until Monday, at school, that I saw Little Doc and had any word about Spider. "He's got an awful heavy cold and he's running a fever," Little Doc said.

"What does that mean?" I asked.

"It means he's pretty sick."

"Has your father seen him?"

"He's been up there twice."

Tuesday brought no change, but at least Little Doc didn't say he was any worse. "My father says he's about the same."

But Wednesday morning Little Doc said, "He's got pneumonia." Even Little Doc said the word in a hushed voice. Pneumonia, in that climate and those days, was so deadly that everyone hesitated to talk about it. It was the dread consequence of a heavy cold, and those with "weak lungs" or asthma were always susceptible to chest colds. Those who recovered from pneumonia were considered lucky to be alive. My mother had it when she was fourteen years old, and she almost died. Her stories about it were so grim that she seldom told them, never when I had even a slight cold.

I was so stunned at Little Doc's news that I went to the wrong room for botany class and didn't realize where I was until the teacher began talking about Hamlet's soliloquy. I left and went to the right room, but even there I heard hardly a word. I went through my other classes in a kind of daze, and after my last class I found Little Doc and said, "We've got to go up and see Spider."

"No," Little Doc said. "I asked my father at noon, and he said we'd better stay away. He said Spider's got an awful high fever and is out of his head."

"Well, there's got to be something we can do!"

"Come on down to the store and we'll see what Dad says."

Dr. Williams wasn't there, but he came in only a few minutes later, looking tired out, red-eyed and haggard. He had been called out at midnight, to a farm fifteen miles up north, to deliver a baby, which was born dead. He'd just got back when he got a call from out west of town where a man had what turned out to be a ruptured appendix. He operated, on a kitchen table, and hoped for the best. Now he had just been up in the north end of town seeing an old lady who had a gallstone attack, and he had gone over to the Miners' for the second time that day before he returned to the drug store. He saw the two of us waiting and said, "Come on back to the office."

We went, and he put down his bag, took off his overcoat, and sat down heavily in the swivel chair at his rolltop desk. He took off his glasses and rubbed his eyes, then turned his back to the desk, began polishing his glasses with his handkerchief, and without looking up said, "I'm afraid I've got bad news about Stanley. His heart can't take the strain much longer. He may not pull through the night."

I felt as though a horse had kicked me right in the pit of the stomach. The room began to swim and I reached for a chair and almost fell into it. Little Doc just stood there, staring at his father, but I saw his hands clench into fists, then slowly relax.

Dr. Williams put his handkerchief away and put his glasses on again. He sighed, then said, "He's got double pneumonia, and a bad heart on top of that—" He shook his head. "He happens to be one of those youngsters who live right on the ragged edge, and it doesn't take much to push them over. A weakness in the lungs and the heart, and no reserve." He paused a moment, then turned to me. "I tried to tell Justin, and I want to tell you, that that hunting trip you three took last Saturday didn't have anything to do with this. He had pneumonia before he ever left the house. If he'd stayed home, in bed, he'd have been just as sick by now! Just remember that, both of you."

"Can we go see him?" I asked.

"No. There's no need for you to be exposed, in the first place. And Stanley is delirious. He wouldn't even know you."

"Isn't there anything we can do?"

Dr. Williams shook his head. "Just see that *you* don't get pneumonia. Though you're both pretty healthy specimens. . . . No, there's nothing you can do for Stanley." And he turned to his desk.

Little Doc and I went out and stood at the big front window, saying nothing for several minutes. Finally I said, "See you in the morning," and went out and around the corner and down to the *News* office.

I told Father what Dr. Williams had said, and he shook his head. "How old is he? Same age you are, isn't he, fifteen?" I said yes. "Too bad. Just too bad. Makes you wonder what it's all about. Some folks outlive any need for them, and others never really get started. And we don't know why. The preachers say it's God's will, and maybe they're right. But it's a peculiar way to run things, if I do say so."

Spider died that night.

The funeral was set for Saturday. Little Doc and I agreed that we weren't going to the funeral. We weren't going to go and watch people cry, and probably cry ourselves, and look at a dead body in a coffin that wouldn't be Spider at all, but just what was left when Stanley Miner died. If we looked in the coffin we would cry, and if we sat there in the church remembering Spider we would think of him the way he was and begin to laugh. We wanted none of the funeral.

When I announced this at home, Mother said, "You can't refuse to go, son. You can't! He was one of your very best friends. What will his family think?"

But Father said, "I don't see why he has to go. If he and Justin feel that way, I think Stanley would say they didn't have to go."

"That's—that's practically irreligious, Will!"

"Nothing of the kind." Father turned to me. "What do you want to do instead, if you don't go to the funeral?"

"Well, we might go out to Verhoff's Dam, or somewhere. Maybe go hunting jacks."

"Go hunting?" Mother was aghast. "During the funeral?"

"Sarah," Father said, "funerals are for family and old folks, like us. I never did think youngsters should be there. Or even fifteen-year-olds. You and I will go to the funeral. You don't have to go, son. You can do whatever you want to."

I don't know what was said to Little Doc. We never talked about it, he and I. I didn't tell him what my folks said. But at two o'clock Saturday afternoon, when they were holding the funeral at the church in Flagler, we were out at Verhoff's Dam. It was a mild day, the snow had all melted, the sun was shining brightly, and we were sitting on the hillside looking down at the sheet of ice on the water above the dam. We weren't talking. There didn't seem to be anything to say. But finally Little Doc turned to me and said, "They must be at the cemetery by now," and I said yes, and we stood up and fired two shots apiece out across the frozen pond. I don't know why, but that's what we did without even planning it.

Then we went back to town, slowly, taking our time. We put up several jack rabbits but didn't fire a shot at them. We didn't even talk until we were almost there. Then Little Doc said, trying to make it offhand, "I've decided I'm going to study medicine." And somehow that brought a big lump in my throat and for the first time all afternoon there were tears in my eyes. Then Little Doc was muttering softly under his breath. And we both sniffled and wiped our eyes and got it over with. Then we went on into town. It was early dusk, and lights were going on in the houses we passed. We went up the side street to the corner where he went north to his house and I went west to mine, and we said, "So long," just as though it was any Saturday in the year, and we went on home.

11

Even with statistics it sometimes is hard to gauge the effects of economic ups and downs. Without them it is sheer guesswork, particularly when human reactions are concerned. And even statistics couldn't have accounted for two qualities that, broadly speaking, marked the character of the people of that time and place: pioneer doggedness and frontier optimism. The pioneer went there determined to stay, in spite of the odds. And the frontiersman, early or late, expected life to be better than it was where he came from.

In any case, there were no statistics about the hail-out of the wheat or the sales in the Flagler stores that fall. But every storekeeper in town was still in business at Thanksgiving, and there had been no mass exodus from the farms. There had been more loss than the real estate men liked to admit, but less than the unhappy old-timer merchants had feared. Business in town was probably no better and not any worse than it had been the year before. I know that when Father tallied up his accounts and paid the interest on his note at the bank he said the *News* had done better than he expected when he bought it. "Not much, but a little. Business fell off in August, right after the hail. It picked up again in September. And October was more than ten percent better than June was."

"Then you don't think we'll go broke," Mother asked, "because I couldn't stand to live in that awful shanty one more night?"

"We haven't gone broke yet," Father said. "We may in another month, of course, but I doubt it. We've got Christmas coming, and I think I can get enough advertising for two extra pages every week till Christmas." The way he said it, he had it all arranged and was quietly triumphant about it.

But Mother said, "After Christmas there'll be January, and February, and everybody will say they are broke. They'll say they spent all they had on Christmas. And then we will have to live on whatever we made in December."

"Probably. But everybody will be in the same boat, won't they? We shouldn't be any worse off than anybody else." And a few minutes later he asked her, "What do you want for Christmas?"

"Christmas? For heaven's sakes! I've got my Christmas present, a house I can keep warm and clean. A place the dust and snow doesn't blow right through like a sieve. Don't you go wasting any money on a Christmas present for me, Will Borland!" Then she added, "Not this year."

It seemed impossible that Christmas was only a few weeks away, but school had been in session three months and in only three more weeks it would let out for the Christmas holiday. I had had my report for mid-term, and my marks were in the 90s for all my classes. There wasn't any talk of cutting me back to the regular freshman schedule. The only class where I was having any trouble at all was Latin, and I finally found what turned out to be my personal key. The teacher kept telling us that Latin would help us understand the meaning of English words. But it didn't seem to help me when she said that "manufacture," for instance, came from the Latin for "make by hand." Even in those days, nearly everything that was manufactured was made by machine. Then one evening it occurred to me that this was all wrong end to. If I started from English I could do much better. "Decimal," meaning by tens, led to *decim*, the Latin word for ten. "Manual," meaning by hand, took me directly to the Latin *manus*. "Renovate," meaning to make over and make new, led to the Latin *novus,* which means new; and so did "novitiate" and "novelty" and a lot of other words. I had a big vocabulary, so I found the clues everywhere I turned. And from then on Latin was easy. Even its grammar was easy because it was logical. I liked logical matters.

I was needed at the office, those last few weeks before Christmas, more than I had been since June, when I was first starting to learn to be a printer. As Father had said, he got the extra advertising, and there was extra job printing besides, Christmas cards, greetings, even personal stationery. I spent all my free time folding papers, cleaning presses, doing the extra chores at the office.

But I knew that things were happening, things that meant Christmas, all over town. There was a feeling in the air that soon became a community sense of holiday. It didn't have anything to do with buying and selling, either. There was Christmas business in the stores, of course, but there was this something-else, too. I suppose you would call it the Christmas spirit.

In most towns this kind of thing usually starts with the churches. But Flagler's principal church didn't have any preacher. After the Gibbses left, the board of the Congregational church took quite a while to decide on a successor, and when one finally was named he couldn't come until after the first of the year. The Congregational church actually was a community church that included practically everybody in town except a handful of Catholics and three or four families of Lutherans. The Lutherans had a tiny chapel in the north end of town, but the Catholics had no church at all; a priest came up from Burlington every few weeks to hold mass in someone's house. Most of the children in town went to Sunday school at the Congregational church, and Sunday school was continued even without a preacher. Plans for a Christmas program actually started there.

Then the Commercial Club, the business men's organiza-

tion, got around to Christmas at the first meeting after Thanksgiving. It started with talk about promoting the town and
inviting the farmers to come in and "enjoy the Christmas
spirit," which meant spend their money in the Flagler stores.
After a little of this claptrap Clarence Smith got up. He was a
real estate man, an influential member of the school board,
and a man with a strong sense of social responsibility. Some
of the old-timers called him a Socialist because he said Flagler
should have a municipal light plant and water system. He got
up and said, in his rather mild way, "If we are talking about
Christmas, gentlemen, I suggest that we forget about promoting Flagler and pulling the farmers into the stores and plan a
Christmas program worthy of the occasion. I rather imagine
that business will take care of itself, with no more than the
usual attention we give it. But Christmas needs our help. Are
you willing to give that help, or are you going to go on talking
about your margin of profit?"

There was considerable muttering, but finally someone
moved that a Christmas Committee be named, with Clarence
Smith as chairman, to do what was fit and proper in assisting
with a community Christmas. There was no discussion, and
the motion was about to come to a vote when Mr. Smith
said, "Unless there is an appropriation, I see no point in naming a committee. I certainly don't intend to go around and
pass the hat." More muttering. Then someone amended the
motion to empower the committee to spend up to one hundred dollars. A voice asked, horrified, "That much?" And
Chris Straub, who ran a lumber yard and also was superintendent of the Sunday school, said, "That's not enough. That's
only about five dollars apiece. I'll double that if the rest of
you will. Let's make it *two* hundred dollars!" There was a gasp,
and there were muttered dissents; but nobody ever wants it
said that he voted against Christmas. The amendment was
passed unanimously, on the record at least, and then the original motion was passed the same way.

That was the first week in December. Things began happening almost at once.

It was announced that there would be a community Christmas program at the church, complete with tree and gifts for the youngsters and Santa Claus in person. The school, the Sunday school, and practically everyone in town was to have a part in it.

Even before the tree came, decorations were planned and begun. The teacher of the primary grades in school came down to the *News* office to get material for paper chains. Father gave her a big package of colored manila strips, an inch wide and cut on the paper cutter. Several mothers made flour paste. From then till the Christmas holiday, the first-graders made paper chains, uneven and paste-smeared, but chains of love and belief. There must have been well over half a mile of those chains.

Other youngsters made popcorn strings. Nobody knows how much popcorn was popped and scorched and sorted and strung, or how many small fingers were pricked sore with darning needles. But yards, rods, furlongs of popcorn strings were made. And cranberry strings. Mr. Hall ordered a full barrel of cranberries, gave half of them to the cranberry stringers, sold the other half to their mothers for holiday sauce.

For the grownups to manage, there were the gifts. Dolls for the girls, tin whistles and rubber balls for the boys. How many there were, I have no idea, but they were wrapped individually in bright packages, and there were several bushels of them.

There was the candy, hard candy, gum drops, stick candy, red and green and frosty white. It came in huge wooden buckets, and it was packed, so many pieces of each kind, in paper bags. Bushels of bags of candy.

There were oranges. Oranges weren't everyday fare, and canned or frozen orange juice hadn't even been dreamed of. The oranges we had, on rare occasions, came from California and they had to be ordered special. Mr. Hall ordered them, ten or twelve crates, and they cost so much I am sure they were paid for out of the money appropriated to Mr. Smith's committee. I know only one crate of them was put on sale. The rest were for the community Christmas.

And, finally, there was the tree.

I don't know where the tree came from, but probably from up in the mountains beyond Denver. It was close to thirty feet high, and of course it was an evergreen, a spruce as I remember. Farther south, down in New Mexico and even in southern Colorado where there were a good many Mexican-Americans, they decorated cottonwoods for Christmas trees. They put cotton on them for snow and gave it glitter with flakes of mica. They hung them with birds and angels cut from tin cans, and they fastened their presents on those trees or put them down at the foot. But most of the people in and around Flagler came from the Midwest and wouldn't have understood such customs. They wanted an evergreen tree. So that's what they got.

The tree wasn't set up, of course, until the last week before Christmas, when school had let out for the holiday. Then it was taken into the church auditorium, put in place beside the pulpit, braced and wired and made as firm and safe as though it had grown there. It was so tall they had to take almost five feet off its top to make it clear the ceiling of the church.

If there were any other Christmas trees in town, I didn't know about them. I don't think there was even one.

Once it was up, the big tree had to be decorated. The paper chains were brought, and the popcorn strings, and the cranberry strings. The women supervised and the men and bigger boys climbed tall ladders to drape the decorations from the very topmost branch all the way down, twig by twig. And even before the decorations were all in place, the question of candles arose. There was always that question, whether it was a public tree or a private one, and when it was a public tree it was doubly important.

Generally speaking, a Christmas tree had to have candles. That was finally agreed on. But were the candles to be lighted? That was the crucial question. Lighted candles meant open fire, and fire in any evergreen is dangerous. A Christmas tree afire in a crowded public building could become a horrible calamity. A tree fire at home was bad enough.

It was agreed, though, that there should be candles, and they were put up, hundreds of them, red and green and white, four inches long, big around as a lead pencil, before the tall ladders were removed. Then came the question: Shall there be lighted candles? Some said, "We don't go if the candles are lit!" Some said, "We won't go if there *aren't* lighted candles!" More wanted lighted candles than didn't want them, but Mr. Smith, who assumed authority nobody else really wanted, achieved a compromise. Only those candles facing the pews and low enough to be lighted from the floor would be lit. And two men would be delegated to watch the candles and put out any fire the moment it started. They would sit in the front row, directly in front of the tree, and have pails of water at hand. There never had been a Christmas tree fire in a public building in Flagler and Mr. Smith wasn't going to have one now. He was an insurance man as well as a real estate man, knew the hazards, and wasn't going to let anything happen.

Meanwhile, of course, the program itself was being rehearsed. Each of the Sunday school classes had a special number to prepare, recitations by groups and individuals were memorized, and two of the high school girls, one of them a Catholic, practiced solos. And Big Ed Schlote, the biggest man in town, over six feet and more than 220 pounds, was preparing for his special performance. Big Ed played the tuba in the town band, sang baritone in the choir, and had a laugh you could hear clear across town.

Christmas fell on a Saturday that year, so the program would be held Friday evening. It was an almost perfect week, with light snow on Monday, then three days of clear, frosty air and sunshine, followed by another two inches of fresh snow Thursday night, as though to freshen the whole world and add a special Christmas sparkle. Friday was clear and dazzling, and there wasn't enough snow on the ground to really interfere with travel, afoot, on horseback, or in buggy or wagon.

It had been an easy week at the office after three weeks of fifteen-hour days. The rush was over. The paper that week was back to normal size, since there was no point in Christmas advertising in a paper that came out on December twenty-third.

Mother went home in midafternoon, that Friday. There was no business to keep her at the office, and she said there was plenty to do at home. Father and I did the usual jobs of the day after publication day, breaking up the forms of ads, distributing the type in the news columns, cleaning the presses. And at a quarter of five, an hour earlier than usual, Father said, "Let's wash up and call it a day." Then he chuckled. "Call it a *week*, this time. Tomorrow's Christmas, and the next day is Sunday."

We washed up and put on our coats, and Father reached for the big hanging lamp to turn it off. But, his hand on the lamp, he hesitated, looked around the office; and an odd smile came over his face. He shook his head slightly, as though not quite believing, before he turned out the light and we went out and he locked the door.

Up on the street, it was already dark but there was the winter glow, the strange light from the snow as though it somehow had caught some fraction of the vanished daylight and held it. The air was crisp and I could see my own breath. It twinkled as we walked through a yellow beam of light from a window with an oil lamp on the table inside. Our footsteps whined slightly in the snow.

We went home, and it seemed to me that the house was

more full of warmth and comfort than I could remember. There was nothing special, really. Mother had supper almost ready, and she was setting the table when we went in. Father kissed her, as always, and hung up his coat, and I hung mine up, and he looked at the fire in the heating stove in the living room, started to poke at it, as always, and Mother called from the kitchen, "Leave that fire alone! I just got it fixed." Father closed the stove door and put the poker down and muttered under his breath. He stood there, back to the stove, hands behind him, and he began to smile again, the same smile I had seen at the office. Mother was humming in the kitchen, her favorite carol, "Silent Night." A few minutes later she called us to the table.

We hadn't more than served ourselves and taken two bites when she asked, "What are you up to, Will Borland?"

Father looked at her, surprised. "Nothing. Why?"

"I see that look on your face. If you've gone and bought an expensive present for me, you can just take it back and get your money."

"I didn't do anything."

"Well, what's that look on your face?"

"I don't know what you're talking about, but I was thinking, down at the office, and since I got home, about how much better off we are than we have been any Christmas I can remember."

"We're not out of debt."

"No. We owe money on the *News*. But that's all we owe. What I was thinking about was—well, that Christmas when I was just out of the hospital."

"I remember."

"And the Christmas after that, and the next one, and last Christmas. Now I'm my own boss, and the paper's making its own way, and—well, I think we've got a lot to be thankful for this Christmas. I have, I know that."

"I have too," Mother said. "Now eat your supper so I can

do the dishes. We've got to dress and be at the church by seven-thirty to get a seat."

Every star there was seemed to be out when we walked across town to the church. It was all lit up and you could see it from two blocks away, its lights gleaming through the windows onto the snow. There was talk and laughter from all directions, for people were coming from all over town. We joined a line going up the front steps four abreast, and when we got inside there weren't more than twenty or thirty empty seats left in the pews. Men were carrying folding chairs up from the basement and setting them up in every vacant foot of space.

The tree, down front, dominated everything. It was magnificent, loaded with paper chains, gleaming with popcorn strings, glowing with the bright red of cranberries. And all over it, from top to bottom, were the candles, bright flecks of color even without flame. At the foot of the tree were heaped the baskets of candy and gifts, covered with colored cloths and looking like mounds of mysterious wealth.

People kept coming. By eight o'clock the church was jammed, every seat taken, every inch of standing room full. On the stage was the Knies orchestra, six pieces with William Knies, who ran the Beatrice cream station, as first violinist and leader. He pronounced the name "Ken-nees," accenting the second syllable, and he gave music lessons, had been trying to persuade Mother to let me learn some instrument. Promptly at eight o'clock Mr. Knies tapped his music stand and the orchestra played "Joy to the World!" The program had begun.

The orchestra played three selections. Then Professor Conley, who had a good reading voice, went to the lectern, opened the Bible to the book of Luke, and began reading. "Now it came to pass in those days. . . ." He read right on through the first twenty verses of the second chapter. "And the shepherds returned, glorifying and praising God for all the things that they had heard and seen, as it was told unto them." He finished reading, and there was a hush as he left the lectern without a word more and returned to his seat.

And then Chris Straub took over, as superintendent of the Sunday school. He said, "Now we will have our program," and he waited there while Bill Kliewer and Ray Thompson lit the candles in reach on the front of the tree, then returned to their seats in the front row, handy to half a dozen buckets of water. Then Chris glanced at his notes and said, "Now I think the girls are going to sing 'Holy Night' for us."

A group of older girls went onto the platform, trying to suppress their giggles, and the pianist struck a chord and they sang "O Little Town of Bethlehem." They returned to their seats and Chris said, "I guess the boys are the ones who are going to sing 'Holy Night.'" A group of ten- and twelve-year-old boys trooped up onto the stage, smirking, and they sang "Deck the Halls." They left, and Chris said, "Well, confound it, we're going to have 'Holy Night' one way or another. Everybody, please, sing 'Holy Night.'" And he turned to the pianist, who nodded and struck the right chords, and everybody in the church stood up and sang that beautiful old song which seems to mean Christmas, all by itself.

After that Chris had a schedule to read, and he summoned various ones to give their recitations—or sing their songs. Then one more carol was sung by everyone. By that time Chris Straub was getting fidgety. He kept watching the door at the back of the church. Just as the carol was ending there was the sound of sleigh bells outside. They jingled, then were quiet, then jingled again, and there was a motion at the outer door. The carol ended and Chris gestured toward the door and said in a stage whisper that could be heard all over the church, "All right, Ed. Come on. Come on!"

The sleigh bells jingled again, the door opened, and in came Big Ed Schlote, red-faced, red-suited, white-whiskered, beaming. He shook the string of bells and started down the aisle. There was a flutter through the room, then little cries of awe and delight from children in every corner. And before Big Ed got halfway down that aisle something happened. It wasn't Ed Schlote in a red suit. It was Santa Claus. You could feel the wave of belief all over the church, in grownups as well as in the children.

He came down the aisle and paused to look at that tree, with all its paper chains and its strings of popcorn and cranberries and all its candles. He looked and he said, "What a beautiful tree!" and his voice was awed. And everybody knew, in that moment, that it was the most beautiful Christmas tree in the world. Then he asked, "Where are Santa's helpers?" and half a dozen men got from their seats and went down the aisle to his side. He said, "There are the presents," and he held out both hands toward the heaped baskets under the tree. "There were so many I had to send them ahead. Take off the covers, please." The men took off the cloths, revealing the heaped baskets of gifts. Then they lined up and each one took a basket and they went with him up the aisle. He singled out every child, called it by name, gave it a bag of candy, an orange and a toy. Slowly he made his way up the aisle, and across the back, and then down the other aisle, his helpers bringing fresh baskets as the loaded ones were emptied. It took forever, maybe an hour, but not once was there a break in that fantastic web of belief.

Finally every child had been visited, called by name, given the precious bag and package by Santa Claus himself. The baskets were empty. The candles had burned down and been snuffed. And Santa Claus stood there at the foot of the aisle, looking up at the tree again. Then he turned and looked out across the crowded church and lifted his hands almost in benediction, and he said, "Merry Christmas to all! Merry Christmas, and to all a good night!" And he hurried up the aisle, out of the door, and was gone, only the jingling of the bells echoing behind him.

There was a final song, "It Came Upon the Midnight Clear," but it was sung softly, almost in a hush. And after that there was the slow exit, that whole big crowd getting itself organized and up the aisles and out the doors, and all without loud talk or confusion or pushing or anything but patience and courtesy and a kind of quiet sense of peace and good will. The spell was still upon us.

Then we were outside, in the clear, cold starlight. Quiet good nights were said, there was the sound of soft laughter, and over everything there seemed to be the echo of bells.

12

I got the usual and expected things for Christmas, a new mackinaw coat, a sweater, socks, mittens. We were a practical family, and when the homestead experience was added to that there wasn't much tendency to spend money on frippery. Father did get Mother a bottle of perfume—*not* the kind Mr. Hall had advertised; and he got a book for me, Ernest Thompson Seton's *Two Little Savages*. I had heard about that book, had never even seen it, but wanted it. Now I read it, fascinated; but it was about a far-off, foreign land, a woodland place, with the trees and plants and brooks and birds and animals of a forest. It wasn't quite as alien as a book about the moon would have been, but almost.

Mother gave me the most unexpected Christmas present of my life—music lessons. She had made arrangements with Mr. Knies for me to learn to play whatever instrument I chose. When she told me, I did my best to show proper appreciation. I liked music, and I was willing to learn to play almost anything but the piano. But there were other things that seemed more important to me. I can't remember what they were, but I knew then. There it was, though: I was going to take music lessons.

Both Mother and Father had what might be called musical impulses, perhaps even talents. Neither of them could play any instrument, but both could sing. Father's baritone was clear and true and he could carry an air accurately. Mother's soprano was beautiful and strong, and though she had never been taught to read music she could follow the notes, knew something of their value, and could hum a tune she had never heard by following the score. From time to time they both sang in the church choir. I never did. Maybe that is why I got the music lessons. Anyway, I thanked her and a few days later went to see Mr. Knies.

He was a pleasant little man with a bristly brown mustache and a slight German accent. He was in the Beatrice cream station, wearing a long white apron, taking samples from big cream cans, putting the samples in test tubes, adding a few drops of acid, then spinning the tubes in a centrifuge turned by hand crank. When he took the tubes out, the percentage of butterfat could be read on the graduated scale on each tube. Farmers were paid for their cream in proportion to its butterfat content.

He glanced at me, said, "In a minute," and finished reading the test tubes he had just centrifuged. Then he wiped his hands on his apron and said, "My new pupil! And what are you going to learn to play?"

I had no idea what I wanted to play. But before I could find a proper way to tell him that, he said, "Well, now, Atwood plays the cornet. Winfield plays the trombone. Miriam plays the cello." Atwood and Winfield were his two sons, Miriam his grown daughter. "But Miriam will be away most of the winter. Why don't—the cello! That's the instrument for you! The cello." He spread his hands, then clapped them together in triumph. "Then we have a quintette all winter, with Mama at the piano and me with the fiddle."

I had no objection. At least with the cello you played only one note at a time. It would be simpler than the piano.

So I became a cellist, simply because Miriam Knies was going to be away most of the winter. The Knieses lived in quarters back of the cream station, and for the first month I went down there two evenings a week to learn how to use the bow, how to run scales, how to read music. Fortunately, my ear was fairly accurate, because the cello has no frets—you guess where the right note should be, put the proper finger on the right string at that point, and use the bow. You can ease up or down a bit to true up the note, but not very far. So I sawed away at those strings two hours a week for a month, and the best I could do was run the scale in three different keys. Mr. Knies said I wasn't getting enough practice and wondered what to do about it. It would be much better, he mused, if I had my own cello. Miriam's cello was much too expensive to let me take it home and practice with it. It probably cost three or four hundred dollars, maybe more, for all I knew. Then Mr. Knies said, "Maybe I could find an inexpensive one in Denver. A used one. It would do to practice on."

I asked how much it would cost. I had fifty-five dollars, money I had saved from my summer pay at the printing office.

"Thirty-five dollars, maybe?" he suggested. "Could you pay that much?"

I said yes, I could pay that much for a cello to practice on. He seemed greatly relieved. He had to go to Denver on business the very next day, he said. He would see what he could do.

He brought back a cello for me, a second-hand instrument, probably from a pawn shop, and not a very good cello to begin with. But a cello. He showed it to me, and he wiped the dust from its belly with his handkerchief, and he gave me the bow and said to try it. I bowed a few notes and said it sounded almost as good as Miriam's. Mr. Knies beamed, then shook his head. "No, no, it's not that good! But for the price—it's really very good for the price, a nice tone." Then he turned solemn and pulled at his lower lip. "I—uh—I have to tell you it cost more than I hoped it would. It cost forty dollars. I knew you only had thirty-five, but I said to myself, 'This is worth the money, this cello. And he is an honest boy and serious about music.' I said, 'He will pay me the extra five dollars when he gets it.' " He smiled at me, hopefully. "You will?"

"I'll pay you right now," I said, getting out my wallet. "I've got fifty-five dollars!"

He gasped. "Oh." He was hurt and couldn't conceal it. "You should have told me. For fifty dollars I could have got a really good instrument, a good—uh—" He took the forty dollars I gave him, counted it, and pocketed it. "Well," he said with a sigh, "we do the best we can, huh? So take your cello home and practice. Maybe we get somewheres yet."

Anyone who has heard a beginner on a violin can imagine what my parents went through the next few weeks. A cello can squeal just like a fiddle but three times as loud and with ten times the resonance. After a couple of days of it, Father left the house every time I started to practice. Mother stuck it out, though it must have been real punishment. But Mr. Knies was right. With my forty-dollar cello I finally began to learn.

Flagler was a musical town, with enough real talent to be tolerant of beginners and serious amateurs but sharply critical of all others. There were two orchestras, that of Mr. Knies, which was basically a family group, and that led by C. A. Anderson, a tall, handsome Scandinavian cobbler and harness maker who also played the violin. Mr. Anderson was moody and temperamental and he played the violin with verve and flourishes. I am sure he was a much more exciting teacher and leader than Mr. Knies. But the temperamental cobbler from time to time publicly announced that if Flagler wanted to listen to "that milkman's tum-tum-de-tum fiddling" it had no need for Mr. Anderson and his music. He would disband his own musical group, glower for a month or two, bitterly and no doubt honestly criticize every musical event in town, then gather his own group and start playing again. Mother preferred his music, even the wild Hungarian dances of Liszt and the strange Norwegian melodies of Grieg, to Mr. Knies' quiet semi-classics. I don't remember being surprised by this at the time, but now, looking back, it strikes me as almost unbelievable. Half German by birth and strict Methodist by upbringing, she should have called such music "heathenish." But there were contradictions in her that I still can't explain. In any case, Mr. Anderson was in one of his glowering, bitter moods when she arranged for my lessons.

But it was unschooled talent that kept cropping up in unexpected places. That, of course, was characteristic of the old frontiers, where people had to create their own amusement, and it continued in the rural areas west of the Missouri right down to the age of vicarious music, of radio, records and tape recorders. Until then, you made your own music or you did without it most of the time.

Only a few weeks after we arrived in Flagler we went to the hotel for Sunday dinner and, to our surprise, found the dining room crowded. Sunday dinner cost 50 cents, 15 cents more than a weekday dinner, so nobody was there to save money. We looked in, saw the crowd, and Mother said, "I wonder if it's a wedding, or what?" Mr. Blancken came past and said, "I'm sorry, but you'll only have to wait a few minutes." Mother asked him what was the reason for the crowd, but he had already hurried away. Before long the dining room began to clear out a bit and we got a table.

We had just started to eat when the music began. Someone was at the piano in the corner of the lobby. Through the doorway I could see only that people were sitting in all the chairs and standing along the walls. And whoever was at the piano was making it do tricks, everything from ballads of the Nineties to dance tunes.

I hurried through my food and excused myself, went to the doorway, and wormed my way inside. There at the piano was a short dark-haired man in a blue shirt with red sleeve garters,

147

a vest but no coat, and blue serge pants so old they had a green shine on them. He had big hands but stubby fingers, and they danced all over the keyboard. As I watched he swung into a dance tune and began to bounce up and down on the piano stool, and he threw back his head and laughed. Then he turned to the woman in the big chair beside the piano and said something and laughed again. She was a chubby little woman, very blonde, and she had a baby in her arms and a toddling little girl at her knee who watched the man at the piano with solemn concentration. Standing beside the little girl was a big dark man who looked like an Indian. Ed Probst, the well digger. Then I recognized the man at the piano—Bob Probst, Ed's brother, who worked with Ed digging wells and ditches and cesspools, any kind of pick-and-shovel work.

Bob Probst played that piano for an hour without a stop. Now and then someone suggested a tune and Bob nodded, went on playing until he reached a place for a break, then switched to the new tune. Finally he played "Little Brown Jug" with a lot of runs and flourishes, and people began to leave. He finished with three loud chords, drew a deep breath, and got to his feet. He put on his coat, took the baby from his wife, who took the toddler by the hand and followed him across the lobby. Ed, who looked like an Indian who had lost his braids, brought up the rear. The concert was over. The Probsts crossed the street to where their team was hitched, got into the lumber wagon with its two spring seats, and left.

About once a month Bob Probst came to town for Sunday dinner at the hotel, which always was free to him and his retinue. People saw him or heard he was in town and gathered to hear him. He ate, then sat down and played. He didn't know one note of music, and he played in odd keys full of sharps and flats. So far as I knew, he never played any other piano. He had none of his own. The story went that one Sunday two or three years before we went to Flagler he sat down at the piano in the hotel and began to play, just like that, for the first time in his life. We heard him play maybe half a dozen times, that summer and fall. Then he didn't play again. I don't know what happened. He and Ed were around Flagler for several years after that, but Bob never played the piano again as far as I know.

Late that winter we heard another kind of music at a country square dance. It wasn't called a square dance because a good many of the farmers out north of town were strict Baptists who disapproved of cards and dancing as sternly as Mother did in her Methodism. They called it a game party, and that made it possible for Mother to accept an invitation to go. Father would have gone with a clear conscience, no matter what they called it. He was brought up as a Camp-bellite, and his church wasn't *that* strict. Anyway, we were invited, Father said he wanted to know those farmers better, and Mother said she didn't mind going. So we went.

The dance—or game party—was held in a big one-room sod house about six miles north of town. It was March, almost spring, and the weather was fairly mild. When we got there the dooryard was full of furniture—everything had been moved outdoors, even the cookstove. The only thing left in the house was an old reed organ, off in one corner. There were benches along the walls, and there were about forty people there when we arrived.

We walked in and for a moment it looked as though even Father didn't know a soul. Then a tall thin man came over to us and smiled, bowed to Mother, nodded to me. "Hello," he said. "Glad to see you here. They're going to have quite a party." It was Dr. Neff, a physician who had been in Flagler I don't know how long. He was one of the old saddlebag doctors who had gone on horseback to remote soddies where men were dying and women were delivering their own babies. I doubt that even he knew how many crucial operations he had performed by oil-lamp light on kitchen tables, or how many babies he delivered without even the help of a midwife.

Now he was saying to Mother, "Have a good time," and with a gesture to Father he turned and was gone. Mother asked, in a whisper, "I wonder what he's doing here."

Before Father could even guess, a red-faced man who seemed to be in charge shouted, "Attention! Attention, please!" and people quieted down enough to hear him say, "I want to introduce some special guests. Most of you know *about* him, but I want you to *know* him. And his wife, and his boy, too. Come on over here, Will Borland! All three of you." Mother blushed with embarrassment, but Father urged her and the crowd made way for us. We reached the announcer and he introduced us one at a time, and there was loud clapping and shouting of welcome.

Just then there was a stir at the doorway and we were forgotten. A wizened old man came in carrying a violin case. With him was a boy about my age with long, ragged blond hair, a freckled face, and a solemn look. Way was cleared for them and they crossed the room to the reed organ. The boy sat down on the stool, pumped the pedals a few times, and struck a chord or two. The old man got out his fiddle and bow and asked the boy for a note. The boy pumped again, held down the key, and the organ groaned the wanted note. The old man began to tune up.

The red-faced man who had introduced us shouted, "Partners all and get ready for the figures!" Sets were formed, six sets of four couples each, all the room would hold. The others, most of them older men and women, seated themselves on the benches.

The old fiddler cleared his throat, bowed a few notes, and said, "We'll start with 'Darling Nelly Gray,'" and he nodded to the boy. The organ began to wheeze, the boy struck the opening chords, the fiddle began to sing, and the old fiddler called, "All hands round and circle to the left." He was caller as well as fiddler. The dance began.

I was fascinated, not so much by the dancing as by the

music. The boy at the organ did what was known as chording. I suppose it was equivalent to a guitar background, or maybe even drums, because it set the beat and provided the background for the fiddle's melody. The fiddler carried the tune while he called the figures. But I never heard anything like the way that boy brought the beat of the music out of that wheezy old organ without once playing a melody note.

The dancing went on, from one dance to another. At the first break the red-faced announcer came over and asked Mother to be his partner. "I don't know how," she protested, but he insisted. "Nothing to it. Just follow the lead, do what the other ladies do." Father urged, and reluctantly she went. And a moment later the announcer's wife asked Father to be her partner. Father was a good dancer, with natural rhythm. Mother would have been too if she hadn't been so deep-dyed Methodist about it. But she did all right, and she danced another set later, though she wouldn't allow herself to enjoy one minute of it.

After two or three sets the dancers began to call for special tunes. One of them was "Possum up a Gum Stump," apparently a favorite of the Missourians in this crowd. The fiddler said all right, he would try it, but he wouldn't guarantee he could keep on the right track. He started in and got about halfway through, then obviously lost the tune. The dancers shook their heads at him, then laughed as he slid off into "The Arkansas Traveler."

Dr. Neff, who had been standing on the sidelines, started across the floor, signaling to the fiddler. The music stopped. People looked around, saw Dr. Neff, and began to talk and whisper, excitedly.

Dr. Neff said to the fiddler, "You kind of lost the tune, didn't you Jim?"

"Sure did, Doc! Lost it like the old dog lost the cold coon track."

"Mind if I take it once through?"

"Be mighty pleased if you would, Doc." And he handed the fiddle to the tall, lanky doctor. Dr. Neff tucked the fiddle under his chin, turned to the crowd, said, "Places all." Then he said to the boy at the organ, "Let's take it in G, Orville."

The boy looked baffled. "I don't know them by name," he said.

Dr. Neff shifted the bow to his left hand, said, "Pump," and reached down and struck the basic G chord, ran the major sequence, up and back. The boy grinned at him. "Oh, that one!" He ran the sequence himself, then ran it with all the minors thrown in. His fingers knew. All he didn't know was the names.

Dr. Neff nodded. "That's the one. Let's go!" He lifted the bow, struck a long, firm note while the organ chords began. Then he was off. You never heard such playing. It was "Possum up a Gum Stump" straight through, simple and clear, and then it was "Possum up a Gum Stump" with flourishes. Then it was "Possum up a Gum Stump" with flourishes, ruffles and embellishments. And the boy at the organ followed him, every note, every turn and flourish. So did the dancers, for the doctor called the figures—sang them, in fact—as he played.

When he finished there was a roar of applause and shouts for "More! More!" He shook his head and let them shout, and he turned to the old fiddler. "Here," he said, "is where you went off," and he played the tricky part again, showing the fingering and the progression. "It's easy to go off, at that place. I do it myself if I don't watch out." He handed the fiddle back to the old man and went over and sat down. The dance was the old man's once more.

Later, on the way home some time after midnight, Mother asked, "Did you know Dr. Neff could play the violin that way?"

"No," Father said. "I didn't know he could play the violin

any way." We were in a livery rig that Father had hired, and the horses were feeling frisky.

"I wonder if he'd been drinking," Mother said.

"Drinking? With that bunch of hard-shell Baptists!" Father began to laugh.

"Well, I hear he *is* a drinking man. I didn't smell it on his breath, but he could have used Sen-Sen, or something."

"I wonder what he drinks. If I thought it would make me play the fiddle the way he can, I might—"

"Will Borland, don't you go talking that way! Not even if you are joking. What would people think if they heard you say a thing like that?"

Father didn't answer. He was having to keep taut reins on the horses. But some of their friskiness must have got into him because I heard him whistling "Possum up a Gum Stump" under his breath. Mother heard him too, and finally she said, "Will Borland, you'd just as well stop trying to plague me. You've tried four times now, and got the tune wrong every time."

"Just how does it go?" Father asked.

She began to hum the tune and went all the way through before she heard Father chuckling. "Well!" she exclaimed. "At least I got it right!" Then, in spite of herself, she laughed with him.

Flagler also had outside music, professional music. There were what were called lyceum programs, a series of lectures and concerts spaced through the winter months. The "talent" was sent out by an agency in Lincoln or Des Moines which made local contracts and laid out schedules and routes as far west as Utah. A group of Flagler business men signed up, guaranteed the minimum fee, then sold tickets to local people. The programs were held in Seal's Hall and always drew a full house.

I remember nothing about the lectures, but two of the mus-

153

ical programs were unforgettable. One was by the Jubilee Singers. We had no Negroes in Flagler nor, as far as I knew, in the whole of Kit Carson County, and few of us had ever heard any real Negro music. We knew Stephen Foster and the minstrel show songs, but they weren't Negro music at all, as we found out as soon as those Jubilee Singers got well under way. There was a chorus of about a dozen men, and there were quartets and soloists. They sang everything from spirituals to ballads, and I had never dreamed of anything like it, the rhythm, the syncopation, the laughter, the sorrow, and those marvelous voices. Before they arrived in town there apparently was some rather baffling correspondence with the booking office, since they would be in Flagler overnight. I don't know what questions were raised, but they didn't bother anyone in Flagler, whatever they were. The Jubilee Singers stayed at the hotel, just like any travelers, and they ate in the dining room there with the townsfolk. Nobody seemed to think anything of that.

The other memorable program was by the Royal Hawaiians. It was the first Hawaiian music I had ever heard, and I wish I could hear it again now. It was the first time we had seen or heard ukuleles or steel guitars. And the program ranged from the War Chant to the hulas, from beach-boy songs to dirges. They may not have been the best company of Hawaiian musicians who ever came to this country, but they had something more hauntingly beautiful than anything we had ever heard. They didn't have any grass-skirted girls to do the hula, and they did none of the heavy-handed clowning that became a standard part of Hawaiian repertoires ten or fifteen years later. They simply played and sang Hawaiian music pretty much the way I imagine it was played and sung in the islands before our tin-pan alley boys began to tinker with it. I know I would have swapped my cello for a ukulele, and I thought then that I would throw in my shotgun, my most precious possession, if anyone wanted to swap a steel guitar.

After the Hawaiians, the cello was a very uninteresting in-strument. And the Knies quintette was dull as ditch water. But I kept up my practice, though not every day, and I played with the group on special occasions at school or church. I never did become a sight reader who could sit down and play anything set on the music rack in front of me. But I became a soloist that spring. Twice I was allowed to play solo parts during informal concerts we gave. Once I played "Traumerei," and the other time I played "The Last Rose of Summer." Mr. Knies evidently decided that even I couldn't ruin those two pieces.

Beyond the fact that I was a slow reader and had a good ear, I never had any distinction as a cellist. My experience with it did give me a basic course in music that I never would have had otherwise. But, just to round off this particular memory, I must report that after high school I found that the college orchestra didn't need my degree of skill on the cello. There was an opening on a small dance band for a banjo player, so I swapped my forty-dollar cello for a thirty-five dollar tenor banjo. A few years later, after I was out of college, I swapped the banjo for a twenty-five-dollar second-hand guitar, and eventually I gave the guitar away. But I still love cello music, especially when played by someone who is at least a good journeyman musician. Casals, say.

13

Winter in a High Plains town in those days was neither as dour as the small-town debunkers painted it twenty years later nor as blithe as the rural romantics said it was. It was winter, with snow and cold and bitter wind. When a blizzard swept across those treeless flats it seemed to come all the way from Saskatchewan, gathering strength with every mile. But few winters brought more than a couple of real blizzards. Snow-storms were more frequent, storms without the high wind and intense cold. And there were intervals every winter when chinooks, relatively warm, dry winds, came rolling out across the plains from the eastern slope of the Rockies and gave us periods of melt and balminess that sustained the spirit. Then we knew that eventually there would be end to winter.

But meanwhile Flagler was, if not quite beleaguered, at least left to its own devices in facing winter's problems. Towns-people shoveled snow off their sidewalks and dug paths to stables, chicken houses and privies. The big road grader was trundled out and pushed enough snow to the sides of the main streets so that what little traffic there was could move: the drays from the depot, the coal wagons from the lumber yards, a delivery wagon or two from the food stores to get groceries to the lame, the halt and the aged. Except where the wind blew them clear, rural roads were blocked until and unless the farmers plowed out or dug out a track. The road to Denver was impassable even for the few automobiles that might have attempted to travel it.

Actually, nobody had yet got the idea that man could, or should, be a gadabout in winter. You lived with winter and let it make the rules. The automobile was going to change all that, but we didn't yet know it. We merely thought that the Model T was a mechanical wonder—which it was—and that with it we could break a few of the bonds of time and distance, but only a few. We didn't own a car, but friends of ours had a Model T. Before I was through college I bought one that had been wrecked in a ditch, rebuilt it, and drove it close to a hundred thousand miles. It was unchanged, mechanically, from the Model T of 1915. It had a magneto but no battery, no starter, no lights when the motor stopped. It had three pedals that you pushed to make it start or stop or go backward. Two small levers on the steering wheel fed the gas and advanced or retarded the spark. There was no such thing known to man, in 1915, as a windshield wiper. When it rained you opened the two-pane windshield and got wet while you looked, or you stuck your head out and looked around the windshield and got soaked. Its folding top—there were no closed sedans until the 1920s—had side curtains that buttoned on, but it was the coldest vehicle ever invented because it went faster than a buggy and had more cracks for the frigid air to get in.

The roads, still designed primarily for horse-drawn vehicles, were plowed open or a track was shoveled through the deepest drifts only where the snow was belly-deep on a horse. If the wind drifted an opened road full overnight it was up to the next traveler to find a way through or around. Travel beyond the immediate vicinity of a town was by rail, and the Rock Island had a rotary plow out clearing the rails after every storm. Even so, trains often were late and occasionally a freight got stuck in a deep-drifted cut and had to wait for a plow and a booster engine to arrive from Denver or Goodland, Kansas.

What I am trying to say is that people didn't live such impatient, fretful lives in those days, at least not in that area. Without electricity, nobody worried that storms might take down the wires. Burning coal, you knew at a glance when the bin was getting empty; it wasn't like burning oil from a tank hidden underground. You kept a five-gallon can of coal oil on the back porch for the lamps. You had a few bushels of potatoes, a bag of onions, a couple of bushels of apples, and a keg of cider vinegar down cellar. You had a forty-eight-pound sack of flour in the pantry, and maybe a hundred pounds of sugar and at least five pounds of roasted coffee beans. You tried to keep a slab of bacon or salt pork hanging in the woodshed. If you were really provident, as a good many townspeople were, you had a case or two of canned tomatoes, canned corn, canned peas, and a fifty-pound sack of dry beans in the pantry. You could last out a couple of weeks of being snowbound, right there in town, if you had to. If you got sick you knew that someone could get to a neighbor and send word to Dr. Williams or Dr. Neff, who would get to your house somehow, no matter how deep the drifts, and give you something to soothe your pain or, in extremity, ease your dying. It wasn't at all like being twenty miles from civilization and a mile from the nearest neighbor. Winter might be long and hard, but you didn't have to face it alone. Others were there around you, within hailing distance. You were a part of a community. You might wish it was summer instead of winter; but it wasn't, so you put up with it. Eventually it would be spring again, *and* summer. It always had been, anyway.

Classes started in the new school building, away up at the north end of Main Street, after the Christmas holiday. Everything was brand new and smelled of paint and varnish and hot new radiators. There were classrooms and offices and a domestic science kitchen and laboratories for the science courses. There was a big auditorium with a stage, and under it was the gymnasium, the basketball court. The school board and the staff held open house the first week and practically everybody was proud and impressed. A few old-timers shook their heads and said it cost far too much, with that theater room and that basketball room, and it would cost twice as much to heat as both the old school buildings put together. But even they finally agreed that there it was, and there was nothing to do but use it and get used to it. And, they added, pay off the bonds.

Winter isn't the best time to open a new school, perhaps, but it does reveal the flaws and weaknesses. Plumbing froze and radiators balked, doors swelled and jammed and ventilators didn't work. And after the first big January snowstorm nobody could get to school until the road men got out the big road grader and plowed a track all the way out Main Street, clear to the north end, which never had been done before. When classes were held in the old buildings, which were in the heart of town, walks were shoveled by the householders and paths were quickly trodden past vacant lots, without any outside help. But the problems were handled, one after another, and everybody made the needed adjustments. Even before classes opened in the new building, three people bought building lots on North Main Street near the school and picked out plans at the lumber yards for houses they said they would start building as soon as frost was out of the ground next spring.

Early in January Father wrote, in an editorial note, "Flagler is on the move. We detect signs of a building boom, and the direction of growth is northward. In fact, we venture to predict that within a very few years our handsome new school building, which some people said was away out in the country last summer, will be in the very heart of town. We also venture to predict that there will be a municipal water tower on the hill just north of the new school in a very few years. But before we plan municipal water we must have electric lights and power. They, too, will come. Plans for the new homes on

North Main Street are another sign of the progress that will make Flagler the Best Little City in Eastern Colorado, a community of tree-shaded streets and municipal power and water."

Father had talked about a municipal power plant before, but that was the first time he advocated a municipal water system. The trees were an old topic. He had something to say about trees almost every week. Father loved trees, often talked about the Nebraska woodland he knew as a boy, and he insisted that trees would grow on the High Plains if they were planted right and given enough water to get them started. He always planned to plant trees, a whole grove of them, on the homestead, but he never did. The few that he did plant were gnawed to the ground by the jack rabbits. Now he insisted that Flagler must plant trees, hundreds of them. "A community of tree-shaded streets" was one of his favorite phrases.

He undoubtedly got his passion for tree-planting from the father of Arbor Day, J. Sterling Morton. Mr. Morton, a native New Yorker, went to Nebraska in territorial days and became a crusading editor in Nebraska City, a town on the Missouri river about forty miles below Omaha. He was also an experimental farmer and forester. And he was a politician. He ran four times for governor of Nebraska, and four times was defeated. But President Cleveland named him Secretary of Agriculture in 1893; he was the first Westerner in that cabinet post. The year after he returned from Washington and resumed his editing and farming and tree-planting, Father went to work for him as foreman of the composing room of the Morton daily newspaper in Nebraska City.

How well Father knew Mr. Morton, I do not know, but he worked on the Morton newspaper about a year, he visited the Morton farm, he saw how Morton planted trees. And he heard Morton's vigorous ideas about the value of trees and his whole theory of farming. I have often thought that Father went to Colorado and took the homestead in part because he wanted to be an experimental farmer, like J. Sterling Morton.

If so, he failed utterly. But he never stopped urging people to plant trees. It became a minor crusade in Flagler.

Until Father's crusade got results, the only trees in town had been the cottonwoods in front of W. H. Lavington's house and in the lot across the street, which was a kind of town park even though it belonged to Mr. Lavington. Those cottonwoods were eighteen inches through and sixty feet tall. According to one story, when Mrs. Lavington came to Flagler as a bride from the East she was appalled by the bleakness of the town, the complete lack of trees. So Mr. Lavington got cottonwood saplings, perhaps from along Bijou Creek fifty miles to the west, and planted them for her, and she watered and tended them the first few years. Her care got them started and they throve, tolerant of heat and able to survive months of drouth. But all trees take a beating in that climate, and cottonwoods are not very tough or durable. Windstorms and blizzards pruned them mercilessly, eventually leaving one-armed, topless, misshapen cripples of almost all those big cottonwoods. A few years after we went to Flagler the trees directly in front of the Lavington house became a hazard to the house itself and had to be cut down. There were tears in Mrs. Lavington's eyes as she watched the cutting. Father's campaign by then had begun to have worthwhile results; there were young Norway maples and green ash and honey locusts along most of the town's residential streets, some of them twelve or fifteen feet tall and beginning to cast a bit of shade. But I know how Mrs. Lavington felt about those cottonwoods, scraggly and beaten though they were. They were shade and leaf talk in a sun-seared land, and they were bird-song and insect chirp and hum. Blackbirds stopped there every spring and chattered about far places, both red-wings and yellow-heads. Robins nested there. Red-shafted western flickers searched for grubs and tapped out resounding messages on the stubs of broken branches.

Father got trees, but getting municipal power or municipal

water or municipal anything was considerably more complicated. After he wrote that editorial about the "building
boom" he thought he saw coming, he wondered why he got
no response to his call for municipal power and water. After a
few days he asked Clarence Smith about it. "I didn't expect
everybody in town to support it, but I didn't expect everyone
to ignore it, either. Why, I haven't even heard anyone speak
out *against* it!"

"At this stage, Will," Mr. Smith said, "you are talking
about a pipe dream. Flagler can't even buy a coal-oil lamp or
a hand pump, officially. Flagler isn't a legal entity. It's the
name of a railroad stop, and a post office, but that's all."

"How about the school?"

"Yes, the school district is a legal entity with the power to
issue bonds, but it's the only legally constituted authority in
town. The post office is a convenience provided by the federal
government. The county takes care of our streets, such care as
they get. But as a community, we are just a settlement that
grew up in the vicinity of a railroad station. Yes, I know this
seems strange since Flagler has been a settlement for twenty-
five years. But it happens to be a fact in law. You and I can
talk till doomsday about municipal lights and water, but until
we incorporate and become a legal municipality we will never
have them."

"But you keep talking about them."

Mr. Smith laughed. "I have to keep up my reputation as a
visionary, maybe even as a Socialist, though you know I'm
no more a Socialist than you are. Actually, Will, what I'm
doing is keeping a spark alive, the idea that some day we *can*
have these things. But first we've got to become a legal municipality. We must incorporate."

"Well," Father exclaimed, "why don't we? What are we
waiting for?"

"That," Mr. Smith said, "is what some of us said three
years ago. We tried then, but there were too many people

who didn't want change. They said they'd always got along with a pump and an oil lamp and they saw no need to make changes just to please newcomers with fancy ideas. The simplest way to block change of the kind we wanted was to refuse to incorporate. As long as we aren't incorporated we can't issue bonds, and without bonds you can't buy such things as a light plant or a water works."

"It just doesn't make sense," Father said.

"Lots of things in politics don't make sense."

"What have politics got to do with it?"

"It's the same old story—change or stand pat. The basic difference between the two major parties, as I see it. Teddy Roosevelt tried to liberalize the Republicans four years ago, and we all know what he got for his pains."

"You know where I stand politically, don't you?"

"Well, I think I do."

"I'm a Wilson Democrat. Locally, I'm for incorporation, and the sooner the better. I'm ready to start campaigning for it right now."

Mr. Smith considered for a long minute. "If I were you," he finally said, "I would wait till next spring. Till April, at least."

"Why?"

"Well, we're right in the middle of winter now, and there's some pretty dreary days yet to come. A cold, raw winter day when your feet never get warm, you head is stuffed up, and the coal bin is almost empty somehow doesn't inspire much optimism. We still remember that bumper crop of wheat that got hailed out. Quite a lot of folks, even those who voted for it, look at that new school we just opened and think how long it's going to take to pay off the bonds. Some days I feel that way myself. But by next April, after we've had a couple of good spring rains and the air has warmed up, the world will look a lot different. It'll be a new crop year, another chance to make that million dollars. And by then folks will be used to that new school building and won't think about the bonds every time they see it."

So Father waited. Meanwhile, he went to Burlington, the county seat, several times and talked to lawyers and political leaders, partly about how to incorporate a town like Flagler, partly about the political situation in the county and the state. He laid the groundwork for the political stand he was ready to take. And, of course, for the political patronage he hoped to get if the Democrats won in the fall elections.

The winter passed, the snow began to melt, and April came to the High Plains. April, on those plains, can be a season all by itself. Mild air begins to flow up from the south, all the way from the Gulf of Mexico and across the whole of Texas. The melt begins. Spring rains come. Melt and rain combine to create shallow ponds in every upland swale and hollow. You go out and feel that air and see that water and you know it was worth enduring the winter just to emerge into this. Ducks come winging in, ducks that really shouldn't be there at all, so far from real lakes and running water. But there they are, huge rafts of them on those shallow ponds, resting, feeding, quacking loudly for a few days, maybe as long as a week, before they move on north, only to be followed by more mallards, more canvasbacks, more teal. That's the way it used to be, the way it was that spring. And here and there were geese, mostly the big Canadas but occasionally snow geese with their coal-black wing tips. Honking as they came over, with a gabble that made you think of a pack of small, feisty dogs chasing a rabbit out at the edge of town. The geese, too, stayed a few days at the big shallow ponds, then went on. And in those days there were other strangers such as snipe and curlew and upland plover, to make our remote inland pools as exotic as the bayous of Texas. And then our own birds came back, the meadow larks and the doves and the prairie falcons, and the bullbats, the night hawks that *yeeped* and soared and made roaring dives in the quiet

evening sky. The half-dozen robins that nested in the Lavington cottonwoods returned and sang all day long. And our
horned larks, most of which had never gone very far away,
sang again, spiraling like the storied skylarks that sang so beautifully in English poetry. Our larks sang beautifully, too, and
in reality, not in poems that used verbs like *wert* and *wingest*.
Sand lilies bloomed, little white stars in the tentative new
grass. Here and there, in specially favored places, were violets,
more yellows than purples. Wild onions shot up, greener than
the new grass, green-hungry cows ate them, and for several
weeks the milk was so rank of onions you couldn't drink it
and even the cream stations in town had an aroma of mild
garlic. On the cactus flats, prickly pear and grizzly-bear freshened, their broad pads fattened as they stored moisture for
the dry weeks of midsummer, and the first small nubbins of
flower buds appeared. Buffalo grass turned the brown winter
hills a tawny greenish tan as its first new shoots appeared.

By mid-April it began to feel like spring, to look like spring.
You could feel it in the air, feel it underfoot right through the
soles of your shoes. You could hear it in people's voices, see
it in their eyes.

Then Father began his campaign for incorporation.

All he said the first week was, "Isn't it time Flagler became
an incorporated community? It seems so to us. We believe we
should have the rights and assume the responsibilities of a
legally constituted town. This is going to be a year of decision in county, state and union, and we should be prepared to
make our decisions as a community too. The only way to do
that is to incorporate as a town." It was a call to action, but
not really a summons.

Nothing in particular happened. Clarence Smith said, "It's
a start. Now maybe we'll see who stands where." But he
didn't bring up the matter at the weekly meeting of the Commercial Club. Nobody brought it up.

The next week Father asked, on the front page, "When

are we going to get started on incorporation? How long is
Flagler going to be a settlement without the right to govern
itself? This spring is not too soon to start. It is time for action."
And he listed the legal steps necessary, which were quite
simple.

The next morning Father met W. H. Lavington in the
lobby at the post office. Mr. Lavington, a square-faced man
with a clipped gray mustache and a square jaw, said, "Good
morning, Will. I see you want to get this town incorporated."
He said it with a half smile.

"That's right, W. H.," Father said. "I think it's time we
did something about it."

"I'm inclined to agree," Mr. Lavington said. "I understand you have been looking into the matter. Why don't you
drop over to the bank and let's talk about it."

There were half a dozen men in the post office at the time,
and they all heard what was said. The word spread: *W. H.
Lavington is in favor of incorporation!* Later in the morning
Father went over to the bank and talked with Mr. Lavington.
It was mostly a gesture, as far as incorporation went, and
Father knew it. Mr. Lavington knew as much about the procedure as Father did. They talked maybe ten minutes about
incorporation, then about business in general, then about how
the *News* was doing. The bank, after all, held the mortgage
on the paper.

Father was there less than half an hour. Then Mr. Lavington said, "Thanks for coming over. I think you're right about
incorporating. It's time we began to run our own affairs. I'm
not sure we're ready yet for a municipal light plant," he said
with a smile, "but we should be in a position to have one if
we want it. I guess the next step is to call a meeting and name
a committee." They shook hands, and Mr. Lavington said,
"Too bad you're not a Republican."

The Flagler *Progress*, which had carefully avoided the topic
until then, came out in favor of incorporation the following

week. And when the subject was brought up for discussion at the next meeting of the Commercial Club, opinion there favored incorporation by a margin of almost four to one.

Clarence Smith stopped in at the office in late afternoon a few days later. "Well," he said to Father, "I guess you are the winner on this one."

"Nothing's won," Father said, "until the vote is in."

"It will get the vote," Mr. Smith said. "There'll be votes against it, of course, die-hards who always hold out to the bitter end. But I'll venture that the margin is just about what it was for the new school. We knew we had that won just as soon as W. H. came out in favor of it."

Father nodded. "I knew it was pretty well settled when I talked to him. Then when the *Progress* came out for it there wasn't any question. The *Progress*, of course, will be the official paper."

"You mean that's the price you had to pay?"

"Oh, no!" Father laughed, made a wry face. "Nothing was said about the *Progress*. Nothing *had* to be said. I was just reminded that I'm not a Republican. I had hoped to keep politics out of it, but—" Father shrugged.

"Will it hurt, not being the official town paper?"

"Some. But I'll manage. The pay for printing town ordinances and other official notices would help, but I'll get along without it. And if the Democrats win this fall in the state and the county, I'll get my share of the county printing. In the long run it'll probably amount to more than the town's legal printing would." Father rolled a cigarette. "Besides," he said, "this means that I'll be completely independent. I won't have to try to keep in with anybody. I can speak my mind."

A meeting was called the following week to consider the matter of incorporation. Everybody in town turned out, it seemed. Several cranky old-timers complained bitterly that some people just couldn't leave well enough alone, that they had to find new ways to run other people's business. There

167

wasn't much said in favor of incorporating the town until
W. H. Lavington got up and said, "I think we should get
started. It will take quite a while to get things done, with all
the legal papers and so on, maybe till next fall. I think we'd
better name a committee tonight to get started." And after
that nobody had to say anything in favor of the proposal. A
vote was taken and it carried by an even greater margin than
the new school proposal got the year before. Then a "Town
Committee" was named to take charge of the whole matter.
There were five members, three old-timers, Mr. Lavington,
Mr. Blancken from the hotel, and Ed Epperson, and two of
the new people, Dave Buck, who came from Arkansas for his
health, and Posey Briggs, whose real name was Elaine and
who was the sister of Spider Miner's mother.

So Father rounded out his first year in Flagler with a victory
that wasn't going to add one nickel to his income. But he cele-
brated the anniversary by going to the bank and paying not
only the interest on the mortgage but a hundred dollars on
the principal. And in the next issue of the *News* he announced
his political stand. He said, "It is time that Democratic principles were put into action all over this country. It is time for
a change in Colorado and Kit Carson County, and it is imperative that Woodrow Wilson be kept at the helm of our
nation. *The Flagler News* will work for and support all those
objectives with all the strength at our command."

He showed the statement of policy to Mother before he
printed it, just as he had typed it out on the old Oliver,
words X-ed out and interlined with pencil. Mother read it,
reread it. Finally she asked, "Are you sure that's the right way
to spell 'imperative'?"

"Yes."

She read it a third time and Father waited impatiently,
jingling the small change in his pants pocket.

"Are you sure this is what you want to do?"

"As sure as I'm alive."

"What if the Republicans win?"

"Then the Democrats will lose. Oh, for goodness' sake, Sarah, I didn't ask you to correct the spelling or ask me if I meant it! All I want to know is whether I made it clear."

"It seems plenty clear to me. All I was asking was what you will do if the Democrats lose."

"If we lose, I won't get any county printing. I don't get any now, so I won't be any worse off."

"That's what I wondered. If you're not going to get any town printing either—"

"Sarah, I have to take that stand, regardless of the county printing or the town printing. I'm a Democrat. I've been a Democrat all my life, and I'm not going to shilly-shally about it in hopes of making a dollar or two by keeping my mouth shut. I'm for the Democratic ticket right down the line, and I want everybody to know it." He took the copy from her, read it to himself again, then said, "That's exactly what I wanted to say."

"Then I guess you'd better say it," Mother said.

14

That was the summer of the beans. It was a wheat summer too, but I didn't have much to do with the wheat. It really began the last week in April, when Mr. Hall brought down the copy for his advertisement late one afternoon and stayed to talk a little while. It was after school and I was at the case setting type, so I could hear everything that was said. Father and Mr. Hall talked about business, and finally Mr. Hall said he needed extra help for the summer.

"What I really need," he said, "is a boy to take up the slack on Saturdays. Help with the chores, stock the shelves, put up orders, run errands. If you hear of a reliable boy who'd like to make some pocket money, let me know."

After he had left I said to Father, "You don't really need me on Saturdays, do you?"

"So," Father said, "you want to work for Bill Hall."

"Well, I thought—" I wasn't sure what I thought, but working in a store seemed, from there at least, more fun than being a printer.

"You didn't work here very much on Saturdays last summer," Father said. "You were out playing baseball or prowling the flats with Justin Williams most Saturdays." Then he said, "No, son, I don't really need you on Saturdays. I had figured you would be playing baseball or something else most of the time. So if you would rather work for Bill Hall than do that, go ahead.'

"What do you think he would pay me?"

"I haven't any idea. I figured on paying you a dollar and a half a day, but only for five days a week. That's all I can afford this summer. Why don't you ask him and see what he says, see if it's enough to make it worth while?"

I went to the store the next afternoon and found Mr. Hall. I told him I might be interested in that Saturday job he was talking about. He looked at me with a smile and said, "I thought I saw your ears prick up when your dad and I were talking. That's fine. How about starting day after tomorrow?"

"Well, I guess I could."

"Good! You know John. He opens the store at seven o'clock. You can help him sweep out and stock shelves. He'll tell you what to do. The morning won't be too busy, but we'll all be kept hopping in the afternoon. It usually isn't very busy after supper, though, and we close at nine o'clock."

I hadn't thought about the store being open after supper on Saturday nights. But I wasn't going to back out now, even before I started. "All right," I said. "I'll be here Saturday morning." Then I mustered my courage and asked, "How about pay?"

"Oh," he put a hand on my shoulder, "don't worry about that. You'll get paid every Saturday night, like everyone else."

And that was that. I just couldn't say, *Yes, I know I'll get paid, but I want to know how much.* Either you are a natural-born bargainer or you aren't. I wasn't.

I went back to the *News* office and told Father Mr. Hall wanted me to start right away, that week. "Just on Saturdays," I said. "I'll work here the rest of the time this summer. And every afternoon after school till school's out."

"Fine," Father said. "As I said a year ago, I don't care what you do as long as you learn the printer's trade. You got a good start last summer, and by the end of this summer you should be a pretty good journeyman printer. . . . Well, what did he say he would pay you?"

"He didn't say."

"Didn't you ask?"

"Well, sort of. I guess he didn't understand. He just said I would get paid every Saturday night, like the rest of them."

"Maybe you should have had your mother talk to him. *She*'d have found out. Well, you will too, Saturday night. And if he's not paying you enough you can always quit."

The big front doors were still locked when I went to the store at seven Saturday morning, but when I went around to the side door I found it open. John Robinson was already there, sprinkling oily red sweeping compound in the aisles. Without any greeting he said, "Get a broom from the back room." He was an older man, maybe as much as fifty, rather florid-faced, almost wholly bald, slightly stooped, with quick eyes and a firm, soft voice. He had been a store clerk for years, maybe all his life for all I knew. He knew the stock in that store from A to Z and knew practically all the customers by their first names. Seeing him about the store you almost felt that Mr. Hall worked for him, not the other way round. He was the senior employee and he had special privileges. An early riser, he always opened the store. He went home about ten and didn't come back till after the noon meal. And he never worked after supper. Someone once asked him why he didn't start a store of his own. With all his friends for customers he would be sure to make a go of it. John shook his head. "I like to work but I hate to worry. I don't mind making decisions if someone else takes the responsibility. If I owned a store I'd have bills and credit and notes and interest to worry about. Not me! I'll sell anything over the counter, but Bill Hall can run the business and welcome to it."

I got the broom and John told me to take one aisle while he took the other. I knew how to sweep, and sweep clean. Mother had finally drilled that into me. Then we went behind the counters with our brooms, and we swept out the shoe alcove and the alcove with women's notions. Finally we had all our sweepings at the door to the back room, and John said, "You take that end and I'll take this," and we swept the back room, gathered the sweeping compound, now black with accumulated dirt, in a scoop shovel and dumped it in the trash barrel to be burned. That was my next job, to burn the waste paper and trash. I felt as though I was starting to be a printer's devil all over again, but maybe on a cleaner scale this time.

After I had burned the trash John said, "Come take a look at the shelves," and he showed me the gaps in the canned goods on the grocery shelves that had to be filled. We walked down the whole line of shelves, all across the back of the store, John barely glancing at them, it seemed to me. Then we went down the back stairs to the basement.

The basement was a huge room, and it was full of groceries. Canned goods, mostly. Cases of canned goods were piled almost to the ceiling in long rows with aisles between them. Everything you could think of, from tomatoes to peas, from sweet corn to baked beans. And Karo syrup in tin buckets, cases of them. Sardines, some canned in oil, some in mustard. Wooden box after box of soda crackers. Pickles: sweet, sour, dill and mustard. Canned fruit: apricots, peaches, pears, cherries, pineapple, some of it put up in gallon cans for the ranch trade. Dried fruit: prunes, raisins, apricots, wooden box after box of them. All the canned and dried things were put up in wooden cases. It was another ten years or more before corrugated cardboard took the place of wood.

John led me down one aisle and back another, pointing to the cases. "Vegetables over here, fruits yonder. Easy to remember. You probably have the idea already. Now, what do we need on the shelves?"

I hadn't the faintest idea what we needed.

"You don't remember which ones needed filling up?"

"I guess I didn't really look."

John grunted, then sighed. "Maybe you'll learn." But he didn't sound hopeful. "Start with the peas," he said, "over there. Take up a couple of cases. Then three or four cases of tomatoes. And sliced pineapple. Always sell lots of pineapple on Saturday. I'll take some baked beans, as long as I'm here."

I worked two cases of canned peas off the nearest stack, shouldered them, and went up the stairs and opened them in the back room. John was right behind me with a couple of cases of baked beans. "I'll put them on the shelves," he said. "You bring them up and open them. Some more peas. And then tomatoes."

We were just well started on filling the shelves when the other clerks arrived at seven-thirty. Mr. Hall didn't come in till eight on Saturdays, but Henry Weidenheimer, who was second in command, greeted me, asked John how I was doing, and, without waiting for an answer, told Jimmy Wallace to lend a hand.

Jimmy had been a combination choreboy and delivery boy, but with my coming he was to be a full-time clerk on Saturdays. He was stocky, dark-haired, about nineteen, a farm boy who was the exception in a family that seemed to have a genuis for bad luck and improvidence. As a boy, Jimmy's father lost two fingers off his right hand in a corn sheller. Then he broke a leg and the bones knitted crooked, leaving him with a gimpy walk. Soon after he moved his family from his native Arkansas to a homestead near Flagler he lost an eye and almost had his throat cut when a strand of barbed wire broke when he tightened it too much while building fence. Jimmy's mother had one crossed eye and a big mole on her nose, and she lost all her front teeth when a cow she was feeding, one fly-pestered day, swung her head to dislodge a particularly painful pest and struck Mrs. Wallace square in the mouth. There were three children when they moved to the homestead, but the second summer they were there a little tornado came whirling across the flats and wrecked their flimsy house. The parents were visiting a sick neighbor. Jimmy, fourteen at the time, was at the well, not fifty feet from the house, getting a pail of water. Jimmy was untouched by the freak storm, but both younger children were killed in the wreckage of the house.

Jimmy seemed to walk a charmed life through an incredible maze of hazards that constantly beset the Wallaces. He grew up unscarred, even with a quiet sense of humor, and with an unobtrusive streak of ambition.

That morning when I started to work at the store, Jimmy took one look at the shelves and dashed to the basement. He came back with two cases of canned corn, put them down in the back room, said to me, "You open 'em and I'll lug 'em," and was gone again. He made five trips while I was opening three cases, then said, "That should about do it," and I knew that without looking a second time he had brought up exactly what was needed to fill the shelves. He and I put the cans on the shelves, then he helped me pile the empty cases behind the store where they were available to anyone who wanted the wood for kindling.

Jimmy was grateful to me because my going to work in the store freed him to learn more about the business. Now he was a clerk. Some day he wanted to be a storekeeper, have his own store. But the day I started he was full of plans for his bean project. Later in the morning, after the townsfolk had been in to do their marketing and before the farm folk arrived, there was a slack period for all of us, and Jimmy told me about his beans.

Two years earlier a few of the farmers out north had the idea that pinto beans might make a profitable crop. Pintos, often called Mexican beans, are brown and white and about the size of kidney beans, half again as big as the familiar white navy beans. They are the basic bean of Latin-American cooking and were then widely used through the Southwest. They grow on a low, bushy plant, much like the ordinary bush beans grown in the vegetable garden for green beans, snap beans. But the pintos are a variety that can thrive in a moderately dry climate. At that time they were yielding fifteen or twenty bushels of dry beans to the acre in an average year. They were relatively easy to grow. Farmers in that area planted them with a corn planter and cultivated them much like corn. When they had bloomed, set pods, and the pods were almost ripe, they mowed the bushes like hay, raked them into windrows, let them dry, and threshed them. The bean straw made good cow feed, and the shelled beans, of course, went to market.

The farmers who grew pinto beans in the Flagler area thought they were a more reliable crop than wheat. In a good year the same acreage of wheat made more money, but in a poor year the beans made more. Jimmy talked to half a dozen farmers who had grown beans, learned all he could about them, and the spring before I went to work in the store he bought two hundred pounds of seed beans and parceled them out among four farmers who were short of seed money but were willing to plant and tend the beans for half the crop. Three of them had good harvests. The fourth one got hailed out. Jimmy sold his share of the crop for a little over two hundred dollars.

"This year," he told me, "I'm going to put out five hundred pounds of beans on shares. Seed beans cost fifteen cents a pound, so that's an investment of seventy-five dollars. If I do as good as I did last year I should clear close to five hundred dollars. That's not bad on a seventy-five-dollar investment, huh?"

"That," I said, "is wonderful! I wish I knew somebody who wanted to plant beans on shares."

"Maybe your dad knows somebody."

"Let's see. For fifteen dollars I could get a hundred pounds of beans, couldn't I?"

"That's right. Seed beans are fifteen cents a pound. But they've got to be planted in the next two or three weeks or they won't make a crop. Mine are supposed to be here on the eastbound freight either Monday or Tuesday. Mr. Hall probably could get some for you by a week from today."

I had half an hour for dinner, as we called the noon meal, following farm practice. I went to the office and walked home with Father, and I told him about Jimmy Wallace and the big profit he made on beans. I said I was going to ask Mr. Hall to get me a hundred pounds of beans and I would find someone to plant them on shares.

"Well," Father said, when he could get a word in. "You've really got the speculator's bug, haven't you?"

"That isn't speculation, is it? It's just—well, just growing beans on shares."

"No, I guess it's no more speculative than growing wheat. But suppose it hails. Suppose there's a drouth. Suppose the bean beetles go to work on them. Then what?"

"Then I guess there wouldn't be much profit. But things like that don't *have* to happen, do they?"

"They do, son. You know what happened to the wheat last year."

"Well, I don't think they're going to happen this year. I'm going to ask Mr. Hall to order the beans. And maybe you can help find someone to plant them on shares. Is that all right?"

"That's up to you. If I hear of someone reliable who wants to plant beans, I'll tell him to talk to you."

Mother was worried about one of her sisters back in Nebraska, when we got home. She had a letter that morning saying that Garnet was sick and the doctor hadn't diagnosed what it was but it might be pneumonia. Mother was so worried that Father didn't mention my beans, and I certainly didn't, after what he had said. Mother could think up twice as many reasons for a crop failure. But when I went home for supper Father asked if I had bought my beans yet. I told him I asked Mr. Hall to order them. Mother asked, "What's this about beans?"

Father said, "Oh, he's going to take a flier in Mexican beans."

"A what? What kind of a flier?"

"I'm getting a hundred pounds of Mexican beans and I'm going to get someone to plant them on shares."

"Oh. Who thought up that idea? Money's hard enough to get. I'd certainly think twice about spending it on beans to give away."

"Jimmy Wallace," I said, "made two hundred dollars that way last year."

"Jimmy Wallace?" She looked at me aghast. "Don't you bring home any of that Wallace luck! We've got enough trouble of our own."

I didn't answer, and she didn't say anything more. I hurried through my supper and went back to the store.

There was the usual Saturday evening crowd, lots of people but not much business. Mostly, the people just stood around and visited among themselves. Mr. Hall laughed and joked with them, and the rest of us began straightening up the goods on the counters, starting to get the store in order again. And finally it was a quarter of nine and most of the people had left the store. Jimmy Wallace and I put the muslin covers over the women's notions counter, and Henry Weidenheimer began turning out the big gasoline pressure lamps in the front of the store. Mr. Hall went to the cashier's cage and came back with a handful of small manila envelopes, each with a name written on it. He handed them out. Everyone else tucked his into his pocket unopened, so I did too. Then we saw that the big front doors were locked, we bolted the back doors, and when Henry had turned out the last lamp we all went out the side door. Mr. Hall locked it, said good night, and I headed for home, hurrying because I wanted to see how much was in the pay envelope.

Father was in the front room, reading the *Denver Post*, the *Record-Stockman* on the table at his elbow. Across the table

from him, Mother was darning socks. "Well," she said, looking up as I came in. "The storekeeper is home. How do you
like working for somebody else besides your father?"

"It's all right," I said.

"Did you get paid?"

I pulled out the envelope.

"How much?"

I opened it, emptied it into my hand. Out came one silver
dollar and one half dollar. I shook the envelope, looked inside.

"A dollar and a half," Mother said. "Is that what he said
he would pay you?"

"He didn't say."

"Didn't you ask, before you started?"

"Well. . . . No."

She gave me one look, then went back to her darning. "I
just hope you learn before you grow up and have to make your
own living. . . . You look tired. Are you hungry?"

"No. I'd rather just go to bed."

I went to my room and went to bed, but not to sleep. I was
tired. I was also angry. Mostly at myself, though also at Mr.
Hall. I decided I would go see him some afternoon after school
next week and tell him either to pay me two dollars or get
another boy. Then I decided that didn't make sense. Besides,
I had already asked him to order those beans. And it really
wasn't very hard work in the store. And I was new at it, didn't
really know my way around. . . . And by then I was so drowsy
I didn't know what I thought. I went to sleep.

I didn't go to Mr. Hall. I went to work as usual the next
Saturday morning, and when Mr. Hall came in he told me
that my beans had come in with the Friday freight. I paid him
for them and kept going out to the back room every chance I
got just to look at that fat burlap bag of beans. When I came
back from dinner that noon, John said a man had been in,
looking for me. I asked who it was and John said, "Ed Paxton." I didn't know any Ed Paxton, but John said he was a

farmer, "sort of. Lives somewhere out north, toward Thurman." Ten minutes later Mr. Paxton came in the store and asked for me.

He was a tall, slim man probably in his late thirties, dark-haired, with a broad smile, a good talker. He had heard I wanted someone to plant Mexican beans on shares. Yes, I said. "Well," he said, "I'm your man." I asked if Father had sent him to see me. "No," he said, "not exactly. I heard someone say it down at the café, said your father asked him to find someone. I've got forty acres of good land laying idle, and I've got time on my hands to plant it. All I ain't got is seed or ready cash to buy it."

"Do you know how to grow beans?" I asked. "Mexican beans?"

He laughed. "Look, son. If I had a penny for every Mexican bean I've grown I'd be a millionaire."

"They've got to be planted in the next two weeks to get a crop."

"I know, I know. I'm all ready to plant. Got the ground plowed and everything. Where's your beans?"

I hesitated. I hadn't been at all businesslike with Mr. Hall. I had to be with this man. "This is on shares," I said. "Half and half of what you harvest."

"Suits me," he said.

I took a piece of wrapping paper and wrote out an agreement: "I, Edward Paxton, hereby make an agreement with H. G. Borland, to plant one hundred pounds of Mexican beans on my land and cultivate and harvest the same, Mr. Borland to provide the beans for seed and to receive half the harvested beans as his share of the crop." That sounded simple enough and still clear enough. I let him read it, and he said again, "Suits me." So I dated it and we both signed it, and I folded it and put it in my pocket. Then I took him to the back room and showed him my bag of beans, and he brought his team and wagon around back of the store, put the beans in, waved to me, and drove away.

I went back inside and tried to put my mind on business, store business. But it was an hour before I could think of anything except Ed Paxton and the beans. The afternoon passed. At supper I told Father and Mother what I had done. Father said, "Ed Paxton," and frowned, puzzling. "I seem to have heard that name, but I can't place it." Mother hadn't a word to say.

That evening, when business at the store had slackened off, I had a chance to tell Jimmy what I had done. "Ed Paxton?" he said. "Oh. Well, maybe it will work out.

"Why? What do you mean by that?"

"I don't know much about him. He came here from Oklahoma, I think it was, a couple of years ago. All I know is what I've heard. They say he's a blow-hard. If he worked half as much as he talks, they say, he'd be a millionaire." Then Jimmy grinned. "But I guess it doesn't take a quiet fellow to grow beans. It may work out all right."

The die was cast. I had bought the beans, signed that "contract," given the beans to Ed Paxton, who said he would plant and tend and harvest them. Now it was up to the weather. I hoped it was only the weather, anyway.

May passed with several good rains. Wheat was doing wonderfully, but few people were talking about "million-dollar wheat" this year. People kept quiet and hoped and waited. Father printed several cautious items about the good rains and the fact that the wheat was headed out, but not much more than that.

The first week in June Father asked me, "How are your beans coming, son?" I had to tell him I didn't know. "Haven't you seen that Paxton fellow to ask him?"

"No. He hasn't been in the store and I haven't seen him on the street."

"Come to think of it, I haven't either. Well, maybe he's busy farming." And that was all Father said. Mother didn't even mention the matter.

Wheat harvest began, a good harvest with virtually no hail. For several days there was a constant string of trucks in from the harvest fields out north to the elevators in town, the dust never settling. And Father at last mentioned "a bumper wheat harvest." Everybody was happy. The store on Saturdays was jammed with people and the farmers were taking out the biggest orders I ever saw, more groceries than it would have taken to feed us, at our house, for two months.

The last weekend of harvest Clarence Smith offered to take Father and Mother and me out to see what he called the best piece of wheat in all of eastern Colorado. They were starting to harvest it on Saturday and would still be at it Sunday. It was out northeast of town. So early Sunday afternoon Mr. Smith came past our house and we got into his Model T Ford and started out to see the wheat.

We saw half a dozen fields of stubble, where the wheat had already been cut, and Mr. Smith told Father who owned each piece and how much wheat had been harvested. And finally we came to this unharvested piece, a full half section, 320 acres, wheat the color of a brand-new penny and standing more than three feet tall. The harvesters were working on it when we got there, and the sight was one of dust, glittering sunlight, sweaty men, and wheat, clean new wheat that came off the combines in a stream like a river of gold. It poured into the waiting trucks, which rumbled off, out of the field, to the dusty road, and away toward town and the elevators.

We stayed and watched for about half an hour. Then we got back into the car and were about to leave when Mother asked Mr. Smith, "Doesn't Ed Paxton live out in this district somewhere?"

"Paxton?" Mr. Smith frowned, then made a wry face. "Oh,

yes, Ed Paxton's land is only a couple of miles from here. Not much of a place, but—well, you know how some people are."

"Would it be too far out of the way to go past it?" Mother asked.

"Not at all." And Mr. Smith took the road north. Two miles and we came to an unfenced weed patch that had been plowed ground a few years before but had been neglected. Just beyond was an unpainted house that didn't look big enough for more than two rooms. Just beyond the house was a well with a hand pump, and near the well was an open shed that apparently served for a stable.

"Let's stop," Mother said.

Mr. Smith was surprised. "Uh—" he said. "All right." And he turned in at the wagon track to the house, drew up in the dooryard. We waited a few minutes, and a woman came to the door. She looked frayed and worn. "You want something?" she asked.

"Yes," Mother called to her. "We want to talk to your—I guess your husband. Edward Paxton."

"That's him," the woman said with a giggle. "I'll git him up."

Another wait, and Ed Paxton came outside. He looked at us and he rubbed his neck, and he said, "Howdy do, folks. I'm sorry to be laid up this way, but—"

"Where are the beans?" Mother asked.

"The what?" He looked at her, startled. Then he saw me. "Oh," he said, "the beans. Well, I'll tell you. It's this way. Back in May, when it was time to get them planted, my woman took sick, and—"

"Where," Mother repeated, "are the beans you contracted to plant on the shares?"

"I was trying to tell you, ma'am, that back in May the woman she took sick and was laid up for most of a month, and time to plant beans come and went—"

"You didn't plant them?"

"Well, now—No, matter of fact, I didn't get out to plant a blessed thing, the woman sick and all. I just didn't, and that's God's truth, I swear it."

"What did you do with them?"

"Well, there's some left. Maybe half of 'em. You see, after she got better, then I took sick myself, and she dipped into them beans, not knowing they was seed beans, just thinking they was beans for eating like, and we lived on beans quite a spell there before I knowed what was happening. So—"

"Bring out what are left," Mother ordered.

"Yes'm." And he went back into the house.

"You don't mind, do you?" Mother asked Mr. Smith. "We'll make room for them here in the back."

Then Ed Paxton returned with the bean sack and less than half the hundred pounds that had been in it originally. "Put it in here," Mother ordered, and he put it in the car. He started to turn away, but Mother said, "You can be sued, you know."

"Yes'm, I know. I know, and I'll pay for them beans just as soon as I get a nickel ahead, I sure will, and don't you worry your head about it one bit."

"Let's go," Mother said, and Mr. Smith drove out of the yard and back onto the road and toward town.

Not another word was said about the beans all the way home. Father and Mr. Smith talked wheat, and Mother and I just didn't talk. Finally we were at our house, and Mother got out, and I took the bag of beans and carried it around to the back porch. Father and Mr. Smith talked for another five minutes. Then Father came in the house. "Well," he said, with an air of forced casualness, "that certainly was a nice trip. And we saw some of the finest wheat I ever saw in my life. Didn't you enjoy it, Sarah?"

"Some of the best wheat, and two of the worst people,"

Mother said. Then she turned to me. "Well, son, I hope you learned a lesson. Maybe next time you won't be so quick to run after easy money. I always say experience is a hard teacher, but maybe the cheapest one in the long run. What are you going to do with the beans you've got left?"

"I don't know. See if Mr. Hall will buy them back, I guess."

"Not for seed beans, he won't. And for regular beans he won't pay more than about seven or eight cents a pound. That's three and a half or four dollars."

"Couldn't we eat them, maybe?"

"Not that many beans, not in five years. By then the weevils would be in them."

I felt miserable and ashamed. I didn't care what happened to those beans. All I wanted to do was write them off, try to forget the fifteen dollars I had paid for them, and never do so stupid a thing again.

By Monday afternoon, though, I mustered my nerve and went to see Mr. Hall. I told him I had about fifty pounds of seed beans left over and asked if he would buy them. He didn't ask any questions. He said yes, he would take them off my hands, but he could pay only six cents a pound because new beans would soon be coming in. There were forty-two pounds of them left. Mr. Hall paid me $2.52 for them.

The wheat crop was one of the best Flagler had yet had. There were piles of wheat on the ground, like tremendous golden ant hills, overflow from the grain elevators which couldn't get freight cars fast enough to ship it out as it came in. Flagler was going to have money in its pockets, at last.

Beans were harvested in late August. There weren't many beans, really; most of the farmers who grew them grew them as a side crop and nobody planted more than forty or fifty acres of them. Besides, there had been a bean blight that year and the bean beetle had appeared in some fields. Jimmy Wallace made only about $250 from his $75 investment in seed. He had expected to make twice that much. But I couldn't work up any tears for Jimmy. At least, he made a profit, a good profit. I lost $12.48.

Mr. Hall gave me a raise the first of July, to $1.75. And at the end of August he offered me $2 a Saturday if I would stay on that fall and winter. But I said no, I didn't really want to be a storekeeper. Besides, I had other things to do on Saturdays after school started.

15

That was the summer of Nell Bainbridge's trouble, and it closed, for me, with the kit foxes. At the time I didn't think there was any link at all between Nell and the foxes, but I have wondered since.

Nell's name really was Cornelia, and though she was a rather plain-looking girl she was one of those you think of as beautiful because they are so full of life and vitality. She was slim, blue-eyed, with reddish-brown hair and a laugh always hovering. Everyone said Nell was fun. She dated various boys but never seemed serious about any of them. She was going on to college, Teacher's College at Greeley. She finished high school in a flurry of parties and then just dropped out of things. The Bainbridges lived a few miles out of town—her father was one of the better farmers, but a stubborn, head-strong man—and Nell simply stayed at home. Then word got around that Nell was "in trouble." I heard it first from the high school crowd. Nell had "got caught," the girls said. The boys said she "got knocked up." Then the talk began among the grownups. Nell always was "a little fast," as the women put it, and now she'd have to pay for it.

People began to wonder when Nell would go away for "a visit with relatives" at a distance. That was the way such matters usually were handled. The girl went away for a visit, had her baby, put it out for adoption, and came home as though nothing had happened. In time she was taken back into the community's social life, though usually with reservations.

But Nell didn't go away, and word got around that she wasn't going. She intended to stay right there and have her baby at home. And her father was going to start a paternity suit. That put a brand new angle on the story. Who was the boy—or the man? And now there was gossip about several married men in town being involved. One underground joke had it that three different husbands had bought one-way tickets to California and were just waiting to see who Jim Bainbridge was going to name when he filed the suit.

Mother thought it was a disgrace to the whole community, everything about the case. "You aren't going to print a word about it, are you?" she said to Father.

"Not unless Jim Bainbridge actually starts suit and it comes to trial. If it comes to court, I don't see how I can avoid at least mentioning it. You can't pretend that a court trial isn't going on. You can't hide it."

I knew what probably would happen, not at the trial but to Nell and her baby, especially to the baby. There had been a similar situation in one town where we lived, though it had happened before we moved there. A schoolgirl became pregnant and her parents brought the man responsible, a married man, to trial and he was sent to prison for a nominal term. The girl had her baby at home and her parents adopted it, gave it a legal name and status. The girl then went away to finish school, became a professional woman, and eventually married. The baby was a boy my age, and when we moved there he and I became close friends. He was a brilliant boy and the grandparents—the legal parents—had money and standing in the community. They carried the whole situation off with decency and dignity. But every now and then some vindictive grownup or angry playmate would brand the boy with that searing word, bastard, and I would see him flinch, turn florid with anger, then walk away. He never fought back, even with words. He had to take it. He took it, right through school. Then he went away to college and changed his given name; and after college he took a job in a distant state, cut virtually all his ties to the past.

Something like that probably awaited Nell's unborn child. But nobody in town seemed to be thinking about that child as a child. The talk was about Nell's disgrace and, of course, the disgrace she was bringing on the town. There was even talk that Jim Bainbridge shouldn't bring a paternity suit, that he should let the matter drop and let people forget it. But Jim couldn't see it that way.

Then, the last week in August, I got involved with the kit foxes. George Sebastian came down to the *News* office on Friday afternoon and asked Father, "You know a kit fox when you see one?"

"Of course I do. We had kit foxes out south of Brush when we were on the homestead there."

"Ever shoot one?"

"No. Hardest thing in the world to shoot. And they can drive a dog crazy, trying to run one down."

"Right." George Sebastian was tall, sinewy, red-faced, with dark eyes and reddish hair and a small mustache. He was something of a dandy, in a rough way. He lived out southeast of Flagler. "But," he said, "I'm going to get me one. Maybe three or four. There's a bitch denned on the hill off east of my house and she had kits there last spring. She's still there, with the kits, and they've been stealing my chickens."

"Never heard of a kit fox taking chickens," Father said. "Sure it's not coyotes, or maybe a weasel?"

"It's them damn foxes," Sebastian insisted. "I'm going to dig them out, and I heard you like animals, maybe you or the boy might want to have one of them kits for a pet. I hear they tame all right, you get them young."

Father turned to me. I said yes, I thought I'd like to have a kit fox for a pet. At least I'd like to be there and decide if I wanted one when they were dug out. Sebastian said to come out to his place the next day, but it was a Saturday and I had to work in the store, so we agreed on Sunday, when I would ride out to his place on my bicycle and help with the digging.

We didn't know George Sebastian except to speak to on the street. He came originally from Oklahoma or the Texas panhandle, took a homestead out on the flats, built up a herd of forty or fifty head of cattle, and called himself a ranchman. His wife was a rather pretty woman, a tall, bosomy blonde whom Mother called "stand-offish." They had two little girls maybe six and eight years old. George was what used to be called "a ladies' man," a term that could be either a compliment or a sneer, depending on the way it was said.

Mother didn't think much of having a kit fox for a pet, but she didn't lay down a flat no. She never had much time or much liking for pets, though I was allowed to have dogs and, now and then, a cat when I was younger. But she didn't like cats. And Fritz was the only dog that ever really made himself a place in her heart. He was practically a member of the family. On the whole, I had no need for wild pets, not even any particular interest in them. I thought that rabbits, ground squirrels, coyotes, snakes, and all the other native fauna were better off, and more interesting, wild and free.

But a kit fox was something else again. Maybe if I had one, even for a little while, I could learn more about its kind. All the way out to the Sebastian place the next morning I kept thinking about those I had known on the homestead. We sometimes called them swifts, or swift foxes. I don't know where we got those names, but they are accepted common names, too. The animal is a true fox, *Vulpes velox*, the smallest fox there is, smaller than most jack rabbits. This is hard to believe because a kit fox has that beautiful full fox tail and long fluffy hair and looks at least twice as big as it really is. It looks like a miniature red fox with unusually big ears and a gray coat, almost silvery but with a golden tinge. It has the same slim, dainty legs as a red fox, the long plumelike tail, and the sharply pointed nose. And it lives on smaller fare, chiefly mice and ground squirrels and small snakes and grass-hoppers. Maybe with an occasional nestling bird or a baby rabbit. It can't run fast enough and isn't really big enough to catch and kill a grown jack rabbit. I doubt that a kit fox would weigh more than half as much as a big white-tailed jack rabbit.

And despite the name "swift," the kit isn't a fast runner. A good rabbit dog could easily outrun a kit fox, but it prob-ably would never catch one. The kit fox runs zigzag, which is the reason it is so difficult to shoot one. It will take off, run-ning low to the ground, and run straight ahead maybe five jumps, then dart off at an angle another five or six jumps, then veer again, and again, keeping it up till it drives a dog crazy. And a man with a gun can't get a bead on anything that runs that way. So there the kit fox goes, zigzagging across the flats until it suddenly vanishes. It goes to ground, and it can get into a hole that seems no bigger than a man's fist. You stand and look at the hole, and you know that's where the kit fox went, and still you can't believe it. The animal looks so much bigger than it really is.

Jake Farley, our homestead neighbor, shot one once, large-ly by accident. He was hunting jack rabbits and this kit fox jumped out of a gully not twenty feet in front of him. Jake shot before he saw that it wasn't a jack rabbit, one of those reflex shots from the hip with a 12-gauge shotgun. He hit it with a load of number 4 shot before it made its first sidewise jump. Jake skinned it out and tacked the skin on his barn, and it was unbelievably small. The carcass, Jake said, when he skinned it wasn't as big as his little gray cat, which was the runt of a litter. "It's them big ears," Jake said, "that make them look so big." We measured the ears and found they were as long as the kit fox's face from forehead to nose tip. If I hadn't known how much smaller a coyote is than it looks, I wouldn't have believed that kit fox was fully grown.

It was a bright sunny morning and the road wasn't rutted, so I made good time out to the Sebastian place. I got there soon after ten o'clock. There was a white frame house with a fence around it to keep the livestock out, and there was an unpainted barn and a big open shed with a corral and a stack yard and three big haystacks. It all looked neat and well kept up. There weren't even any loose chickens, as there were on most farms. There was a flock of Plymouth Rocks, but they were penned, with their own coop, out beside the barn. At the house, there were white curtains at the windows and they all seemed exactly alike, even tied back just so, and the green window shades were all at exactly the same level, one-third down from the top.

There was a friendly dog, one of those woolly black-and-tan shepherds, as we used to call them. He was outside the fenced dooryard and he came to bark at me and wag his tail. He followed me up to the dooryard gate. I waited there a moment or so, and then the door of the house opened. Mrs. Sebastian appeared, tall and starchy looking, her blonde hair drawn back so tight it seemed to stretch her forehead. She had a dress that buttoned all the way up to her chin. She looked at me a moment and asked, "Yes?" then said, "Oh, you came to help dig out the fox, I guess. Mr. Sebastian is out at the barn." And she closed the door. I saw the two little girls, blonde as their mother, peeking out one of the windows, but when she closed the door they drew back and pushed the white curtains into place again.

I went on out to the barn. Mr. Sebastian was cleaning the stalls where he kept his two saddle horses. The horses were out in the corral, and Sebastian was using the pitchfork almost viciously. He saw me and stood for a moment, his square jaws knotted, his knuckles white as he gripped the fork handle.

Then he said, "Hello," in a slightly hoarse voice and picked up half a forkful of bedding with the fork and threw it through the open door behind him onto the manure pile. He hung the fork on its pegs on the barn wall, took a deep breath, and let it out slowly before he smiled at me and said, "Nice day out. If it wasn't for women it would be a good world." Then he laughed, a kind of dry chuckle, and said, "Let's go get that old bitch fox."

We went to the tool shed and got two long-handled, round-pointed spades and a couple of gunny sacks. The tool shed, like the barn, was neat and orderly, as neat as the house and the dooryard. Almost fanatically neat.

Sebastian called the dog and we started out across the flat to the east, toward the top of the rise half a mile away. About half way there was a shallow swale, and as we approached it Sebastian said to the dog, "Go chase that bitch out of there, Tuffy. Go get her!" Tuffy perked his ears and headed for the swale, at a lope. Sure enough, he put up a kit fox, probably mousing in the tall grass. The fox took off, the dog yelped, and the chase was on. I had seen it happen many times, the dog's initial rush, the fox's sharp dodge just as the dog was about to close in, the zig and zag, the dog's bewilderment and frustration. But Tuffy kept on, and the fox dodged to safety, time after time, working toward the top of the rise all the while.

We stopped and watched, and Sebastian shook his head and muttered, "That bitch! Just like them all. Let you get all ready to take them and then duck right out of your hands. You think you've got her, and then—there she goes!—then she slams the door in your face."

The fox had reached her den, vanished, gone to ground.

Tuffy was still at the hole, tongue out, panting, from time to time thrusting his muzzle down and sniffing, when we got there. I would swear that hole wasn't six inches in diameter. It had a low mound of bare earth around it, not high and doughnut shaped like a prairie dog hole but broad and low and bare of grass. I looked around for chicken feathers, but there wasn't a feather in sight. Father probably was right. The fox wasn't taking the Sebastian chickens. Coyotes maybe, but not kit foxes.

"Well," Sebastian said, "here she is, right down this hole. All we got to do is dig her out. You want to start?"

I began spading the sandy soil, following the burrow which led down at a sharp angle a little way, then flattened off. I opened a trench about a foot and a half wide, just big enough to work in. Sebastian watched in silence for a time, then said, "I heard that Bainbridge fellow is set on starting a bastardy suit."

I didn't answer, just went on digging and tossing the dirt onto the pile alongside the trench.

"Now that's a damn fool thing to do," he went on. "If that girl of his is going to have a baby, why don't he do something about that? Send her away, or something. You know her?"

"Yes," I said.

"Hot stuff, huh?" He laughed, a tense kind of laugh.

I saw no need to answer.

"Used to see her around town," he said, "before she quit going to town. A hot little bitch. You can spot them, the way they walk, the way they look at you." He licked his lips and spat and said, "I'll take it a while."

I backed out of the trench, glad to let him take over. If he was digging he probably wouldn't be talking. I didn't like his kind of talk. It made me feel uncomfortable, not quite nauseated but uneasy inside. He dug for maybe fifteen minutes and began to sweat as the sun got hotter. Finally he said, "All right, you take it a while," and he climbed out. I went down the trench and started digging again, and Sebastian lit a cigarette and turned to stare at the house, muttering something I couldn't hear. I hadn't dug five minutes when I came to a fork in the burrow. I cleaned out both openings, told him what I had found, and asked which fork to follow. He wasn't listening. I asked him again and he said, "What? Oh. Oh, it forks. I don't know which one to follow."

"Maybe the dog would know," I said. "Maybe he could smell which one."

But the dog had left, gone back to the house, probably, not interested in watching us dig a trench. Sebastian called a couple of times, "Hyah, Tuffy, hyah, Tuffy!" and gave up. Then he laughed. "Let me get down in that ditch. I'll find out which one that bitch is in. By God, I can sniff one out as good as a dog can!"

I climbed out and Sebastian got into the trench, down on his hands and knees first, then flat on his belly, and sniffed at both holes. He sniffed loudly, seemed to relish it, finally rolled over on his side and said, "Both of them got a lot of that smell!" He turned and sniffed again, drew a deep breath and held it, then let it out with a long, "A-a-a-ahh." Then he got to his knees. "She's in there, all right, one place or the other. Give me a shovel." I handed him a shovel and he went to work, following the original burrow. The trench was down about four feet and now had to be widened so one could work in it comfortably. He began widening it, working fast and breathing hard. He paused to catch his breath and said, "When we get through, we're going to have to put this dirt all back. Fill the damned hole so a steer won't fall in and break a leg." He resumed digging, but after a few shovelfuls said, "But like my old man used to say, that's what holes are for. To be filled." He laughed to himself and went on digging. And a few minutes later he said, "You better start on that side tunnel. It smelled pretty hot, too. She's got to be in one or the other." So I started digging out the branch burrow, and there were both of us tossing dirt out like badgers digging out a prairie dog, except that badgers toss the dirt out behind them and we tossed it to one side.

Every now and then Sebastian stopped digging and got down and sniffed at the burrow he was working on. Each time it seemed to give him new energy. In the next half hour we had dug at least ten feet of the main trench and close to five feet of the side trench. He got down and sniffed again and announced, "I'm really close now!" He was excited, breathing hard. He dug a few more shovelfuls, undercutting so he wouldn't have to move so much dirt, then sniffed again and reached in with one arm. He thrust his arm in full length and shouted, "Got her! By God, I've got her by the twat!" And an instant later he yelled in pain and pulled back his arm, got to his knees. His hand was bleeding from several small punctures and two long scratches. He stared at it an instant, there on his knees in the trench, then sucked it clean and spat out the blood. He grabbed his spade, thrust the handle into the hole, felt for a moment, then jabbed viciously. There was a whimper of pain. He jabbed again, and when he drew out the spade the handle had blood on the end. He sucked his hand again, cursed loudly, then got to his feet and dug furiously. I saw two eyes and a small black muzzle only a few inches back in the hole, and a small mouth half open, front teeth broken, jaws bleeding. Sebastian tossed a shovelful of dirt out of the trench and suddenly the kit fox leaped free just as he was poising the spade for another jab at the soil. She shot between his legs as he jabbed. The spade caught her tail, cut it clean a couple of inches from its base. It lay there, still bushed, as her feet spurted dirt in her desperate rush.

Sebastian yelled, spun around, slapped at her with the spade. But she was out of the trench, running. He flung the spade at her, leaped from the trench, screaming, "You dirty bitch! You bitch, you bitch!" But she was gone, down the slope away from the house, toward the long shallow draw to the east. She dodged, zigzagging, but she seemed to waver as she ran, off balance, almost staggering, without the plume of a tail to steady her. But she went down the long slope and around a little shoulder of the hill and was gone. And when

I looked down into the trench again, that length of her tail was just a hairy bit of bone and skin that oozed a drop or two of blood onto the yellowish, sandy soil.

Sebastian had sworn himself hoarse. He picked up his spade, came back to the trench, glaring at me, and began digging at the side burrow. I got out of his way, stayed out. He dug for another half hour and opened the burrow to what must have been a kind of nesting room, big enough to hold several young foxes. There he found two kits, almost fully grown. Unlike their mother, they made no attempt to escape. They cowered back in the burrow, and Sebastian simply clubbed them to death with the back of the spade, then dragged them out and stomped them.

He was red-eyed by then and covered with sweat, his shirt dark and wet and muddy from the dirt he had wallowed in as he got down to sniff, his pants wet with sweat almost to his knees. He got out of the trench, looked at me almost surprised, and began shoveling the dirt back in. I helped, from the opposite side. We shoveled dirt back into the trench for twenty minutes or so. Then he paused, looked back at the house, and said to me, "Finish filling this in." He looked at the house again and said, "I'm going to take her, and really make her like it!" and he set off toward the house, dragging the long-handled spade. A few minutes later he took the spade up in his hand and carried it, the long handle foreward, and threw back his shoulders and laughed so loud I could hear him two hundred yards away.

I finished filling the trenches and went down the slope to the barn, where I left the spade. Then I got on my bicycle and started back to town. As I passed the fenced dooryard at the house, the two little girls stood at the gate and watched me. There wasn't a sign of anybody at the house, and the shades were drawn in the windows of the room at the back. The little girls looked frightened, but they didn't say a word, didn't wave or make a gesture. They just stood there at the gate, wide-eyed, and watched me ride past and out the long lane to the main road.

It was midafternoon when I got home. I had taken my time and stopped twice to get things back in place. The first time, I thought I was going to vomit, but I didn't. I thought at first that it was the heat getting to me, so I sat with my back against a fence post for ten minutes or so and cooled off. Then I felt better. The second time I knew it was George Sebastian, and I got that one straightened out enough to live with.

I got home and Mother got me a sandwich and a glass of milk and asked, "You didn't get a kit fox to make a pet out of?"

"No. The mother got away, and he killed the two young ones."

"Probably just as well."

Father put aside the *Denver Post* long enough to ask, "Didn't they give you any dinner?"

I shook my head.

"That's funny. George Sebastian never struck me as tight-fisted that way. She didn't either."

"Did she have nice things in the house?" Mother asked.

"I don't know. I didn't go in."

"You had quite a visit, didn't you?" Father said, and he went back to his newspaper.

"That's about what I expected," Mother said. "He's got a look in his eye I never did like. She's probably got to watch him like a hawk. Well, next time you'll know better."

There were no more questions, and there was no need to tell them what happened. I wasn't altogether sure myself what happened, really. All I knew was what I did and saw and heard.

Eventually Nell Bainbridge had her baby, a boy. Dr. Neff delivered it, and when the most eager gossip in town got up her nerve to ask him who the baby looked like, he said, "I couldn't really say, Ellie." And then, as Father told the story to Mother and me, the doctor said, "Looked a good deal like you did when you were born. Except we tucked it in for you, but we left his dangling."

Mother stiffened and blushed. "That sounds like him! Probably been drinking when he said it." She tried to hide the little smile of amusement with a frown, but it lifted the corners of her mouth.

Jim Bainbridge filed the paternity suit, naming a young man from Kansas who had worked at odd jobs around Flagler for a couple of years. The defendant hired a lawyer from Burlington who was known for slick practices. When the case came to trial the lawyer summoned two livery stable loafers and a farm hand from down near Seibert, who all swore that they "had relations" with Nell. The prosecution challenged the character and veracity of all three witnesses, but the case was lost on a basis of reasonable doubt. And even those in town who had said the suit was a disgrace to the community declared that the verdict was a disgrace to the court. But Jim hadn't the money to appeal it.

Father printed a brief item on an inside page when the suit was filed. He gave the decision a few more lines but an equally inconspicuous place in the paper. But a few weeks later, when the defendant found that he was no longer wanted in Flagler and went back to Kansas, Father printed the item on the front page and headed it "Wes Jones Leaves Town." Which closed the case, at least as far as the proprieties were concerned.

16

Julius Gunter and Woodrow Wilson never knew it, but they saved *The Flagler News*. I didn't know it either, and Mother didn't, though she probably had her suspicions. If Wilson hadn't won the presidency and Gunter the governorship in November of 1916, Father probably couldn't have kept the paper going another year. He had built it up, doubled its circulation, almost doubled its advertising. But he started from virtually nothing, and he had to buy new type and new equipment. He kept putting money back into the paper, but he couldn't get ahead. W. E. Hall's front-page ad pulled him through the first winter, and he hoped that the good wheat crop that second summer would boom things enough to carry the *News* along. It didn't, because the political campaign created too many uncertainties.

The campaign was crucial because everybody seemed to wait and see how it came out before spending their money. There wasn't any increase in advertising, and the job printing slacked off. The other paper in town, the *Progress*, didn't gain much advertising either, but it didn't seem to be having any problems. Ed Gibson, the owner, wasn't in debt the way Father was. And of course he was on the same side of the political fence as the old-timers, the Republican side. If they favored either paper, they were going to favor the *Progress*.

Father, both a newcomer and a Democrat, had a mortgage and interest to pay, and he had no reserve. Interest could run as high as fifteen percent, but he was considered a good risk and had to pay only ten. But even that could add up to a heavy load. And if you missed an interest payment the bank could call the loan and sell you out. The bankers in Flagler were Republicans. But Father kept saying, in print as well as privately, that the county, the state and the nation needed a Democratic victory in November. Both state and county had gone Republican in 1914. By September Mother was saying that if the Democrats didn't win this year Father certainly would be out in the cold. Father gave her a wry smile. "I'm not exactly getting sunstroke now." And he didn't change his stand. By then he was in so deep he couldn't have backed out if he had tried.

I was aware of the political campaign, but I wasn't involved. From the first week in September I was absorbed almost totally in school and football. Schoolboys, even high school students, didn't then think they could run the government or dictate to the school.

There were major changes at school that year. Until then it had been essentially a rural grammar school trying to do the job of a high school. Even the new building hadn't changed the ideas and organization it housed. But that summer the Conleys resigned and the school board hired an energetic, athletic young man from Iowa as principal. Robert Ward had been teaching in Nebraska and was eager for the administrative job. His sister, Phyllis, was hired to teach Latin and English classes. And Amelia Alexander, daughter of a local lumber dealer, was hired to take charge of the science courses and the domestic arts, as they were called—cooking and sewing for the girls, carpentry and cabinetmaking for the boys. Some people laughed at the idea of a woman teaching boys how to use a hammer and a saw, but we boys soon found that she was a better cabinetmaker than anybody else in town. I made a cedar chest in her class that we still cherish, not because I made it but because it is a beautiful piece of work.

With the changes, I had to explain all over again why I wanted to take six courses instead of the usual four. But Professor Ward—he acquired the title with the job—cut me off before I was really well started with my argument. "Go ahead," he said, looking at my record. "You didn't seem to have any trouble last year. You'll be a full-fledged senior next year, and if you keep your grades up you'll be eligible for a scholarship." Then, almost in the same sentence, it seemed, "We are starting a football practice next Monday and I want to see you there." Professor Ward, it turned out, had been an all-conference tackle in college. He was going to coach us. Leon Lavington wouldn't have much time to spare from business, but he would help.

So while Father and most of the other grownups in town were deep in politics, we boys in high school were deep in football. Professor Ward got enough boys out to have a complete scrub team, but he drilled us hard on fundamentals, just as Leon Lavington had. "You will win as many games recovering fumbles," he said, "as you will trying to run tricky plays. Learn to fall on a fumble, and learn to hold on to that ball. Learn how to block and tackle hard enough to bring your man down. Once you learn those things you won't need more than a dozen simple plays."

So we learned, adding skill to knowledge from the year before. We had lost only three players by graduation, but one was our quarterback. After trying several of us at that position, Professor Ward moved Hugh Quinn—we all called him "Irish" —up from fullback and gave him the job. Irish hadn't much imagination and he used the same pattern of plays over and over, but we won games just the same. The other team always saw the play pattern Irish was following by the time the second half began, but by then we usually had at least two touchdowns more than they did. And we were a good defensive team—we hung on long enough to win.

We won our first game, against Limon, by two touchdowns. We beat Hugo by a touchdown and a field goal. Then we went to Akron, eighty miles north of Flagler, up on the Burlington railroad. Akron had a good team, with a Negro halfback who was a deadly tackler and a hard, fast runner. But we were lucky. They fumbled the opening kickoff, we recovered on their twenty-yard line and went in for the touchdown. Late in the first quarter they fumbled again and we recovered at midfield, and Irish carried the ball on an end run that went in for another touchdown. But in the second half that Negro halfback ran all over us. He made three touchdowns, the third one with only four minutes left in the game. But Karl Pearson, one of our tackles, blocked the extra point. On their kickoff we took the ball back almost to midfield. Our first two plays got nowhere. The next play in Irish's pattern was up the middle, but I told him before we lined up that I thought I could get clear if he would throw one as far as he could. I knew he could throw a pass almost fifty yards. So when Akron massed to block the expected drive over center I went as far and as fast as I could downfield. Irish faded back, waited maybe four seconds, and really threw that ball. I caught it like a punt, so I wouldn't drop it, and had only five yards to go for the score. Nobody was anywhere near me. Then I kicked the extra point, and that was the game.

The Akron halfback was the first Negro player we had faced. There weren't any Negroes in our area, probably because the dry-land flats had no appeal to them. There certainly wasn't any sense of discrimination that I was ever aware of, against any minority. One of our tackles was a half-blood Indian, and Hugo had a full-blood Indian. Nobody seemed to care or bother about your color or race or religion. We were so unaware of such matters, in fact, that during my first year in college I asked a boy named Finklestein what nationality he was.

He had asked me if my name wasn't Swedish, and I said it was Scotch-Irish, that the Swedish version had a "u" in place of the "a." Then I asked about his name, and he looked at me, stunned, and demanded, "Are you trying to be funny?" I said no, and he said, "I'm a German Jew." I said I had one German grandfather, and he asked, "Jewish?" I said, "No," I don't think so," and he laughed at me, that half-sad, half-derisive laugh, and said, "You would know. Believe me, you'd know."

The Akron game made the season for us, though we still had two return games to play, with Hugo and Limon. We lost to Hugo by a touchdown, but we beat Limon by two touchdowns. Then, despite warnings from Leon Lavington that we would get trounced, we begged Professor Ward to get us a game with Burlington, the county seat and a school three times as big as Flagler's. Burlington had the first Saturday in November open, so they came to Flagler and trounced us, just as Leon had said they could. I forget the score, but they really put us in our place by playing their scrub team the whole final quarter.

Meanwhile, of course, the political campaign went on hard-fought. Father went down to Burlington a couple of times to discuss issues and strategy with the county's Democratic leaders. Candidates from both parties came and went, shaking hands, pointing with pride, viewing with alarm, making promises. One group of Democratic candidates for state offices toured the east end of the state and made a point of stopping in Flagler to see Father. It was a kind of fraternal visit since one of them was Charley Leckenby, owner of the Steamboat Springs *Pilot* and candidate for state auditor, and another was James R. Noland, a Denver newspaperman and candidate for secretary of state. Also with them was Leslie Hubbard, candidate for attorney general and a lawyer from the Western Slope whom Father had known the summer he spent as an editor in Pagosa, the summer he came home with typhoid fever and nearly died.

This visit added considerably to Father's local prestige and helped his standing in the county's Democratic councils. After that, every Democratic candidate who visited that area stopped at the *News* office to see Father. Inevitably, he was a little puffed up by all this. He had worked for recognition, and now he was getting it. One evening at the supper table, late in October, he quoted something somebody, maybe Leslie Hubbard, had said about him. He bragged a little about his own standing in the county's Democratic organization, as a man feels free to do at his own family dinner table. But Mother, who was both a realist and a skeptic, listened with tightening lips and finally said, "You are talking like a politician, Will. I don't care what you say, you're still a country editor, and you owe the bank almost a thousand dollars."

Father looked at her, surprised, and asked, "Don't you realize that after we win this election I can practically write my own ticket in Burlington? Maybe even in Denver."

"Fiddlesticks! If the Democrats win you'll probably get some of the county printing, but that's all. They come around now and slap you on the back and give you campaign cigars and call you Bill, but they're all looking out for Number One."

"It's good to have important friends," Father said stiffly.

Mother smiled. "Important? As Ma used to say, their dirty socks stink just like yours do."

Father said no more. He liked people, wanted to believe the best of them. He was a good deal of a romantic and sentimental to the point where tears came easily. Mother, thoroughly practical, had an intuitive sense of motives that made her habitually skeptical. She distrusted most politicians, and most of them didn't like her, maybe because they sensed that she knew about their dirty socks.

The campaign was virtually over by the Saturday that our football team was humiliated by the team from Burlington. The following Tuesday was election day. By then there wasn't much real doubt about how Colorado would vote. The Republicans had won in 1914, but this time the Democrats claimed victory "by at least 50,000." As it turned out, they won the governorship and most of the other state offices by a margin of about 35,000. President Wilson, however, doubled that margin in the state, though nationally the election was very close, so close that President Wilson went to bed on election night thinking that he had lost to Charles Evans Hughes. Not until late the next day, when all the returns were in from the Far West, was the Wilson victory assured. For the first time, a presidential candidate who lost in the East was elected by the votes from the West. Something was happening to the balance of power in the United States, something that few people understood. The Old Order was passing. Looking back now, it seems to me that the five years from 1915 to 1920 were a belated transition from the nineteenth century to the twentieth. I don't recall that any historian ever made a point of this, but I feel sure something of that kind happened. Perhaps it would be most obvious to those of my generation who lived in the swiftly changing West at that time.

What mattered at that moment, however, was that Colorado and Kit Carson County went Democratic, and Father was on the winning side. I don't remember what Father said to Mother about it, or if he said anything. But I do remember that for quite a while he walked with a trace of a swagger and wore his soft black hat at a more rakish angle. Physically he was a small man, just under five feet seven and about 150 pounds; but after that election he stood tall in local and regional Democratic councils. The only public office he ever held was as a member of Flagler's nonpolitical town council, but some years later he got the notion he would like to be county treasurer. He said as much to the county chairman, who shook his head and said, "I wouldn't try it, Will."

"Why not?"

"You'd get trounced."

"This is going to be a Democratic year."

"Yes, I think so. But you'd still lose."

"Why do you say that?"

"Don't ask why. Just take my word."

"I *am* asking why."

The chairman hesitated, then said, "Your wife."

"What! *I'm* going to be the candidate, not Sarah!"

"All right, Will. You asked for it. Your wife thinks politicians are the scum of the earth, and she makes no secret of it. You'll get knifed, believe me, and that's the reason. Now don't get me wrong—I happen to like her, but she's made *me* feel awful cheap a time or two."

So Father never became county treasurer. He was consulted about appointments and legislation, and he served a term or two as county chairman. When the Democrats were in power he was welcome in any office in the capitol building in Denver. But that was later. Now he was the spokesman for the young Democratic majority in Flagler, and his newspaper had a degree of prestige. Inevitably, the local advertisers came to him, once the election was over. At last the *News* had the edge over Ed Gibson's *Progress*.

That was the best Christmas season Father had had, and the change for the better carried right over into the new year. Father was making money, enough to begin to lay some aside for the better equipment he had been dreaming about. He had talked to me occasionally, at the office. about what he wanted to get, but it all had the someday-maybe aura about it. By the first of March, however, with inauguration day at hand, he told Mother that he had decided to buy a flat-bed press "and make the *News* a real newspaper."

Mother was surprised, and she was skeptical, as usual. A new flat-bed press would cost a lot of money. She wasn't sure just how much, but she doubted that it would be wise to put that much into a new press just now.

She said her say, and Father said, "I'm not going to get a new press. Not when I can practically steal a second-hand one that's just what I want."

Mother stiffened. "What are you talking about?"

"That little Miehle down at Stratton. I've had my eye on it quite a while, wondering when Guy Ray would get to the point where he'd have to sell it to meet his mortgage. Well, he's there now."

"Are you sure?"

"Positive. Bob Wilkinson told me yesterday, in Burlington. Bob said Guy wanted to borrow five hundred dollars, said he had to have it by the middle of next week."

"How do you know he'll sell the press?"

"He offered it to Bob, but Bob doesn't need it. His paper has all the equipment he can use. There's only one hitch."

"What's that?"

"Getting it moved. If I try to get the Miehle people to come out from Denver, they'll charge a fortune."

"I should think somebody else could move a press."

"I think so too," Father said.

That afternoon he went over to Ed Malbaff's blacksmith shop across the street from the livery stable. Ed Malbaff was a big dark-haired man who could make almost anything out of iron and who had an uncanny sense of how machines operated. Thirty-odd years later his son Bill, who had inherited the blacksmith shop and branched out into automobile repairing, was called out one day to see if anything could be done for an army airplane that had been forced down a few miles from town with engine trouble. Bill had never seen an airplane engine, but within two hours he had that plane in the air again. When someone asked how he did it, Bill said, "Just figured it out, like my old man would. He probably would have had it fixed in less time, though. He always said I was a little backward."

That's the kind of blacksmith Ed Malbaff was, and Father knew it. They talked for ten minutes or so and Ed said, "Let me take it apart, get Ory to haul it up here, and I'll put it back together."

The next day Father went to Stratton, which was twenty-two miles east of Flagler, and made his deal with Guy Ray, who owned the *Stratton Press*, a typical run-down small-town newspaper. Ray was a good enough printer, but a casual sort of man who lived a casual life. He had almost no job printing and barely enough advertising to pay his paper bills. Pinched by an overdue mortgage, he had to raise money somehow. I don't know how much Father paid for that press, but it was only a fraction of what it would have cost new.

It was called a Pony Miehle and printed two pages of standard newspaper size at a time. Being a Miehle, it was one of the best presses made, and since the *Stratton Press* had only a small circulation it was hardly worn at all, though it had been there at least ten years. But it was caked with dirt and grease, as I saw the next weekend when I went with Father and Ed Malbaff to take it down and load it onto Ora Groves' truck. It was so dirty that we washed it down with gasoline and scraped it with putty knives before we loosened a bolt. Then Ed spent almost an hour going over it, asking Father or me to turn the drive pulley half a turn or a whole turn, watching how every part moved or was moved upon. Then he chalked numbers and arrows and other strange signs on the major pieces.

Finally Guy Ray, who had been watching all this and fidgeting nervously, came over to Father. "Will, I've got to tell you something about that press. It doesn't run right."

"This is a fine time to tell me! What's wrong with it?"

"I don't know. I never could find out. I went to the Miehle people up in Denver once and asked them, but they couldn't tell me. And I—well, I'm not a crook. I had to tell you."

"You've been printing your paper on it, haven't you?"

"That's right. But it'll only run about half speed. Try to go any faster and it acts like it's going to tear itself apart."

"That doesn't make sense," Father said. "Ed!"

Mr. Malbaff, who was about to start loosening bolts with his big wrenches, came over to them.

"Guy says there's something wrong with the press," Father said.

Ed shifted a big quid of tobacco in his cheek. "Um-hummm," he said. "I saw that half an hour ago." And Ed went back to work.

Guy Ray watched him a moment, then said to Father, "If you want to back out of the deal—I don't know what I'll do, but—"

Father went over to Ed and asked, "Anything bad, Ed?"

"Couple of loose bearings," Ed said under his breath. "I'll take them up when we put it back together."

Father went back to Ray and said, "The deal's still on. But I do think you ought to set us up to a good meal over at the hotel at noon."

It was a Saturday, and Ora Groves made three trips before he had moved the whole press to Flagler. And it all had to be taken down to that basement room, with the only way in down the outside stairway. The stairway, open at the top, was about four feet wide and offered no obstacle, but it was impossible to get any but the smaller parts through the door. So they took out the big window, which was more than five feet square. Then they rigged a block and tackle and backed the truck up to the curb, hoisted the press sections out, lowered them down the open stairway onto heavy skids and through the big window opening. Some of the sections, Mr. Groves said, weighed close to a thousand pounds.

The last load wasn't in the office until eight o'clock that night, and we were all dog-tired. Ed Malbaff came along with the final load, and when the last piece had been lowered onto the skids and through the window he said, "Put the window back in and be here at seven-thirty tomorrow morning. We've got a day's work ahead of us."

Mr. Groves laughed, but it was a weary laugh. "What do you call what we've been doing today, Ed?"

"Today," Ed said, "was the easy part, taking this thing to pieces. Tomorrow we've got to put it back together."

The next day was Sunday, but we were all there before eight o'clock. By ten o'clock we had the frame in place, plumb and solid. By noon the press was two-thirds assembled. By three o'clock Ed said, "Let's see what happens when you turn that drive pulley." We turned it, and the bed of the press moved the way it was supposed to, the cylinder turned, the grippers closed. "Hold it," Ed ordered. He made an adjustment.

At five o'clock Ed Malbaff said, "That's it, Will. We'll change your line shafting tomorrow and you'll be all ready to print papers."

"How about the trouble Guy Ray had with it?" Father asked.

"Oh, that. I fixed that two hours ago. The take-up on the main bearings had been shimmed, for some reason, and the shims hadn't been taken out after they settled in. I took out the shims and drew them down where they should be, and that was that."

So Father called it a day and sent everybody home. The next morning Ed came and hung a new line shaft and put on the right size pulleys. They cut and laced belts. Before noon they had the Fairbanks-Morse running the new press. Full speed, too. Ed made a few more adjustments and said that would do for now.

When I went to the office after school, Father started the engine, threw in the clutch on the press, and stood with me, just watching it run, without a form or a line of type on its bed, just running free and to no purpose at all. It ran as smooth as Mother's New Home sewing machine, and it wasn't any louder than the big Gordon job press. It was, as father said, a jewel of a press, beautifully made and a fine piece of machinery.

We stood and watched it, and for maybe five minutes Father couldn't bring himself to throw out the clutch and stop the engine. Then he came back and looked at the press again, put his hand on the feedboard and said, half to himself, "Now I've got me a real printshop. A newspaper and a press to print it on, the best press made."

He turned to me. "You didn't know I was practically broke last summer. Nobody knew, not even your mother, but I didn't know whether I could hold on till after election. Early in September I was so near broke I went to W. H. Lavington and laid the cards on the table, told him exactly where I stood. He made me a personal loan, enough to live on till after the campaign, with nothing but a personal note. He said he didn't want to see the *News* fold up. Said the town needed it."

Then he added, "It's all paid back. I paid it back before Christmas."

And I was sorry, in a way, that he had told me. It was his secret. Now I know he had to tell someone and, at the time, he didn't want to tell Mother. I know, too, why he was so outspoken, almost defiantly truculent, during that political campaign. He was fighting for his life, at least for the life of his newspaper.

17

That had been a busy fall and winter for me. In addition to everything else, I was the operator who ran the projector in Flagler's first motion picture theater.

Motion pictures had been shown in Flagler before 1916, but only now and then, when an itinerant came along with a few rolls of well-worn film, a projector, and an electric generator, all in an old truck that wheezed and bumped from one small town to the next. Motion pictures were dependent on electricity for the carbon arc lamps in their projectors, and relatively few small towns in the West had electric power plants, so the itinerants had to have their own portable generators. Motion pictures really were no longer a novelty, though they certainly weren't common in rural areas. I saw my first movie in 1908 in the little Nebraska town where I was born. It was that early classic, *The Great Train Robbery*. It was shown by traveling exhibitors who hired an empty store building and made temporary benches by laying planks on nail kegs. The place was jammed and the picture was dim and jerky, but it was a marvel of the day. It probably was an old copy of the film, which was made originally in 1903. I was surprised, years later when I read a book on the history of the motion pictures, to see that one of the actors in that historic film was G. M. Anderson, who a few years later was widely known as "Broncho Billy" Anderson, the star of early Western movies.

I wouldn't be surprised if Flagler had a visit from that same film, certainly from others of that period. But the town had no movie theater or regular program till Manzal Gromer started one. Mr. Gromer owned one of Flagler's lumber yards and had his hand in several businesses, including hardware. That may have been how he got involved with motion pictures—a Denver hardware wholesaler may have sold him the equipment. All I know is that he bought a second-hand projector, a five-horsepower Fairbanks-Morse gasoline engine, and a generator. He signed up with a booking agency for films. Then he rented Seal's Hall for Saturday afternoons and nights, built a cubbyhole projection booth at the back, put up a screen on the miniature stage, built a shed out back for the engine and generator, and put in the necessary electric wiring.

Thus Flagler got not only motion pictures but an electric street light, the lone bare bulb Mr. Gromer installed at the stairway entrance to Seal's Hall on Main Street. There was another bulb at the head of the stairs, where he put the ticket booth, and there were three bulbs in the hall itself, not counting the one in the projection booth. The hall already had folding wooden chairs and an old upright piano. Mr. Gromer found a local woman who could play an incredible number of pieces from memory. So he had everything he needed except an audience, and as soon as he announced his first show the audience came from all over town and the nearby area.

For the first two weeks Mr. Gromer ran the projector himself. Then he decided that he had more important things to do, such as counting the cash, or taking tickets, or keeping order among the younger customers. Besides, he was a restless man, and running a movie projector is a stay-put job. So he came down to the *News* office late one Friday afternoon. He was a big, broad, red-faced man with a booming voice. "Will," he shouted to Father, "I want someone to run my moving picture projector. You know anyone, or am I going to have to advertise?"

"Offhand," Father said, "I'd say you will have to advertise." Then he grinned. "What kind of a job is it, anyway?"

"Simple," Mr. Gromer said. "Nothing difficult about it. Anyone who can turn a crank can do it, if he has any mechanical sense at all."

"That sounds easy enough."

"Well, it's easy all right, but it's got to be somebody responsible. He has to watch what he's doing. That carbon arc can be dangerous, and the film burns awful fast if it gets started." He paused and looked across the shop to where I was making ready to print envelopes on the little job press. "How about that boy of yours?" He asked. "He must be handy with machinery, and I guess he tends to business, doesn't he?"

Father turned and motioned to me. I went over to them. "You probably heard what Mr. Gromer was saying," Father said to me. I nodded, and Father left us, went over to the job press to finish the make-ready I had started. And to leave it to me to make any arrangement with Mr. Gromer.

"Well," Mr. Gromer said, "how about it?"

"I'd like to try it if—"

"Fine, fine! Tomorrow afternoon, and—"

"No, I can't work Saturday afternoons till after football season. I can work Saturday nights. But—"

"When is the end of this football season?"

"November."

He thought a moment, frowning. "Well, I guess I can run the afternoon shows till then." He turned and shouted to Father, still at the job press, "What do you think would be a fair deal, Will?"

"You two work it out," Father said.

Mr. Gromer turned back to me. "Since you won't be working afternoons for a while, let's see how it goes evenings. You'll see the show for nothing, of course."

"Mr. Gromer, I like to know what a job is going to pay before I take it."

Mr. Gromer frowned, then shouted to Father, "I've got a tough customer here, Will. He wants to know how much I'll pay before he does a lick of work."

"Good idea," Father said, but he kept out of it.

"Since you're only going to be working half time," Mr. Gromer said, "we'll have to start at half pay."

"All right. How much will that be?"

"Well, let's see. This isn't really work, you know. You just stand there and turn the crank, keep the carbons set right." He hesitated, waited. I waited too. Finally he asked, "How much do you think you're worth?"

"A dollar a show," I said, setting it high so I could bargain.

"A dollar a show! Good Lord Jehoshephat! Will," he shouted, "I guess I'll have to advertise! This boy wants all my profit just for standing there turning a crank."

"Write out what you want in the ad," Father said, still at the press. "It'll cost you twenty-five cents a line."

"Holy Moses! I sure walked into a den of thieves." Mr. Gromer turned toward the door, then shook his head and turned back to me. "Seventy-five cents," he said. "And if you let the film get on fire even once, out you go."

"Seventy-five cents a show," I said. "A dollar and a half when I work both afternoon and night."

Mr. Gromer made a grimace of pain, but he said, "All right. Come over to the yard about nine o'clock tomorrow morning and I'll go over to the hall with you and show you how to run the projector." Then he turned to Father and shouted, "Better let this boy run your business, Will. He'll make a go of it. He sure knows what makes the mare go!" And he left, with a completely surprising wink at me.

I met him at the lumber yard the next morning and we spent an hour in the projection booth, going over the details of the job, setting the carbons for the arc, threading the film in the projector, cranking it at just the right speed, changing reels, feeding in the slides at intermission, rewinding. And, time after time, the necessity of guarding against fire.

Mr. Gromer had brought the films for that day's shows, which came by mail in flat, round tin cans the size of a reel, about twelve inches in diameter. Before he could run the first reel and show me all the routine of the job, we had to rewind that film. He showed me how to start it, on the spindles fastened to a small shelf at the side of the booth, which was built of fireproof building board. I started rewinding, and we struck the first of half a dozen breaks in the film. Mr. Gromer swore under his breath at the first break, swore softly at the second, and before we finished the reel was shouting imprecations on the projection man in Limon, who had failed to mend the breaks. I learned, eventually, that virtually every reel of film we received had at least two breaks in it, and I became an expert at mending film, if at no other phase of the job. It was old, badly worn film to begin with, and most of the men who ran those small-town movie theaters were either inept or didn't give a hoot. And never did we receive a reel that didn't have to be rewound before it could be shown.

I learned the fundamentals of the job that morning, then dashed home to get a bite of dinner at noon, hurried up to school and into my football uniform, played a game of football that afternoon, went home, did the household chores, such as carrying out the ashes from the stoves, bringing in kindling and coal, seeing that the water bucket was full, running to the store for some item Mother needed. Ate supper, almost too tired to eat, and was at the movie theater by seven o'clock.

That first evening Mr. Gromer either stayed in the booth with me or was close by all through the show. But I went through the four full reels with only minor lapses. I forgot the advertising slides which opened the show, and had to be reminded. Those slides were vitally important—they brought

Mr. Gromer ten or fifteen dollars a week. Then I got the "Ladies Please Remove Your Hats" slide in upside down, which provoked laughter, whistling and stomping. But after that I ran the first reel, a comedy with Louise Fazenda, Chester Conklin and Ben Turpin, that incredibly cross-eyed zany. I had no trouble with that reel. Then I started the three-reel feature film, something presumably high society and dramatic, with Francis X. Bushman and Beverly Bayne. The first reel went all right, but I got the third reel on next and ran it several minutes before I knew something was wrong. Mr. Gromer came hurrying back to the booth, banged on the door, and told me in a stage whisper that could have been heard down on the street that I had the wrong reel on. I stopped it, put in the slide saying, "One Moment, Please," and switched reels, making sure I had the loops properly large and the intermittent sprocket threaded right. Then I started in again, and there were cheers and laughter as the picture picked up the story where it had been broken at the end of Reel One. Otherwise, it was an uneventful evening.

After the first couple of weeks I began to feel like a professional. I could mend film perfectly with the cement that smelled like bananas, match frame to frame so there was scarcely a flicker. I could pace the cranking of the film exactly right without having to watch the screen. I could tell when the carbon pencils of the arc were getting too short to last through another reel, and I could replace them in no time. I made it routine to rewind all the reels after I had shown them, mending any breaks that showed up, for the convenience of the next exhibitor, hoping that eventually the fellow who had those films before we got them would do me the same favor. He never did.

I don't think I had seen a dozen movies before that winter. But I began to catch up with what had been made and shown over the previous five years. Some of the films we got were all the way back to the Al Christie days in New Jersey, which was around 1911. We showed *Caprice* that winter, with Mary Pickford and Owen Moore, which was made by Adolph Zukor in 1913. We showed another 1913 picture, *The Squaw Man*, whose star was Dustin Farnum. But the highlight of that whole winter was the relatively new *The Birth of a Nation*, the first of the "epic" films. We ran it in the spring of 1917, and it was so much of a drawing card that Mr. Gromer held it over and showed it a third time on Monday evening. The stars were Lillian Gish and Henry B. Walthall, but the huge cast also included Mae Marsh, Ralph Lewis, Elmer Clifton, and Wallace Reid, who played the blacksmith, and Raoul Walsh as John Wilkes Booth. We hadn't many Civil War veterans in Flagler, so there wasn't much to-do about the picture's rather obvious Southern bias. A few middle-aged people from Ohio and Michigan objected, but they were outnumbered by farmers from Missouri and the half dozen older ranchmen who came from Texas originally.

The program usually consisted of a comedy, nearly always a one-reeler, a two-reel feature, and a serial that ran one reel a week. In Deems Taylor's pictorial history of the movies I find him saying that *The Perils of Pauline*, with Pearl White, came along in 1917; but I distinctly remember showing episodes of that thriller series in the winter of 1916. Another similar serial was *The Adventures of Kathlyn*, starring Kathlyn Williams. The "Pauline" series, as I remember, was the pioneer in the suspense serials. It piled the perils on Pearl White and it left her, at the end of each episode, either literally or figuratively clinging to the crumbling brink of a cliff with a bottomless chasm beneath her. Sometimes she was in a roaring torrent being swept toward falls higher than Niagara. Sometimes she was trapped under a fallen tree in the path of a forest fire. Always, she was in a perilous predicament from which there seemed to be no escape. From this movie serial came the expression that still survives as the term for an incident of high suspense—a cliff-hanger. And you never knew until the next episode, next week, how she escaped. But she always did escape.

Another series that we ran was the horror serial. It also was one of a whole school of the scare-you-to-death serials, which were almost as violent as the television fare of today. The one we ran that winter was *The Clutching Hand*, and its chief terror element was a mysterious something or somebody with a grisly, taloned hand that reached out of the shadows and caught someone, usually a villain, by the throat. This was technically a retribution serial, which probably was its moral excuse—that grim, throttling hand was the hand of justice. But it certainly was a nightmarish bit of justice, and if the youngsters of that era didn't have bad dreams, it wasn't the fault of *The Clutching Hand*.

The comedies got the biggest hand, of course, except for the occasional special feature. Keystone Comedy was the big one at that time, with the famous Keystone Cops and the Mack Sennett bathing girls. Years later, when the Marx Brothers were making their mad comedies for the screen and mingling zany antics with wild, bottompinching chases of pretty girls, I thought how much they owed to those old Keystone comedies. Mabel Normand got her start there—incidentally, she is credited with throwing the first custard pie. There was a whole bevy of pretty girls in the minimal bathing suits then allowed, and Ben Turpin, Paddy McGuire and the two Conklins, Chester and Heinie, chased them all over the lot. Charlie Chaplin was just getting well started; he had joined the Keystone Company only in 1914. But he had enough of a reputation that a skinny young man with a bashful smile had begun to imitate him, even to the tiny mustache, as "Lonesome Luke" in a comedy series. It wasn't until a couple of years later that he discarded the mustache, put on horn-rim glasses, and struck out on his own line of comedy under his own name, Harold Lloyd.

The Western already had begun to make a place for itself.

"Broncho Billy" Anderson was starring in Westerns as early as 1912. By 1914 the iron-faced William S. Hart was coming along, with his two-gun brand of heroics on horseback. Hart was a big drawing card by 1916.

Let's see. There also was fat, grandfatherly John Bunny, one of the drollest of the comedians of that day and a tremendous boxoffice attraction. There was Roscoe Arbuckle, called "Fatty," who started as a Keystone Cop and became a featured comedian but was no match at all for John Bunny. Arbuckle's popularity ended overnight a few years later, a consequence of a scandalous Hollywood death. There was an extra girl named Gloria Swanson, who had minor roles in many of that year's pictures. There was Theda Bara and the whole category of "vampire" pictures. Theda Bara was starred in *Cleopatra* in 1917 and made it one of the worst pictures, the most dismal even by that day's standards, of the era.

And there were the romantic actresses. I doubt that it was because we were so naïve, or so young, or so starved for romance that we loved those film queens. They were young themselves, and somewhat naïve, and certainly full of romantic dreams. Mary Pickford was a major star at fourteen. Bebe Daniels and Lila Lee and Constance Talmadge were leading ladies at fifteen. Most of those girls who had the big romantic parts were under the age of twenty, and few of the glamorous bathing girls were as old as eighteen. By the time the girls reached the age of twenty-two or twenty-three they were practically old hags, at least in movie terms.

The ones who held my loyalty and shaped my dreams at that time were the Talmadge sisters, Norma and Constance. Connie—I knew them so well that I called them by their familiar names, to myself at least—Connie was blonde, a bit dizzy, very much the comedienne, although she could carry off a serious dramatic role with the best of them. Norma, Connie's older sister by a year or two, was brunette, just chubby enough to be cuddly, and had a sweet wistfulness that could break your heart. Norma was usually straight romance or drama, with a minimum of comic flummery. I laughed at Connie, who was the happy-go-lucky good companion; but I sighed and dreamed over Norma. When she began having Conway Tearle as her leading man more or less regularly, I hated Tearle's guts. There was a third sister, Natalie, who also was in pictures. But Natalie never registered with me. She was just another actress.

Inevitably, the girls in town were aware of those girls on the screen every weekend at Seal's Hall. Not only of the girls, but of the town boys who watched those girls on the screen and compared the girls in town with them. It is hard now to know whether I became aware of girls, both on and off the screen, for the first time that winter, or whether the town girls made themselves apparent to me for the first time. As girls, that is, not just as classmates or as occasional companions at Sunday school parties and birthday celebrations. Or maybe, approaching seventeen, I was growing up. Boys, and girls too, didn't get pushed into dating at ten and eleven in those days, and rarely did they "go steady" until they were out of high school. Anyway, I did become aware of girls as girls that spring and winter.

Helen Hall, W. E. Hall's young sister, was one of the first. Mr. Gromer had hired her to sell tickets at the movie house, so we were fellow employees. We sometimes met on the street on our way to work and walked the rest of the way together. She was a year older than I, a petite blonde with a beautiful smile. Within a month after the movies began running every week she began to look a little like a blonde Bebe Daniels. To me, at least. She changed the style of her hair and began rouging her lips the way the girls did in the movies. But I never had a date with her, never asked for one. There always was someone ahead of me.

Mabel Seal was another who seemed to me to follow the movies rather personally. She was the daughter of J. H. Seal, the owner not only of Seal's Hall but of the land with the pond on it in the north end of town. Mabel was petite too, but on the rounded side; she made me think of Norma Talmadge. She had graduated the previous spring and went with the older group when she dated. But she wasn't much interested in dates, or didn't seem to be. She went to Denver that spring and got a job, and married someone she met there. I kept thinking of her every time I saw Norma Talmadge, thinking Mabel Seal could have been a movie actress if she had only gone to Hollywood.

Marjorie Miner, Spider's older sister, who was in the same graduating class with Mabel Seal, was as blonde as Connie Talmadge, and in some ways prettier. But Marjorie could no more have made a fool of herself, even to make people laugh, than she could have spread her arms and taken flight. She was bigger than the other two girls, and certainly never dreamed of being a Mary Pickford; but for a while she did wear her beautiful blonde hair in long curls. Then she put it up on her head again and settled for being Marjorie Miner.

Most of the other girls in town were too big or too small, too old or too young, to be noticeably influenced by those movie stars except in minor matters. The older girls aped the film stars' hairdos, when they could, and the younger girls tried to ape their gestures and their manner of speaking. It was inevitable. As I said elsewhere in this book, we were in a period of change, of transition from one era to another, and the motion pictures were an agent of change and an early pioneer in the processes that would, in another decade or two, be bringing a degree of uniformity to the various parts of America that thinned out and slowly dissolved so many of the local and regional patterns of life and personality.

Change came, and was absorbed, and life broadened somewhat, I suppose. Women's dress fashions changed as well as their fashions of hair style and facial makeup. It was that winter that the crepe de Chine shirtwaist came to Flagler, and with it the colorful camisole that made the sheerness of the shirtwaist properly, but still provocatively, modest. That, too, was the era of the hobble shirt, and that strange phenomenon was commonly seen on the streets of Denver, we were told. But nobody in Flagler apparently cared to risk either her neck or her reputation in such a skirt, since there were relatively few sidewalks off Main Street, and the footpaths and cowpaths that were common elsewhere were not exactly ideal for a woman who had to mince along in a hobble skirt. Nor did any of the girls in Flagler dare appear in the slit skirt that followed the hobble; the slit sometimes showed the wearer's leg—it was still a *limb* in the cities, but we who lived close to the land and to the facts of rural life knew a *leg* when we saw one, and we called it a leg—the slit skirts sometimes showed a leg almost to the knee, a really scandalous exposure.

So I became aware of the girls, but I didn't go courting. I was busy, for one thing. If I wasn't playing football or basketball or practicing for the 440-yard race in track, I was studying, or I was working at the *News* office. Besides, I still had no clear status in school, for I was less than a full-fledged junior and more than a sophomore. I was almost automatically cast in the role of a lone traveler. It was a role I had had for quite a while, and it had been ingrained in me during the lone years on the homestead. The year in Brush had weakened it somewhat, but there I had had boys for my companions, the usual boy society of that age group at that time, which had no particular interest in girls. I still had the idea that if I was going anywhere in life, I would have to go alone. I was sure I wanted to go somewhere, and I was almost equally sure I could travel faster by myself.

Perhaps I would have been less sure of all these things if Little Doc Williams hadn't felt the same way. He, too, was going somewhere, and he hadn't the time to waste on girls. We never discussed it then, but it must have been implicit in our attitudes. Some years later we did talk about it, and Justin —he was no longer Little Doc but a full-fledged doctor—Justin said, "Maybe you are right about you being a loner, but I wasn't. It was just that I wasn't seriously interested in girls. After all, we grew up in the country, and I had access to Dad's medical books. We knew the difference between boys and girls. There wasn't any urgency to find out things we already knew. Besides, there were a great many important things to learn, both in school and out. And I think we had a pretty good sense of time. We knew there would be time for girls later. As there was, of course."

I suspect that he was right. But I know that it was the movies that gave me my first broad look at the world of make-believe and the sentimental dreams that became so much a part of life in the next few decades. I know that it is an old, established custom to speak of the late war years and the 1920s which followed as a time of forthright realism when the romantic notions of the Nineties were finally laid to rest; but I am not at all sure that is true. I would say, rather, that we were being transported from the candy-coated fables of the late Nineties to the lacquered and gold-plated fables of the Twenties. And the vehicle that was taking us was war.

Woodrow Wilson had been re-elected to the pious boast, "He has kept us out of war!" But on February 3, 1917, only three months after that election, we broke diplomatic relations with Germany over unrestricted submarine warfare. On March 12, only eight days after Wilson's second inauguration, the notorious Zimmermann papers were intercepted, revealing a German plot to get Mexico to enter the war and attack the United States. On April 6 the Congress, at the President's request, declared war on Germany. On May 18 all men between the ages of twenty-one and thirty were registered for selective conscription. On June 5 the first members of the American Expeditionary Force landed in France.

There in Flagler we were aware of all this in a kind of remote, impersonal way. We read the news. Those over twenty-one registered for the draft. But there I was, projecting motion pictures, week after week, that showed the antics of Fatty Arbuckle, John Bunny, Ben Turpin, Louise Fazenda; that showed the never-never land of William S. Hart and Pearl White and Theda Bara and Constance and Norma Talmadge.

Remote as it was, however, Flagler wasn't alone on this. All over the United States people were watching those shadows on the screen, those candy-coated fables, while the furious storms of the twentieth century were rumbling like distant thunder on the battlefields of Europe.

18

Though we were not totally unaware of the war, it didn't dominate our lives or make anywhere near the impact it did back east. The only major effect in our area was that the price of wheat went up to the highest it had ever been. The *News* carried a column of war news each week, a syndicated summary prepared in Denver and a part of the preprinted "patent insides" of the paper. We knew the Germans were giving the British and French a hard time and we knew that submarine warfare was making it difficult to remain neutral. When President Wilson asked for a declaration of war, Father printed a first-page story about it.

When recruits were asked for, maybe half a dozen young men from our area went to Denver and signed up. I remember only one of them, a devil-may-care young cowhand from one of the outlying ranches. He went to Denver, joined the Marines, and when he had a leave a few weeks later returned to Flagler and spent almost the whole day parading up and down Main Street in full dress uniform, even with a cartridge belt and a pistol strapped on his hip. When it was almost time for the westbound train on which he was returning to Denver he went down to the depot and, with a crowd of maybe a dozen loafers and curious youngsters watching, fired two clips of cartridges from that big black automatic pistol. He aimed at somebody's stray dog a hundred yards or so away in the unfenced pasture south of the depot. The closest he came with all that shooting was about two yards from the dog, but he kicked up a lot of dust and made a lot of noise. Then the train came in, the cowboy Marine yelled "Yip-eeeee!" and got on board, the grinning conductor said to anyone listening, "He's off to catch Kaiser Bill, I guess," and laughed, shouted, "All aboard!" tossed his metal step into the vestibule, and signaled the engineer. The train rolled out and that was the last we ever saw of that cowboy in his parade uniform of the United States Marines.

That summer, however, we had a chance to look a long way into the future, though nobody knew it at the time. All the way to World War II and beyond, in fact.

It was early June, a beautiful day with the mildness of early summer all around. It was a slack day, a Friday, after the paper was printed for the week. Mother had taken the day off to do the week's washing, and I was helping Father break up the forms and distribute the type back into the cases. I was at the case, slowly distributing type, and Father was at the stone, whistling softly to himself as he worked. Then I saw this man come down the stairway, a tall, broad-shouldered man in a dark suit and wearing a soft hat over iron-gray hair. He looked important, a man of affairs, somehow. He came in, glanced around, said to Father, "You are the editor?"

Father wiped his hands and came to the front of the office. "I'm the editor. My name is Borland. What can I do for you?"

"My name is Buck," the stranger said. "I spent a year or two in this neighborhood some years ago. Before you came."

"I've only been here a couple of years."

"I have come back on a—an unusual mission. I hope you will keep my confidence. It will be best for all concerned, for me, for the Army, for the government, for everyone, if you print nothing about me or what I do here."

I saw Father's surprise. Most strangers who came to the office wanted a story in the paper about themselves or a puff for their business.

"What I am here for," Mr. Buck said, "is not wholly secret, but it does have its confidential aspects. May I speak freely?"

"Of course."

Mr. Buck glanced at me, and Father said, "That is my son, Mr. Buck. He can hold his tongue as well as I can."

"Well," Mr. Buck said, "I have invented a device that will put an end to war. Not only the present war, but war for all time. I am here to test and perfect it, with the blessing of high officials entrusted with the safety of our country. I do not expect the layman to understand, but you are obviously an intelligent man who can grasp the fundamentals. I have invented a flying torpedo which can deposit a high-explosive bomb at any strategic point even twenty miles away. It flies through the air. It can be directed from the ground. Half a dozen of my flying torpedoes could devastate an enemy army. And without the loss of one man on our side. It is this device that I am here to test and about which I request your silence."

Father stared at him for a moment, then asked, "With high-explosives, did you say?" His voice was tense.

"I am testing it *without* explosives," Mr. Buck said firmly. "There will be no explosions of any kind. No one will be in danger. My tests will be only of the vehicle itself, its flight and directability."

"What is this vehicle?" Father asked.

"An aeroplane. A small aeroplane which can be directed to its destination from the ground. It has no human pilot."

"Suppose it should strike a house."

"That is precisely why I am here. There are large areas of vacant land here, with very few houses. I am making arrangements to conduct my tests out west of Flagler, and the aerial torpedo will be directed away from town. Moreover, its test flights will be limited to a mile or two at most."

"You can be sure of this?"

"Absolutely. My dear man, this is no pipe dream or hare-brained idea. This is a device that high-placed army men have examined and which, when my final tests are completed, will be turned over to the government. It is for your ultimate safety as well as mine and that of everyone in this whole country. Right now it is as nearly foolproof as any flying machine can be made." He paused and smiled. "Will you keep my confidence? Can I rest assured that you will print nothing about me or my tests in your newspaper?"

"As long as you do not endanger the town or anyone in the area, yes. Beyond that I can make no promises."

"Thank you. Thank you, *sir!*" Mr. Buck thrust out his hand. "And if you wish to witness our preliminary tests, I will be glad to have you on hand. If all goes well, we should have the runways completed and ready for our initial flight by Sunday afternoon."

He left the office and Father stood there speechless, watching him go up the steps two at a time. Then he said, "Well, I'll be damned!"

He came over to the case where I was at work. "You heard what he said." He shook his head and glanced out the big window and up the stairs again. "You never know, when a man talks like that, whether he's a nut or a genius." He got out papers and his bag of Bull Durham and rolled a cigarette. When he had it going he said, "I didn't recognize the name at first, but he fits the description to a T. Doc Buck, they called him. I don't know where he got the 'Doc,' but he used to have a place out east of town. Never did any farming. Always was tinkering with machines. Built a tractor that wouldn't run and a windmill that wouldn't pump water. But this idea he's got now—well, it makes sense. An aerial torpedo could be quite a weapon."

I had the afternoon off and nothing special to do, so I got on my bike and looked up Little Doc. He was at the drug store, but he had the afternoon off too, so we decided to go down to Verhoff's Dam. But as we went down the back street past Alexander's lumber yard I saw Doc Buck talking to Mr. Alexander while a couple of men loaded boards onto an out-of-town Ford truck. And Little Doc said, "I guess they're taking lumber out to build the tracks for Doc Buck's flying machine."

I was dumbfounded. "How did you know about that?" I asked.

"Everybody in town knows it, I guess. Why? Is it a secret, or something?"

"It's supposed to be a secret."

Little Doc laughed. "They drove into town last night with the flying machine right out in plain sight on that truck. And he was around town this morning telling everybody he was going to end the war in Europe with it."

"Where is the flying machine now?"

"I don't know. Probably out at the old Elgin place. That's where he's going to try to make it fly."

Little Doc obviously knew even more than I did about this. "Why don't we go out to the Elgin place and look?" I asked.

So we rode out the Arriba road four miles, then turned south on an overgrown trail. A man named Elgin had homesteaded there about ten years before, had plowed a few acres, built a little frame house and a sod barn, lived there long enough to prove up, then had moved away. One of the real estate men in town had the land for sale. We had been there a few times, hunting rabbits. The house was just a weatherbeaten shell, windows gone, several boards missing from the roof. And cottontail rabbits had burrowed under it from all sides. We always could count on getting a couple of cottontails there.

We rode into the forlorn dooryard and, as always, flushed a cottontail that scurried and disappeared under the house. The buffalo grass had healed most of the scars of tenancy, leaving only the path to the pump, which now lacked a handle, to the old privy, which had no door, and to the sagging sod walls of the barn. A big clump of cactus near the privy was in bloom. There weren't many places left where cactus throve, so we went to look. There were both prickly pear and grizzly-bear in this clump. The prickly pear was loaded with yellow blossoms big as tea roses and that marvelous cactus-yellow, rich and waxy looking. The flowers on the grizzly-bear were a bit smaller and a bright rose color, one of the most luscious pinks I know. I hadn't seen such a show of cactus blossoms since the second year on the homestead, when the whole school section east of our land burst into cactus flowers the same week.

We went to look and admire, and to mark the place for a later trip when the juicy, oversweet, seedy prickly-pear fruit would be ripe. The fruits on the grizzly-bear weren't worth trying to eat; they were too spiny and they hadn't much taste anyway.

From the cactus bed we could see the flying machine out back of the barn. We raced to be the first to touch it. Neither of us had ever seen an airplane, though we had seen plenty of pictures. This was an airplane, all right, though a miniature. It had a wingspread of no more than twelve feet, and like all the planes of that day it was a biplane. Its two wings were of canvas stretched over a wooden framework and braced with wires tautened by turnbuckles. Its fuselage was like the body of a big night moth, fat and tapering, and it too was of canvas over a wooden frame. In its nose was an automobile radiator with the Ford ensign in plain sight, and beneath the radiator a shaft stuck out. It had no propeller. Inside, directly under the wings, was a Ford engine, just like the four-cylinder engine in any Model T touring car.

We were so entranced with the flying machine that we didn't hear the truck until it had almost reached the barn. Then we jumped back, feeling as guilty as though we had been caught in some kind of theft. The driver of the truck yelled, "Get away from that torpedo!" then grinned at us and drew the truck to a stop. He was a stranger but a friendly person. We could look at the flying machine all we wanted to, he said, just so we didn't touch things. He even got out and showed us how it worked.

"The propeller," he said, "goes here, on this shaft. Put water in the radiator, just like a car, measure the right amount of gasoline into the tank. Set the flaps on the wings, like this. Set the rudder, to guide it. Then wind it up, with the propeller, to start the engine, and away she goes! . . . You don't believe it? Well, you'll see."

"Can we watch?"

"Tell you what. You help unload this lumber and I'll give you a pass so you *can* see."

That seemed like a wonderful idea.

"We're going to build a track right down the slope, see? So we've got to put the boards where we'll build the track. I'll drive and you two unload the boards, six at a time."

That's what we did, unloading the boards six at a time until the truck was empty. Then we rode back to the barn. The driver took a grimy notebook and a pencil stub from his pocket, asked our names, wrote them on a blank page, and under it wrote, "Pass these two gentlemen free," and signed it J.C.R. His name, he said, was Jake. I never did hear his last name. He tore out the pass and handed it to me and asked, "You going to be out here tomorrow?"

"I thought the flight was Sunday."

"That's right, Sunday. But we'll be building the tracks tomorrow and tuning up the torpedo. Just thought you might like to help, see how a big inventor does these things."

We said we would be there the next day, and he suggested that we put our bikes in the truck and ride back to town with him. My hands were full of slivers, but it was a small price to pay for having a part in a historic event. Some day we would be able to tell folks that we helped test the machine that put an end to war.

Back at the office I told Father what had happened and what we were going to do tomorrow. He wasn't at all excited. He asked me if I didn't remember the fence in *Tom Sawyer*.

I remembered, but this didn't seem like the fence at all. I told Father so, and he smiled and said, "All right, take tomorrow off and go out there and help Doc Buck. But you needn't tell your mother unless she asks what you are up to. I'm not sure she would understand how important this aerial torpedo is."

Mother apparently hadn't heard about Doc Buck. She didn't mention him, at least, and I didn't volunteer anything. The next morning I went down to the shop with Father as usual and did the morning chores. About eight-thirty Father said, "I guess I can handle things now, if you want to go. How are your hands?"

"They're all right," I said, refusing to admit how sore they were.

"There's a pair of old work gloves on the shelf over there in the corner."

I put the gloves in my pocket, took my bike, met Little Doc at the drug store, and we rode out to the Elgin place. It was another beautiful June day, and Little Doc said, "I hope tomorrow's like this." I did too, because tomorrow was test day for the torpedo.

Half a dozen men were at work. We left our bikes at the old barn, took a quick look at the flying machine, then went down the slope to where saws and hammers were making a lot of noise. Doc Buck was there, overseeing things, telling Jake what he wanted done. Jake relayed the orders to the workmen, but Doc Buck himself came over to us. Before he could tell us to go away I took the pass Jake had given us from my pocket and showed it to him. He glanced at it, looked at us with a half smile, and said, "All right, boys. You can move some of that lumber on down the slope and hand it to the carpenters as they need it."

We worked the rest of the morning, carrying boards, fetching tools, acting as carpenter's helpers. By noon the crew had built parallel troughs halfway down the slope, twin tracks spaced to take the two bicycle wheels that served as the flying torpedo's landing gear. They looked like miniature flumes to carry irrigation water, six inches wide, four inches deep, and held in place by two-by-four cross members beneath, like railroad ties but spaced about ten feet apart.

We had brought no lunch, but the workmen shared their sandwiches with us, and when we had eaten we went back to work. By late afternoon the track was finished. It extended close to four hundred yards down the slope, and the final two sections were up on legs so it looked like a gigantic schoolyard slide for little kids. "That," Jake said, "is to give the torpedo a lift into the air at take-off."

Doc Buck had inspected the track, measuring its width with a carpenter's rule and getting down on his knees to sight down it and gauge its pitch. Finally he said, "That's a good job," and he and Jake went back to the flying machine beside the barn. They tinkered with it, made adjustments, cranked the motor, got it running. But it ran rough, so Jake changed a couple of spark plugs. At last Doc Buck said, "That'll do till tomorrow," and said we'd done enough for one day.

Jake assembled the workmen, who climbed into the truck. He and Doc Buck got into the seat, but before they left Jake said to us, "Ten o'clock tomorrow morning." Then he started the motor and they drove off. Little Doc and I, dog-tired, got on our bikes and followed, lagging far enough behind to let the truck's dust settle. It was a long ride, twice as far as it had been coming out that morning.

At the supper table that evening I wondered why Mother kept looking at Father and me with a strange, tight smile. Doc

Buck and his aerial torpedo hadn't been mentioned, but obviously something was up. Finally she said to me, "I suppose you want to skip Sunday school tomorrow."

"What?" I pretended not to understand.

"Oh, I know what you've been up to."

I glanced at Father, automatically.

"No," she said, "your father didn't tell me. He didn't have to. I've got eyes and ears. You needn't think you put anything over on anyone, either of you."

Father cleared his throat but didn't say a word.

"All right," Mother said. "As long as you've come this far, you might as well go the rest of the way. I won't try to stop either of you. You can both go out and watch that fool thing tomorrow."

We ate in silence, both Father and I. I was embarrassed and felt guilty, and I suppose he did too. By now Mother was smiling a maddening little secret smile. At last she couldn't keep it to herself any longer. She got up to clear away the dishes and she said, "As a matter of fact, there isn't going to be morning church *or* Sunday school tomorrow."

"What's that?" Father asked.

"I met Reverend Moore on the street this afternoon and he said there wouldn't be any services tomorrow. He said so many folks want to go out and watch Doc Buck make a fool of himself that he had decided to cancel services." She looked at Father and laughed. "I told him he needn't bother to tell you, that I would." And a moment later, "You didn't think I wouldn't find out, did you?"

Father sighed. It seemed to be a sigh of relief. "No. We just didn't want to worry you." He shook his head. "Apparently more people know what's going on in secret than if I'd printed handbills. I begin to wonder if he's going to charge admission."

By nine o'clock the next morning the Arriba road was a solid cloud of dust. Everybody in town—all the men and boys at least, and quite a few women—was on the way out to the old Elgin place. Horses and buggies, wagons, automobiles, trucks and bicycles were on that road, and at least a dozen boys were on foot. Dr. Williams offered to take Father along in his car. Little Doc and I rode our bikes.

By ten o'clock there were at least two hundred people at the flying machine track, lined up on both sides. At least fifty others were gathered at the barn, watching Doc Buck and Jake make their final preparations. Someone said they had been there, tinkering with the aerial torpedo, since six o'clock. I wormed my way into that crowd and watched Doc Buck tauten the brace wires, set the wing flaps, check the water in the radiator, measure the gasoline. Jake put the propeller on the shaft, tightened the bolts, and gave it a tentative turn.

"All right!" Doc Buck finally shouted. "Make room!"

The crowd fell back. Doc Buck at one wing tip, Jake at the other, wheeled the aerial torpedo down the slope to the head of the track. They set the wheels in the track, Jake put blocks in front of them, ordered everyone back again, and spun the propeller. He had to spin it a dozen times before the motor started. Doc Buck set the controls, let the motor idle, timing it with his big gold watch. At last he shouted, "Back! Everybody back from the track! In exactly thirty seconds the aerial torpedo will take off!" He adjusted the controls again, the motor roared, the whole machine shook and began to creak and strain. Doc Buck looked at his watch, shouted, "All right, Jake!" and Jake kicked the chocks out of the way, the machine began to move. With Jake at one wing tip, Doc Buck at the other, it rolled down the track, faster and faster. It outran Jake and Doc Buck and they stood watching, their faces alight.

The crowd, which had been almost wholly silent, began to shout, a great shout of amazement and excitement. But the shout died to a groan before it really gathered volume. The aerial torpedo's motor sputtered, coughed and died. The propeller idled to a stop. But the machine, its tail now bouncing along the ground, rolled on down the track, leaped a little way into the air of its own momentum, and sank to the ground with a splintering crash not ten feet beyond the end of the track.

Doc Buck was running toward the wreckage. Jake was shouting curses and running after him. The crowd surged after them, but Doc Buck turned and shouted, "Back! Stay back. God help us!" Someone in the crowd cried, "It's going to explode!" and the crowd turned upon itself and stumbled and milled, trying to run back up the slope.

But the machine didn't explode. It simply lay there like a stricken bird, one wing crumpled, the propeller splintered, one of its bicycle wheels crushed beyond repair. Doc Buck looked at the wreckage. Jake was examining the motor. Doc Buck looked around, at those of the crowd who hadn't run away in panic, and said quietly, "Gentlemen, you have just witnessed such an incident as plagued the Wright brothers time and again. But remember, they surmounted every obstacle. I, too, shall proceed with my testing. Fortunately, this aerial torpedo is not the wreck it appears. My good assistant and I will have it back in working order by three o'clock this afternoon. And now, if a few of you strong men care to help, we will take this stricken machine back up the slope and proceed with repairs."

There were enough strong men to get the aerial torpedo back on the tracks and support the side with the broken wheel. Slowly they trundled it back up the slope. Jake brought tools and spare parts from the truck and went to work.

The crowd began to disperse, some muttering, some laughing. Father came to me and said, "I am going back to town. Do you want to stay?" I said yes, I would stay. He nodded. "I'll tell your mother. Just get home in time for supper."

Only a handful of people stayed, most of them boys and younger men. They stood around and talked and waited. Noon came and went. Doc Buck and Jake replaced the broken wheel, anchored the motor more firmly to the supports from which it had been shaken, put on a new propeller. At last, in midafternoon, they put chocks under the wheels, started the motor, let it run for perhaps fifteen minutes. There was a leak in the radiator, but only a dripping leak, apparently not enough to matter. Both Doc Buck and Jake ignored it.

Finally they wheeled the machine to the head of the track once more. This time there was no need to shout a warning. There was no crowd, not more than twenty spectators in all, including us boys. The sun was a good half way down the western sky.

Doc Buck's shoulders had begun to sag. He squared them and looked around, hopeful, a man who needed an audience. The shoulders sagged again and he turned back to the flying machine, set the controls, and said, "Go ahead, spin it," to Jake. Jake spun the new propeller, and the engine, now warm from its trial run, started the first time. Doc Buck advanced the throttle till the engine roared and the flying machine seemed to lunge at the chocks under its wheels. "Let's go!" Doc Buck shouted, and Jake kicked the chocks away. They trotted down the slope, one at each wing tip as before. And, as before, the aerial torpedo gathered momentum, ran away from them. This time the motor roared, the propeller hummed, and the machine rocked down the track at maybe twenty miles an hour.

We stood and watched, and I held my breath. The aerial torpedo swooped into the last dip, was lifted by that final rise of track, shot into the air, and was flying. It flew just about a hundred yards, losing altitude steadily. Then it came down, with a crash and a rending screech. Both wheels collapsed. The propeller spun on for a moment, flinging chunks of sod before it dug in and splintered. Then the motor died and the whole machine went over on its back, a slow somersault that ended with a *whoosh* and a rending of canvas.

There was no groan from the handful of spectators. Hardly a word was said. They just stood and looked for almost a minute, then they turned and walked away, back up the hill to their buggies or their automobiles or their bikes. And they rode off in silence.

Doc Buck and Jake walked down the slope, Jake with the weary gait of a tired and disillusioned man. Doc Buck's shoulders didn't seem to sag as much as they had before the start of that last disastrous run. His head was high.

They walked down the slope and looked at the wreckage. They stood there several minutes, not saying a word. Then Jake came back up the hill and got the truck and drove it down to the wreckage. He rigged a windlass and skids and hooked a chain around the motor, which had been torn completely free of the flying machine. He and Doc Buck turned the crank on the windlass and slowly pulled the motor up and into the truck. Then they drove back up the slope, gathered Jake's tools, looked around for anything they might have overlooked, and drove out the dusty road to the highway and turned west, away from Flagler. I followed them on my bike, and I turned east at the highway, toward town.

Mother was setting the table for supper when I got there. Father was in the front room reading the Sunday newspaper. He looked up but said nothing.

Mother said, "Better get washed up, son. Supper's almost ready." Then she said, "It didn't fly, did it?"

"No," I said. "It didn't fly." And I washed up for supper.

19

That was the summer the Chautauqua came to Flagler. It was the Standard Chautauqua, whose headquarters were in Lincoln, Nebraska. Father knew somebody in the main office, a friend from the year he spent in Omaha as a salesman for Barnhart Brothers & Spindler, a printers' supply house, the year I was six years old. He had an amazing range of friends in all kinds of businesses and professions all over the Midwest. That spring he had talked about Chautauqua to various of the Flagler business men, and finally he wrote to his friend in Lincoln and asked if Standard was laying out a Chautauqua circuit for that summer that could include Flagler. He soon had an answer saying it could be arranged and enclosing a fat packet of promotion material telling what Standard Chautauqua had to offer and explaining "How You Can Bring Chautauqua to Your Town." At the next meeting of the Commercial Club, Father brought up the subject, passed the literature around, and said he was going to propose that the club sponsor Chautauqua in Flagler that summer, and would ask for a vote by club members at the next meeting. The time came and his proposal was passed unanimously, thanks to the persuasive literature from Standard. A few weeks later a field man came out from Lincoln, got the signatures he needed on a contract and a guarantee, and the Chautauqua program was assured.

Traveling Chautauqua programs were an outgrowth of an

annual series of religious seminars begun at Chautauqua Lake, New York, in 1874. Chautauqua Lake was a summer resort with a strong religious inclination, and the original purpose of the meetings and lectures there was to improve the teaching in Sunday schools and religious training generally. Before long the assembly plan was broadened to include cultural subjects aside from religion. And from the few days of lectures and discussions it became a summer assembly that lasted several weeks and was supplemented with home reading programs during the fall and winter. Various local "Chautauqua assemblies" were established, modeled more or less on the original Lake Chautauqua program. But few of them could attract the impressive lecturers who made the original seminars famous.

Meanwhile, a Scottish immigrant named James Redpath, an astonishingly energetic young man who threw off sparks in all directions, went through a career as New York journalist, pamphleter, Civil War agitator and partisan, and public school educator, and finally got around to the lecture business. He founded a booking agency in Boston that became known as the Redpath Lyceum Bureau. He booked such men as Horace Greeley, Ralph Waldo Emerson, Henry David Thoreau, Bayard Taylor, Wendell Phillips. And to those he added humorists—Mark Twain, Josh Billings, Petroleum V. Nasby— and a number of poets who read from their own works. Then he booked musicians, individually and as small groups, and miniature theatrical and opera companies. His bookings were made primarily for the fall and winter months, when people had time and inclination for such cultural diversion. They were the basis of what became the lyceum circuits, which provided small towns with five or six programs a winter, scattered over the cold indoor months. The programs were held in local opera houses, churches or schools.

Finally someone, I am not sure who, launched the summer Chautauqua program, which provided five or six continuous days of enlightenment and entertainment, programs much like those on the lyceum circuits, and traveled from town to town performing in a big tent instead of a hall. It wasn't Redpath, though his name was used for one of the major Chautauqua circuits. That fantastic Scotsman, once his lecture bureau was going full tilt, dashed off to Ireland to lead an uprising against English landlords, came back here to edit the *North American Review*, and died a violent death under a street car in New York City in 1891. But he had assembled the elements of the summer Chautauqua. All that was needed was someone to assemble them, and someone did. Several someones, for there were at least half a dozen Chautauqua circuits by 1917.

The system probably was much the same with all of them. The Standard people required that a local group, such as Flagler's Commercial Club, sponsor the Chautauqua program and guarantee a minimum fee. For this the company promised to provide five days of culture and entertainment, two programs a day, as well as the big airy tent, the seats, stage and all necessary equipment. The sponsors were given books of season tickets to sell, and if they sold enough to cover the guarantee they received a part of the income from single admissions sold at the gate.

Flagler's dates were in late June, on the outward swing of the company from Lincoln. But Father began the promotion for the Chautauqua the first week in May. Season ticket sales were under way before school was out; literature distributed to school children put the pressure on parents to buy tickets so that their children wouldn't be deprived of the greatest cultural feast that had ever come to town. The technique, undoubtedly old even then, has come right on down into the color-TV age: Plant your message in the minds of the youngsters and persuade them to sell it to their parents.

Along with this, of course, were all the other persuaders, in the local newspapers, from the church pulpit, and in every public forum. And since this was the first time around for Flagler, there were no disgruntled customers from last year who could complain about the quality of the programs. So by the first of June the ticket sales had covered more than ninety percent of the guarantee. Success was certain.

With his new press, Father was publishing what we thought was the best-looking newspaper in the county, perhaps in all of eastern Colorado. His local advertising had almost doubled. Prosperity, once the uncertainties of the election were resolved, brought a new spirit of optimism to the whole area. Actually, most of the prosperity was a result of wartime inflation, but nobody talked about that and probably few really knew what was happening in terms of economics. Neither farmers nor storekeepers went far beyond the fact that two-dollar wheat put money into a good many people's pockets. With money in their pockets, people were eager to buy. It was as simple as that, and it added up to prosperity.

I remember hearing Clarence Smith, who was neither uninformed nor naïve, and certainly not a wild-eyed dreamer, say that eastern Colorado land was better than a gold mine. He explained it this way:

"Two years ago I sold a half section, three hundred and twenty acres, to this man from Kansas for twenty dollars an acre. He had it all plowed and seeded to winter wheat for something less than five dollars an acre. From that land he harvested sixty-five hundred bushels of wheat, say twenty bushels an acre. Now, that land cost him six thousand four hundred dollars. The plowing and seeding cost him a total of sixteen hundred dollars, making a total investment of eight thousand. His sixty-five hundred bushels of two-dollar wheat brought him thirteen thousand dollars. His first crop, then, paid for his land, his labor, his seed, and gave him a net, over-all profit of just about five thousand dollars. And he still owns the land, free and clear, which is worth more today than he paid for it. Show me a gold mine that will do as well."

Regardless of the economics or the mathematics, which were pretty well blown away in the dust storms a few years later, there was this sense of prosperity. And *The Flagler News* benefited. Besides the increase in local advertising, in which the competing *Progress* shared only to a minor degree, Father had a regular flow of legal notices. The Democrats were in power and the *News* was an official county paper. Legal notices paid very well indeed.

School ended the last week in May, and we had a few days of complete freedom, when Little Doc and I went out to Crystal Springs and to the waterholes along the river on the Rumming ranch and dogpaddled enough to say we had been swimming. Then Doc Buck arrived and we got involved in his tests. But we knew Little Doc was going to work in the drug store that summer and I was going to work at the *News* office at least a part of the summer. I hoped to find some job before school started that would toughen me up for football, my last year of it in high school. But just now we were drafted into the Chautauqua organization, to help set up the tent and then to help the crewman supervise sports and games for the younger boys.

The crew and equipment arrived on a Sunday, on the early afternoon passenger train from the east. We were at the depot to meet them. The superintendent, who would be in charge of the programs, we had been notified, would be Albert Sorenson, who was taking an advanced degree at the University of Nebraska. The crewman, in charge of tent and equipment, would be Eddy Logan, who had just finished his freshman year at Creighton University in Omaha.

The train pulled in and only two people got off, the tall thin one who introduced himself as Al Sorenson, and the stocky younger one who said he was Eddy Logan and then dashed down the platform to where the trainmen were rolling and tumbling bales and bundles of equipment out of the baggage car. There were three tons of it, in all, and the trainmen fumed and swore at anyone who had the gall to ask them to handle three tons of excess baggage. Eddy Logan ignored the complaints and checked the bales, bundles and big black trunks as they were unloaded, finally insisting that one bale of canvas was still missing when the trainmen said it was all there. He insisted until they found it, though the train was almost fifteen minutes late as it finally got under way again toward Denver.

Ora Groves was there with his truck, and we helped load the gear, get it all moved to the Chautauqua grounds, the vacant halfblock back of the Congregational church, where Eddy Logan had each bundle and bale put exactly where he wanted it. Then he got a gray wall tent out of one trunk, we helped set it up, and he and Mr. Sorenson went in, with their suitcases, and changed from their travel clothes to work clothes. That tent was to be their bedroom.

The next hour was one of the best demonstrations of how to get a complicated job done with ignorant volunteer labor that I ever saw. Mr. Sorenson said at the start that Eddy Logan was the boss of that job, and Eddy organized the volunteers in six crews, set them all to work, coordinated them, and never raised his voice. I decided that afternoon that if I ever was in a position of responsibility I wanted to be a boss like Eddy Logan.

He chose the site for the big tent, got a tape from one of his big black trunks, drove marker stakes for the center poles, measured off three guy stakes for each center pole, set crews to driving stakes, showed two other crews how to drive spikes in the end of four-by-four quarter poles and two-by-four wall poles. The local committee had been asked to provide two thirty-foot telephone poles, four-by-fours for quarter poles, two-by-fours for wall poles, planks for the platform stage, and timbers for its foundation. All this material had to be moved to the places where it would be needed.

Typical of Eddy's method was the way he taught the stake

crew to drive stakes. Every one of the volunteers for this job was a big husky man, Big Ed Schlote the biggest of them all. Eddy Logan was about my height and didn't weigh a pound over 140. But he took a sixteen-pound maul, handed one just like it to Big Ed, and said, "Want to put down a couple of guy stakes with me?" Big Ed grinned, swung the maul as though it were a croquet mallet, and said, "Sure." Eddy tapped a four-foot guy stake to start it, nodded to Big Ed, swung the maul, brought it down squarely and drove the stake four inches, caught the rebound, and started his second swing as Big Ed came down with a terrific blow that hit the stake head off-center, glanced, spun the maul in his hands, and almost jerked him off his feet. Eddy's second blow landed an instant later, drove the stake another four inches.

Eddy stopped, looked at Big Ed's right hand, where blood oozed from beneath two fingernails, the flesh pulled loose by the twist of the maul handle. Big Ed flushed, wiped his fingers on his overalls, said, "All right, let's go." But Eddy said, "Take it easy. Let the hammer do the work. And don't grip so tight. Like this," and he swung again, deliberately let the maul fall of its own weight, merely guiding it, struck the stake squarely, and drove it another three inches. "See?" Big Ed nodded, and they started again, and they put that guy stake down within a foot of the ground with another dozen blows, nicely alternated between them. Big Ed learned, and so did all the others; and the guy stakes were driven as fast as Eddy measured and set them out. That's the way he worked, and everyone there was eager to help, to do whatever he suggested.

The wall poles and quarter poles were finished. The two center poles were lugged into place, ready to rig and raise. Eddy had holes bored for the ring bolts, attached the blocks, put the bail rings in place, tied the guy ropes, and checked them twice. Then he assigned two men to each guy, got the huskies to start the center poles, one at a time, get them off the ground while the men at the guys steadied them, then hoisted them on up. Both poles up, he clove-hitched the guys, tightened them, and doubled the hitches. Then he had the crews distribute the sections of the brown tent top, showed how to lace them, starting at the center and not walking on the canvas. He laced the two peaks to the bail rings. He had the stake crews drive enough wall stakes to anchor the tent when it was hoisted. Then he took two men with him and crawled under the canvas to one center pole and hoisted that peak halfway up. They moved to the other pole and hoisted the other peak. Then they took the peaks on up to their proper height, and suddenly there was a tent, a big brown tent with two peaks, covering an area twice as big as all of Seal's Hall.

After that the wall stakes had to be driven, the wall ropes tightened, the wall poles set in place and the quarter poles, which hoisted the tent into a series of lesser peaks all the way around. And finally, that afternoon, Eddy Logan chose a select crew to help him trim the set of the center poles, tighten the guys till they almost hummed, snug the wall ropes, and finish the job. The big top was taut as a drumhead. By then it was almost six o'clock. We helped Eddy move the bedroom tent up close to the big top, and he thanked us all and said, "To-morrow we'll set up the platform and the seats, so better bring your hammers. We've got a lot done this afternoon."

W. E. Hall had come to watch the final hour of work, and he invited Mr. Sorenson and Eddy Logan to his house for supper. But Mr. Sorenson said, "Thanks, but can't we make it tomorrow? We're too dirty to be fit company anywhere to-night. And I might add, we're a little tired, too. Right, Eddy?" And Eddy said, "I am." So they went down to the café across the street from the hotel and sat at the counter, like farm hands, and ate hamburger, which was just about then starting to be called Salisbury steak, and fried potatoes and canned peas and custard pie. And went back to their gray wall tent and made up their beds, on folding canvas cots, and washed in water carried from the pump at the church, and went to bed, too tired to bother with the gasoline lamp they had.

The next day was easy, really. The platform stage was made of planks laid across a cribbing of timbers. Folding chairs were brought from the church and from the Odd Fellows' Hall, and wooden benches were built to supplement them and make room for more than three hundred people in the tent. The curtains were hung for the dressing rooms. A piano was brought from the church and Mr. Knies spent two hours tuning it after it was moved. And Eddy Logan and I hung lines of Chautauqua banners across Main Street, from rooftop to rooftop, twenty lines of them, and made the street almost as gay as Fourth of July. It was during that job that I got to know Eddy well enough to ask questions, because he was skittish about high places. He let me do the roof climbing and admitted that he got dizzy if he was more than ten feet off the ground.

Eddy told me about the circuit, how it was organized, where it went, about his job. In addition to being responsible for the tent and all the equipment, getting it set up, torn down, moved, and taking care of it night and day, he spent a part of each morning organizing the boys, those twelve years old and under, into teams to play games and hold track meets. He needed local help with that, and that was going to be one of my jobs. The last day of Chautauqua he would hold a track meet for all those junior boys and give out Standard Chautauqua medals to the winners.

And he told me about the crews and their schedule and circuit. There were seven crews and tents. Each one spent five days in a town, then had two days to move and get set up. When a crew moved it leapfrogged all the other crews, and every day a crew was moving. The talent—the singers and musicians and lecturers—went from one town to the next every day, usually late at night or in the morning, and put on two programs a day, one in the afternoon, the other at night. The talent had one day off every week. The circuit we were on started in western Nebraska, swung down into Kansas, through Flagler, on to Simla, then to Florence, down near Canon City, on over to the Western Slope, back through the northeastern corner of the state, across the northern tier of Nebraska, and ended in Iowa at the end of August.

That day, on the early afternoon train, the Junior Girl arrived, the third member of the crew. Her name was Doris Carter, she was a junior at Nebraska Wesleyan in Lincoln, she was blonde and tall and skinny, and not at all pretty. But she was so pleasant and so pleased with life that you couldn't help liking her. Eddie Logan called her Sis, said she was like a sister to everyone on the circuit. Her job was to organize a morning story hour and play games with the little children, those up to about eight years old. There were seven Junior Girls on the circuit, but the company rotated them so that none of them was with any one crew more than a week at a time. Sis Carter was to stay with the Clarence Smiths while she was in Flagler. We took her up there, and before the afternoon was out she had enlisted four high school girls as helpers and had gone all over town and, like the pied piper of Hamelin, won the heart of every little boy and girl in sight.

The next morning, opening day of Chautauqua, practically every youngster in town was at the big brown tent. Miss Carter and her helpers took charge of the young ones. Eddy Logan, Little Doc and I had twenty-two boys on our hands. Eddy took charge, divided them into two teams, and we started off with a baseball game, Little Doc managing one team, I the other, and Eddy umpiring. After they had played four or five long innings we switched to track and field events, keeping the two squads as competing teams. It was like trying to manage two tribes of wild young Indians, but we did it. We gradually wore them down and ran them ragged. By noon, when we sent them home for dinner, they were dragging their feet. So were Little Doc and I, but Eddy laughed at us. "How would you like to do this five days a week all summer, and spend the other two days tearing down, moving, and setting up the tent?"

We dragged home, ate, and were back for the afternoon program, where we could at least sit down. On the ground, if nowhere else. Flagler was jammed. The hitch racks on Main Street were full; teams and wagons, buggies, even trucks were parked there. And there were wagons or buggies on almost every vacant lot in town, and family picnic dinners. By one-thirty the big tent was jammed, every seat taken. By two o'clock, when the program was to begin, people were standing all around the tent.

The opening day talent, a lecturer and an instrumental quartet, had arrived on the early morning train and been quartered at the hotel. The musicians were to put on a full program in the afternoon and that evening would give a kind of overture before the lecture, the topic of which was "The Challenge of Today."

Clarence Smith, who was chairman of the Chautauqua Committee, opened the program. He made his remarks brief. He welcomed everyone, said he was glad to see so many people present, that he was sure that everyone knew what Chautauqua meant to a town, thanked everyone who had helped the committee bring Chautauqua to Flagler, and said, "Now I am going to turn things over to the talented young man who will be in charge of this platform and the whole of Chautauqua here for the rest of this week. Albert Sorenson."

Mr. Sorenson stalked onto the stage, all good will and joviality. He thanked Mr. Smith, thanked the audience for its welcome to him, then said, "I always like to open our first program with a word from the church. Will Reverend Moore please come to the platform?"

Adna Moore, the preacher who had been in charge of the Congregational church since the first of the year, was conveniently near the front and seated on the aisle. He went to the platform, a distinguished-looking elderly man with a head of iron-gray hair and twinkling eyes. Of Scottish blood, he spoke at times with a faint burr. After many years in urban pulpits in the East and South, he had come to Flagler to get back to the simplicity of village life, since he had grown up as a small-town boy. He was the best preacher Flagler had ever had. Now he looked out over this Chautauqua audience and smiled, and he said, "This Chautauqua week is certain to be a tremendous success. It has to be, for it opens this afternoon with the McLeods, and that's verrra, verrra nice." He rolled the r's magnificently. And when the ripple of chuckles had died he said, "And now I would speak a few words more solemnly. . . . Bless this gathering, dear Lord. Give thy benediction to these programs we are about to hear. Give us grace, and add thy inspiration to those who come to instruct and entertain us. We ask it in thy name, the name of God. Amen." And he left the platform.

Mr. Sorenson, who had stood with bowed head, waited for the slight rustle to subside in the audience, then said that it was a great privilege to be in Flagler, "with all you good people," and he wanted everyone to meet his two assistants. He summoned Doris Carter and Eddy Logan from the wings, introduced them by name, they took their bows and applause, and Mr. Sorenson said, "We have a musical treat to start our week, an afternoon of musical enjoyment. This evening we have more music, and in addition we will have food for thought and inspiration, a lecture by the distinguished Dr. Philip L. Masterson. This evening I will tell you about tomorrow's programs. But right now it is time to get started with Chautauqua—your Chautauqua! . . . Ladies and gentlemen, I give you the Musical McLeods!"

Four people, two men and two women, came hurrying on-stage, beaming, the men in white jackets, the women in fluffy white dresses. The older man, who had a trumpet in his hand, said, "May I introduce our company?" He bowed to the pianist, a middle-aged blonde. "My wife, Jean Ramsey McLeod, who was practically born at the piano. . . . Mary McPherson"—and he bowed to the other, younger woman—"who is a McLeod by birth"—he turned to the other man, a beetle-browed, dark-haired man with a trombone—"and Jock McPherson, related to Mary McPherson by marriage, so to say, he being her husband." Mary had taken her seat at the set of drums and traps, a female drummer, no less. "And I," said the older man with the trumpet, "am *the* McLeod. Sandy McLeod. . . . Now we know each other."

All in their places, Sandy McLeod signaled with his left hand, put the trumpet to his lips, and they struck up "The Star-Spangled Banner." It brought the audience to their feet, and before the instruments were halfway through the first verse voices took up the words. The tent rang with the national anthem, on through the first verse and through a second. And when the music had stopped and the audience was in the seats again Sandy McLeod said, "Thank you." And a moment later they began their afternoon program with "The Little Gray Home in the West," played with a trombone solo the second time through, and with Sandy himself singing the third time through.

Chautauqua had begun. The Musical McLeods gave us a little of everything that afternoon, including a fully costumed imitation of Harry Lauder singing "Roamin' in the Gloamin'." And that evening they played numbers from light opera before the distinguished Dr. Masterson delivered his sonorous words on "The Challenge of Today."

The second day brought a six-person light opera company, which put on a program of vocal music in the afternoon and in the evening played a condensed version of Victor Herbert's *The Fortune Teller.* For the third day there was a musical trio and a humorous lecturer. That was the day that the circuit supervisor, a Mr. Hovey, arrived. I heard about him that morning, from Eddy Logan, who said his boss was in town, the man who was in charge of all the crews and who did the hiring and firing. Eddy didn't seem worried, however, and I forgot about Mr. Hovey until dinnertime, when Father looked at me with the held-back smile that meant he had something special under his hat.

We had just sat down at the table and Mother was passing the meat. Father gave me that look and asked, "How is it going at Chautauqua these mornings, son?"

"All right, I guess."

"You like what you're doing?"

"Well, yes. Of course I do."

Father nodded and glanced at Mother, who was frowning in question. She evidently didn't know, any more than I did, what he was leading up to.

"Would you like to be doing it again next summer?" Father asked me.

"Well, I suppose so, if we have Chautauqua again. We will, won't we?"

"I mean all summer. Not here, but on the Chautauqua circuit."

"Will!" Mother exclaimed. "You don't mean—"

"Yep, that's what I mean. Dick Hovey is in town. I've told you about Dick. He was in Council Bluffs when we were in Omaha. Well, he's one of the officers of Standard Chatauqua now, Circuit Manager. He came down to the office to see me, and we got to talking, and—well, the upshot was that if you want to have a job as crewman with Standard Chautauqua next summer, it probably can be done."

I didn't know what to say. I was dumbfounded. I thought how everybody liked Eddy Logan, even the talent, and how he was getting around, seeing the world, meeting people. I thought of myself as another Eddy Logan, and yet as still being me. I was tongue-tied.

Mother spoke up. "He's too young to be away from home all summer."

"He's past seventeen."

"With actors and such people. I don't know—"

"If you can find a nicer bunch of people than those Chautauqua folks, I'd like to meet them."

"It seems like sending him away from home."

They were talking as though I wasn't sitting right there at the table with them.

"He'll be starting college a year from this fall. He'll be away from home then."

Mother nodded, slowly, then exclaimed, "Oh, this is so sudden! Does it have to be decided right away?"

"No." Father turned to me. "I told Dick I'd see what you say and let him know."

"I think I'd like to go," I said.

"You don't have to decide today. But if you do want to go you'd better get your application in before September. It's a kind of an honor, really, getting a job with them. Most of their crewmen are in college, Dick tells me. You'll be just out of high school."

Mother dabbed at her eyes with a handkerchief, then left the table and went into the front room. Father watched her go, then drew a deep breath and looked at his plate for a long moment. When he looked at me again I saw a mist in his eyes. "It's hard for her to realize you aren't a little boy any more," he said. Then, with a smile, "Sometimes it's even hard for me to."

20

Flagler got its municipal power plant that fall. The first municipal election had been held in April, almost a year after the committee was named to proceed with incorporation; it took that long to complete all the legal steps. Finally, though, almost everybody in town turned out and voted for the town's first officials. The first mayor was A. J. Lockwood, a man from the same part of Nebraska we came from, a business man with a hand in ventures as varied as a lumber yard and a cattle ranch. Five trustees, the equivalent of a town council, were chosen: J. H. Seal, whose son had married W. H. Lavington's daughter; Henry Blancken, the hotel keeper; Win Reynolds, a carpenter; I. N. Moberly, cashier of "the other bank," not the Lavington bank; and "Uncle John," J. W. White, a hardware dealer and an old-timer.

At their first meeting the trustees chose William Knies as town clerk and named the *Flagler Progress* the town's official newspaper. That was no surprise. It was a part of the price for support for incorporation. It no longer mattered to Father because the *News* was official county paper in the west end of the county. And, Father told me some years later, he knew then that the *Progress* was losing ground.

Soon after the election, the proposal for a municipal power and light plant was brought to a vote and won. Bonds were authorized and work was begun before the end of summer on a brick powerhouse where a big diesel engine was to be installed to drive the generator. Poles were set, lines were strung, houses and offices were wired for the new era, the age of electricity.

Inevitably, there was objection, first in public meeting, then in private after the dissenters were outvoted. With change, life would inevitably follow new patterns. But basically the objections were as much financial as traditional. Taxes always hurt, and old ways always die hard. Flagler never had been a cow town in the sense of being a major shipping point for trail herds. But it had been a ranch town and it had its own traditions, though most of those traditions now were preserved at the livery stable and the blacksmith shop, the two principal loafing places in town, even more generally favored, especially by the older men, than the barber shop.

The livery stable really wasn't a forum. It was more of a hideout for poker players, an arena for fist fights, and a source of supply for thirsty citizens. The town's young bloods settled their quarrels in bruising, bare-knuckle battles there, where an unwritten law against kicking, kneeing, eye gouging and all such foul play was enforced by the onlookers. One of the bloodiest fights I ever saw was held "down at the barn" between two high school boys, "Red" Weller and Joe McBride. Over a girl, as I remember, who wanted nothing to do with either of them after the fight.

Both town and county were "dry" under local option, but a thirsty man could always buy a pint "at the barn," which was a kind of branch store for the town's principal, if not only, bootleggers. They were two brothers, and they ran a laundry and dry-cleaning establishment at their mother's house. She, a widow, did the washing and ironing. And periodically the brothers filled a wash tub with gasoline, sloshed woolen dresses and blue serge suits through it, and hung them on the line till the worst of the odor had blown away. Then the mother smoothed them with her iron and that was that. Between times the younger brother, who owned a big Packard, drove up to Wyoming and came back with a carload of liquor, which the two boys cut and doctored with what was reputed to be licorice and tobacco juice. Then the older boy peddled it to regular customers and left a supply "down at the barn" for transients and occasionals.

Nobody bothered them particularly, except when the older brother went on a binge every two months or so. The younger brother didn't touch the stuff, but the older one, once he started, tried to drink it all. Deep in his cups, he would turn on his mother. But she, a wiry little woman all spunk and gristle, kept an iron stove poker handy for such emergencies. At a certain point in the spree she laid him out properly, then called the local deputy sheriff, who carted him off to jail to sober up, pay a fine for disturbing the peace, and go free. As far as I know, neither brother ever was arrested for bootlegging. Eventually they quit and moved away, about the time the livery stable closed for good, a victim of the Model T Ford.

Ed Malbaff's blacksmith shop was an altogether different kind of gathering place. I wish I had known my Grandfather Borland's blacksmith shop; but he died before I was born. Two of his sons were blacksmiths, though, and I knew their shop for a time before we moved to Colorado. It was a gathering place for townsmen with time on their hands and countrymen in town for a purpose. Ed Malbaff's shop was the same kind of place and, like my uncles, he dominated it absolutely.

Longfellow's poem about the village blacksmith may have been true of New England, but it didn't fit the men or places west of the Missouri river. Those shops I knew were all indoors, in thin-walled, dry-roofed, cavernous places, dark as dungeons and looking like the hell described in Sunday school. They were places of soot and coal dust, echoing hammer and ringing anvil, glare and flame of fire in the forge, awesome showers of sparks that burned like coals when the white-hot iron was being hammered into shape, clouds of stinking steam from the quenching tub when the hot iron was thrust in to cool. The blacksmith "a mighty man was he," to be sure, but those "muscles of his brawny arms" were black with coal dust and so was his face, so was his hairy chest, though seamed with white runnels where his "honest sweat" plowed furrows through the grime. He was a Titan who could wrestle a stallion into submission—legend says that my grandfather once floored an obstreperous Percheron with his fist. A bull of a man, who could outswear a cavalryman or build a wagon; who could tell stories better than Rabelais or forge a butcher knife; who could build a whole grist mill, as my grandfather did, or move and reassemble a printing press he had never seen, as Ed Malbaff did.

Ed ruled his huge, dark cavern of a shop with a hand of tempered steel. Small boys could go there and watch and listen to their elders, but only if they kept out from underfoot and never repeated the language they heard there, or the stories. Grownups could come and sit and talk or listen, but a man's welcome cooled if he failed to respect the difference between profanity and obscenity. Profanity was tolerated, even embellished, by the proprietor, if it had some semblance of meaning and rhythm. Ed once told a fumbling, foul-mouthed lout, "Shut up and stop trying to swear till you learn how to put the words together right. You get everything you say ass-backwards." Vulgarity was allowed up to a point, at which Ed drew the line clearly and emphatically. After just so much filthy language Ed would lay down his hammer, point a calloused forefinger, and say, "You! Either shut up or go on out to the privy and don't come back."

At one time or another almost all the town's idlers and men at loose ends could be found at the blacksmith shop. Among them were old-timers who had been in that country when it was young, before the railroad was built. Mike Quinn qualified because he helped build the railroad. And Mike was a veteran of the Civil War. After the rails were laid, he worked for the railroad as a maintenance man, was head of the local section gang for years. He was full of stories about the old days, at least half of them true and all of them rich with Irish wit and Irish brogue. When he told a whopper, most of his listeners knew what it was. As the one he told about how he used to be a great foot racer, how he kept in trim by running down coyotes, which he butchered to keep his family in meat. That was a wheeze, first because nobody could picture Mike, big, brawny, white-mustached and with a game leg that needed a cane, as a foot racer; and second because everyone knew his wife, a little woman all spunk and gumption and rawhide and sharp tongue, who would have gone out and butchered a range steer, anyone's steer, and dragged it home by the tail before she would have fed her family coyote meat. But when he talked about how they built the railroad, Mike Quinn was listened to with attention and respect.

Simon Rumming was another who qualified. I have spoken of him elsewhere in this book, of his coming up the trail from Texas as a cavvy boy and finally settling on the Republican in the early eighties. Simon Rumming was a man with a soft voice and a winning smile, a one-eyed man who, some said, could charm the blackbirds down out of a cottonwood tree. He was reputed to have been a great horseman, though I never saw him on a horse. Now and then someone would get him to talk about horses and riders, though, and he would chuckle and bob around on his nail keg—nail kegs were the favorite seats, and the regulars each had his own, properly branded with his initials; Simon would rock on his keg and say, "These rodeo riders, how long do they have to ride a horse before the horn blows? Ten seconds? Why, they couldn't even have got a *job* with the outfits in the old days. Many's the frosty morning I had to ride a horse, pitching and bucking his best, for ten *minutes*, till he got the vinegar worked out of him. They all did it. A horse that didn't give you fits on a frosty morning wasn't considered worth his feed. And a man who couldn't ride such a horse couldn't hold a job."

Simon had seen what probably was the last buffalo in the county. "It was in eighty-seven," he said. "I was up on Hackberry Creek, north of Vona, looking for cattle—I was working for the K. P. outfit, then. And I saw this old buffalo bull. I couldn't believe my eyes, at first, till I rode closer and sure enough, that's what it was. Big and mangy looking, he sure was a sight. So old his teeth probably were worn down so he could hardly eat a good mouthful. Even the Indians didn't want him, he was so old and tough. I certainly didn't want him either, so I rode around him and went about my business. But that afternoon, on my way back, I met a couple of folks from Vona and I told them about that old bull, and they got all excited. And a couple of days later I heard that Doc Hoyt went out and shot him. I don't know why. The hide wasn't worth taking, and the meat couldn't be eaten. Anyway, that was the last buffalo ever seen in Kit Carson County, maybe in this end of the state."

Once in a while George Epperson would stop in, usually to get a piece of work done, maybe a plow share sharpened, or occasionally while his wife did the shopping. George was a brother of Ed Epperson of the original Town Incorporation Committee, and his wife was Mike Quinn's oldest daughter. He had a cattle ranch southwest of Flagler, but he wasn't much of a talker. He was one of those who sat and listened. And he caught flies. That's a strange thing to say about a man, but it is true. George Epperson was the only man I ever knew who could reach out and catch a sitting fly. Strangers seeing him do it stood goggle-eyed, and even the blacksmith shop regulars sat entranced to watch him. He did the same thing at home, on the front porch of his ranch house. A visitor would be sitting there, talking, and George would see a fly buzzing around. He would hold out one hand, let it alight there, then slowly reach out with his other hand and catch the fly, just as though it had been mesmerized. And all the time go on with his slow, easy talk, once you got him started, about life there in the eighties, which according to him was just ordinary ranch life.

Most of the old-time ranchmen had worked as riders for the big outfits when they first came to that area. And most of them had seen buffalo, some had shot buffalo, a few had eaten buffalo steaks, which they didn't care for. Tougher than beef, they said without exception. Actually, the buffalo were virtually wiped out by the hide-and-tongue hunters by 1886. After that there were rumors of herds persisting in the Dakotas and even in Minnesota, but they were false rumors. There were a few left in little bands, maybe as many as a dozen, in isolated pockets and brushy margins along the rivers, but the Indians and the trappers killed them without any fanfare. Leaving only such old, toothless specimens as the one Simon Rumming saw in '87.

By 1915 the buffalo were a memory, and a dim one at that. But their brittle white bones and peeling black horns were still there on the flats. I have here in my study a buffalo horn I picked up south of Flagler in 1931, the last one I ever saw lying there in the grass. I have no doubt that those who said, in Ed Malbaff's shop, that they saw live buffalo were telling the truth. But when they vanished they vanished completely. And the slaughter that wiped them out, down to those few tiny last-stand groups, was still evident as late as 1910, when the big homestead wave occurred. There were so many whitened buffalo bones on the flats that homesteaders gathered them and hauled them by the wagonload to Benkelman, Nebraska, and sold them to agents for fertilizer companies in Chicago. I don't know what they were paid for those bones, but some said they bought their winter groceries with bone money. And it was said that at times there was a pile of buffalo bones ten feet high and a quarter of a mile long at Benkelman, waiting shipment to the fertilizer factories.

I knew and particularly admired four of the real old-timers, Charley Farr, Bill Strode, Albert Fisher and John Verhoff.

All were still active ranchmen and none of them had much time for loafing, at the blacksmith shop or anywhere else. When I say I knew them I mean that I knew them to speak to, and they knew me by name; and now and then I heard them talking about the past at the office, for they all knew Father, stopped in to visit with him once in a while.

Charley Farr was the dean of the active cattlemen, oldest of these four and looked up to by the others. Bill Strode called him a man with a lot of courage and good, sound judgment. Albert Fisher said Charley was "the best ranchman, and the best boss, in the state." Both Bill and Albert had worked for him when Charley was foreman of the Hash-Knife outfit, one of the biggest, with headquarters near Deer Trail.

Charley was born in Illinois in 1860, came to Colorado with family friends in a covered wagon in 1877, and started work as a cowboy down on the Arkansas river. Within ten years he was foreman of the Hash-Knife. A few years later he struck out on his own, with a homestead on the Republican river just north of Crystal Springs as his headquarters. That is where he still lived when we arrived, a beautiful ranch with plenty of good valley hay and crop land and upland grass for pasturage.

I remember Charley Farr on a horse, a tall, handsome man with a generous mustache and a face that belonged in a Remington painting of the Old West. He was proud of his horses and his saddle and, unless he came to town for groceries or a load that called for a wagon, he always came on horseback. I can still see him, the superb western horseman, on a big sorrel horse with four white feet, his saddle creaking, his bit chains tinkling, the horse prancing, Charley straight as a poker, his gray hat jaunty, his plainsman eyes squinted like those of an old-time sailor who also knew the far horizon.

Charley's younger son, Duncan, was a classmate of mine in high school and went on to college with me. Quite a horseman himself, Dunc was the high jumper on our high school track team and set a county record that stood for years, five feet nine inches, or thereabout. Charley was as proud of Duncan as he was of his best saddle horse. But when he talked of the old days, which was not often, it wasn't about buffalo or range wars or cattle thieves, but about cattle, and hard winters, and starving Indians, and homesteaders who came and choked the really big ranches to death with barbed wire.

Bill Strode was fifteen years younger than Charley Farr. He didn't reach Flagler till 1887, barely in time to see the first train come through. But he was born in Texas, practically grew up on a horse, and was a full-time cowboy at the age of fifteen. Albert Fisher, a year younger than Bill Strode, also came to Colorado as a boy and became a cowboy at an early age. But Albert was a horseman, a bronc rider, as he sometimes said. He got work breaking horses to the saddle, with roundup trips thrown in, of course, just to keep him busy. Albert married Bill Strode's sister and the two families were linked even more closely. As late as 1916, when Albert was forty years old, he still was considered the best bronc rider anywhere around.

John Verhoff, only eight years younger than Charley Farr, came to Colorado from Kansas as a boy of sixteen and went to work as a cowhand. Six years later, in 1894, his brother Lanch came out from Kansas to join him and they took homesteads on the river southeast of Flagler, about ten miles upriver from Charley Farr's place. John built a rock and sod house, got married, and settled down to ranching for himself. He had eight children, including two sons just a little younger than I was, and he owned a large acreage of valley land and cattle to eat its grass and alfalfa. He built the dam where Little Doc and Spider and I went to watch the ducks and the herons and the frogs, hoping to irrigate some of his drier acres. But when the dam was full the acres never needed irrigating, and when they needed water the water behind the dam was too low to flow off into the irrigation ditches.

None of these four, as I said, was a loafer at the blacksmith shop, though all went there occasionally to get a job done that was too difficult for their ranch forges. And now and then they contributed another paragraph to the oral history of the area. In later years I heard various stories about those men, most of them patently apocryphal. Like the one about Charley Farr and the whip socket. When Charley bought his first Model T, the story went, he took it down to Ed Malbaff and had Ed put a whip socket on the dash; said he wouldn't feel comfortable in the dang thing without a buggy whip handy. Pure fabrication, of course. Any man who could sharp-shoe his own saddle horse could fasten a whip socket on a Model T if he really wanted one there. Another such tale was about John Verhoff. John, the story went, when he first built the big dam wanted Ed Malbaff to build him a water wheel to install in the spillway and drive a generator for electricity. Another fabrication. John Verhoff had no more interest in making electricity than he had in going to the moon. He was a ranchman, and a ranchman's whole being was wrapped in cattle and feed for those cattle. John Verhoff outlived the other three as well as all those who had personal nail kegs at the blacksmith shop. He outlived Ed, for that matter. He didn't die until March of 1969, when he was in his ninety-eighth year.

Another of the old-timers who spent little of his leisure at the blacksmith shop had a ranch on down the river from Charley Farr's place. One of his sons was also a classmate of mine, but he never finished high school. The father was a wiry little man so sunburned that some said he was part Indian, and his silence and reserve added to that story. But he had no Indian blood in him, though his children did. They were half-bloods. The mother could have posed for one of those William Henry Jackson photographs in front of a tepee. She was copper-skinned, dark-eyed, with beautiful black hair that she always wore in two long braids bound at the tips with yarn. And she wore the full blouse and wide, billowing skirts that go with the traditional Indian squaw. She was said to be a full-blood, from Oklahoma, but she spoke better English than some of the women in town who had twelve grades of schooling. Her voice was soft and she laughed easily but almost silently.

She came to town once a week, always driving a team of bay horses hitched to a lumber wagon. Sometimes she brought her little girl, sometimes her husband came with her, but usually she came alone. She went to the stores, did her buying, and then, every time she came to town, she went to the town library. It was only a small library with no more than twenty-five hundred or three thousand volumes, and it was open only two afternoons a week. But her visits to town were always made on library days. She returned the books she had borrowed the week before, browsed the shelves, chose three or four more volumes, checked them out, and went back to her wagon. She had read most of the fiction, the librarian told me some years later, and had gone on to biography and history. If she had come to town alone, she always started home with an open book in her hands, the reins held loosely. The horses knew the way home.

Twice I was at their ranch, stopping for a drink of water when I was prowling the hills along the river. Each time she welcomed me with a smile and gave me a glass of fresh buttermilk and squares of gingerbread. "Boys need something inside besides water," she said. In later years I wished I had had the courage to get acquainted. But I never knew her beyond those brief encounters. She died a quiet, peaceful death, I was told, about ten years later. And nobody in town, not even the librarian, knew any more about her than I did.

One man who might have told remarkable stories, who was, in fact, a strange story himself, probably never set foot in Ed Malbaff's blacksmith shop. That was LeRoy Cuckow, who owned the boxcar house where we lived when we first arrived in town. Mother spoke of him as "that dirty old man" and didn't even like to pass him on the street. He made me think of Fagin in *Oliver Twist*, tall, lean, slightly stooped, with a thin face, hawkish nose and deep-set eyes that always seemed hostile or defensive. He wore a scraggly dark beard, and his hair, thin on top, hung down over his greasy coat collar. He walked with a kind of loping gait and his clothes hung like the clothes on a scarecrow. And, as Mother said, he was dirty, physically dirty. He lived in the office at his garage, along with five or six feisty little dogs. There was an old iron bedstead at the back of the office, with a mattress and a rat's nest of grimy blankets where he and the dogs slept. There was a kerosene stove on which he did his cooking, and it always had a frying pan with traces of egg and pancake batter on it. The office smelled of kerosene and dogs and motor oil and sweat. So did Cuckow.

Where he came from, I never knew. He had few friends and he made no confidences. Somehow Father learned that he was a veteran of the Spanish-American war, had been wounded in one leg, and had some kind of dysentery that never was cured. On top of that he must have had tuberculosis, for he had one of those tombstone coughs you could hear a block away. He was a sick man who simply clung to life with his grimy hands and wouldn't let go. Small boys teased him, and he sicked his dogs on them. Some townsmen laughed at him, some sneered. A good many farmers went to his garage to buy the things he advertised in the *News*—kerosene at 11 cents a gallon, axle grease at 5 cents a pound, engine oil at 34 cents a gallon, asphalt roofing paint at 75 cents a gallon, linseed oil at 80 cents a gallon. Some days the customers had to get him out of bed, where he slept in a grimy suit of long underwear, to get them what they needed, often racked by that ghastly cough till he could hardly stand.

But even then he was a glaring figure of defiance. Defying death, of course, which had been at his heels almost twenty years, ever since that war. He kept on defying it another three or four years. Then he died in his bed, and a paper among the litter on his office desk had a scrawled note. "Notify my sister," and it gave her name and address, back in Illinois as I remember. Dr. Williams, called when the garage mechanic found Cuckow stiff in his bed, sent a telegram. Word came back to bury him there in Flagler, sell his possessions, pay for the burial, and send any leftover to the sister. This was done, and only two things remained of LeRoy Cuckow to remind the town of his life there. One was the store of gossip about him, the untold stories he could have verified or scotched but never did. The other was his dogs.

The feists were the only ones in town who mourned the strange man. Disposessed at the garage, they roamed the town, scavenging for a living, occasionally scuttling back to the empty garage, whining and then howling in chorus. Finally the deputy sheriff was told to do something about them. He tried first to catch them, but it was like chasing greased piglets. When he finally did corner one it was so vicious he didn't dare lay a hand on it. So he got his gun and hunted them down, one by one, and killed them, all six of them.

LeRoy Cuckow, to nearly everyone's surprise, had been in favor of the municipal light plant. Those backing the proposal weren't sure they welcomed his support, knowing how many people disliked him, particularly the women. But there wasn't anything they could do but accept it. At the livery stable the loafers, all against change of any kind, gloated, saying, "If old Cuckow is for it, that'll swing enough votes the other way to kill it." But at the blacksmith shop Ed Malbaff said, "I'd take support from Cuckow's *dogs*, if they could vote. We need that light plant."

One of the most stubborn die-hards said, "Mark my word, Ed, they'll tax you right out of business, the way they're going."

And Ed said, "That's what you said when we voted to build the new school. Remember? And that's what you said when we voted to incorporate the town. Times are changing, Jim. We killed off all the buffalo and most of the Indians some years back. Or didn't you know? God knows you been bragging about it long enough, you *should* know. Why, Jim, we don't even plow with oxen any more!"

Jim wasn't convinced, nor were quite a few others. But before the snow flew again the loafers at Ed's shop were saying what a marvel electricity was. Just look at the way it ran that triphammer Ed built for himself! Only now and then would one of them shake his head and say, "It ain't like it used to be, not with that diesel engine thumping away in the powerhouse. A man can't rest comfortable in the daytime any more, and sometimes he can't sleep at night, with that infernal thump-thump-thump going on."

21

I toughened up for football that year by working for the railroad. In mid-July the company sent a crew to Flagler to put in a whole new water system at the depot, including a big steel tank to replace the old wooden-stave tank down beside the tracks. The new tank was to be up the slope from the depot and a new main would have to be laid. Pick-and-shovel help was needed. Father said he could spare me, since late summer was a slack time at the office, so I went down to the depot and asked the crew boss for a job. He took me on as a general laborer at 46 cents an hour. Big money.

There were nine of us in the crew, only four from Flagler. The boss, who was a master plumber among other things, put me on the ditch crew. I can't remember ever being more tired than I was every night the first week or so on that job. We dug ditches two feet wide and six feet deep. Fortunately, the soil was all ancient sediment, laid down about a hundred million years ago when that land was ocean bed all the way to the Rockies. No rocks in it. But when I shunned pick-and-shovel work in later years it wasn't for snobbish reasons. I had been there. I had dug my ditches.

Two weeks after we started digging ditches the boss started laying pipe. He needed two helpers and I was one of the two he chose. It was a dubious honor. We had to carry sections of cast-iron pipe from the pile to the ditch, and each section weighed close to two hundred pounds. We had to lower those sections into the ditch, with ropes. Once the pipe was in the ditch we had to get down in there and level it at a proper pitch, with the boss himself standing over us. It was back-breaking work, and we fried as the sun bore down on us in the ditch without a breath of moving air.

The pipe in place, the boss started calking the joints with oakum. I showed too much interest in that job; within a couple of days he had me calking joints with oakum. And when the oakum was all in and driven down, he set us to melting lead which had to be poured into those joints, using a flexible "dam," over the oakum. That lead had to be driven in and expanded with calking chisels, and I did my share of that, too. My muscular forearms are in part a consequence of using a calking hammer on that water line; some nights my hands and wrists were so sore and tired I could hardly hold a knife and fork. But we laid those mains, and calked them, and got the job done. And to the best of my knowledge those mains never had to be dug up for repairs. By Labor Day I was all ready for football. No matter how Professor Ward drove us, it was going to be a cinch now.

I was a senior that fall, a full-fledged senior at last, and I had to take only four subjects. But after the first week I had so much free time that I asked if I couldn't take a course in advanced English that was being given for several graduates, Marjorie Miner among them, who weren't starting college for another year. That took up some of my slack time. I joined the debating team. And there was football, of course.

This was going to be my last year of high school football and I wanted it to be special. I secretly hoped to be chosen captain of the team. I hadn't mentioned it, and wasn't going to, but I thought I had earned it. I had scored more points than anybody else on the team last year.

Professor Ward called us together the third day of practice, after we had got into uniform and before we went out onto the field, and said we were going to elect a captain. The boys looked around and I just stood there, waiting. But nobody said a word. Professor Ward laughed and asked, "Aren't you going to have a captain this year?" And one of the Johnson boys, Ab I think, said, "I nominate Irish Quinn." There were shouts of "Yeah!" and "Sure!" and someone made it official by saying, "I second the nomination." Then silence. Professor Ward asked, "Any more nominations?" Silence again. "All right, then, all in favor of Hugh Quinn say 'Aye.'" And everybody said, "Aye." I felt as though I'd been socked in the solar plexus.

I knew I had to get outdoors before I started heaving. I pushed over to Irish and slapped him on the back and said, "Congratulations, Captain," and ran up the stairs and out the side door and down onto the field. I felt the cold sweat and the lightheadedness, but I trotted down the field, belched a couple of times, and felt better. Then the rest of the squad was on the field and I heard Irish yell my name and turned and saw him throw a long pass that I had to sprint and leap to catch. I returned it with a drop kick that went a good fifty yards. Then Professor Ward called us together and started the same old drill, the fundamentals, and I began to feel all right. It didn't matter, really, not being captain. Irish was quarterback again, and he was better than last year. Besides, he had the knack of leadership. He would be a good captain. Probably better than I would have been. For my own pride, I had to say "probably."

By the next day things were back in place. I was pretty much a loner, and the loner doesn't make a good leader. I probably would go right on being a loner. That's the way I grew up. And next spring I would be through high school. Next summer I was going away, to be a crewman on the Chautauqua circuit. I didn't need to be captain of the football team.

That afternoon, during our last period, Phyllis Ward, who was senior class sponsor, called a class meeting. We went to her home room, all eleven of us, five boys and six girls. Miss Ward said, "I called you together because it's time you organized. As seniors, you are the most important class in school, and you should elect your officers. Let's start off with nominations for class president."

There wasn't any hemming or hawing. Later I heard that it had all been agreed on beforehand. Duncan Farr nominated me and the nomination was seconded at once by Lora Moore, the preacher's daughter. Then Little Doc moved that the nominations be closed and Irish Quinn seconded the motion. Miss Ward called for a vote and I was elected by one short of unanimity. I was so amazed that I couldn't even speak.

Miss Ward said, "Now that you have a president, he had better take over the meeting," and I had to go up and take charge. I said my thanks and said what a total surprise it was, and Pearl Robb, the only boy I ever knew named Pearl, said, "You got to be a senior in two years and it took the rest of us three, so maybe you can set a good example, or something." I knew just enough about parliamentary procedure to get a secretary and a treasurer elected, and then we adjourned and Irish Quinn and Duncan Farr and Pearl Robb and I went down to the locker room to suit up for football practice.

At supper, when I told Mother and Father about the class election, Mother said, "That's nice, but don't let it go to your head." Father said, "I'm proud of you, son."

"Who nominated you?" Mother asked. I told her it was Duncan Farr, and she asked who seconded the nomination. "Lora Moore," I said.

"Oh. So now she will expect you to take her to the class parties."

"Of course not!" I said. "She always has a date. She doesn't need me to ask her."

Mother smiled. "You'll learn, some day." Then, "Lora's a nice girl. But don't get serious about her. Or any girl, yet. I was only eighteen when your father married me, but he was almost twenty-one."

I puzzled over what Mother had said about Lora Moore, and it didn't make sense to me. Even if I had a chance, I had no notion of dating Lora regularly. I wasn't dating anyone, really. I took this girl or that one to Sunday school parties and picnics and birthday parties, but nearly always in a group. Anyway, football season was starting the next Saturday, and football didn't leave much time for one to think about girls.

We played six games that year and we lost only one, and that by one touchdown. I had two big days, one against Hugo when I scored two touchdowns, kicked a field goal, and kicked four extra points. The other big day was against Akron, and that was my defensive day. I played defensive left end and everything happened right for me. I was able to get through every defense they tried and I caught their ball carrier for a loss four times, recovered two fumbles, and blocked a punt. The only scoring I did was three points kicked after touchdowns, but it was the best game I ever played.

We played our last game the second week in November, and the school held a football banquet the Saturday before Thanksgiving. Team members were allowed to bring girls, but before I got around to asking anyone all the senior girls had dates. So two days before the banquet I asked Marjorie Miner, who was in the advanced English class with me. We knew each other, not only because she was Spider's sister but because in a town like Flagler and in a school that size you know virtually everyone. I don't know how many there were in high school at that time, but all four classes couldn't have totaled more than sixty. The two previous graduating classes had totaled only thirteen. There simply weren't any strangers among us.

Marjorie went to the banquet with me, and the surprise of the evening was when Professor Ward presented miniature

gold footballs, watch charms, each engraved with the player's name, the school's initials and the date, to each of us
seniors. That was before the school gave athletic letters, so it
had special significance for us. It was a very sentimental evening, as all such banquets are. That was one reason, I suppose, that it was followed by a series of dates with Marjorie
—she had shared that evening. Several times Little Doc borrowed his father's car, dated one of the Kliewer girls, and the
four of us went to parties together. But Little Doc wasn't particularly interested in dating, and by the end of January I
was losing interest too. Marjorie knew it. When I didn't ask
her for a date for almost three weeks she went out of her way
to tell me how busy she was, how little time she had. I said
I had been busy too, of course, and that was that. Not exactly a spat, but almost.

Then Mother said, "I guess you and Marjorie have had a
falling out." She hadn't commented before. She liked Marjorie, or had always seemed to; but the way she said it now
seemed almost triumphant. It made me bristle. But I held
my tongue, simply said no, we hadn't had a quarrel.

Mother smiled that all-knowing smile. "Just as well. You
two were getting pretty thick."

I bit back my answer, knowing that anything I said would
just prolong an argument I didn't want. I didn't know what
was going on in Mother's mind, but whatever it was it was it
didn't need any further fueling, especially from me. I went
over to the drug store, found Little Doc, and we agreed to
go to the movies that evening, just the two of us. I had quit
running the projector the previous summer, so we would have
to pay our way. But a Norma Talmadge picture was on.

Nothing was said about Marjorie at supper, but I thought
from their looks that Father and Mother had been talking
about something that involved. me. Father kept watching
Mother and kept the conversation general and harmless, and
Mother was more tense than usual, and quieter. But we got

through supper and I said I was going to the movies and added, pointedly, "Little Doc and I, and nobody else." Mother was on the point of saying something, but Father cut in and said, "Run along. Enjoy yourself. Nobody is going to sit up waiting for you." He glanced at Mother as he said that, and I grabbed my jacket and got out of the house quickly.

We went to the movie, Little Doc and I, and afterward went over to the drug store and he made sodas for us both. We sat there talking about the picture and I said, "Who does Norma remind you of, right here in Flagler?"

"Who?"

"Mabel Seal."

"Hey, she does, a little! What do you know!" He grinned. "I'll bet Norma can't hunt ducks the way Mabel can, though."

And I remembered Mabel with a shotgun, at the pond in November. I had watched her, from up on the hill near the school, because she was such a good wing-shot. "How old do you suppose she is?" I asked.

"Mabel? About Emp's age. He used to date her once in a while. She went to Denver, you know. And got married. And divorced."

I nodded. I had heard the gossip, too. And the stories that went around school. At school they said it was an impulsive marriage that didn't work so she got out. None of the young folks blamed her. But among some of the town's older women, and more tight-laced younger ones, divorce was rated almost as sinful as bastardy.

We said no more about her, and I went on home a few minutes later. Nobody was waiting up for me, but Father called from the front bedroom, "Is that you, son?" I said yes and good night, and went to my back bedroom. And lay awake, thinking first about the movie and Norma Talmadge and then about Mabel Seal. I was surprised at the things I remembered about her. The way she laughed, how she walked, the tones of her voice. And when I slept I dreamed about Mabel and Norma, all mixed up.

The next day when I went downtown to get the Sunday *Denver Post* I stopped at the *News* office before I went home. I had a key, and I went in and got out the subscription list and went through the Denver subscribers till I found her name and address. I copied the address and that evening, with the excuse of having some writing to do, presumably homework, I sat in my room and wrote a letter about the weather and what was going on at school and how the pond looked after the February melt. I mailed it to her the next morning when I got the office mail.

Getting the morning mail had been one of my daily chores, a part of helping Father open the *News* office and get the day started before I went to school. Some days, in the past, I had forgotten the mail, but from then on I didn't have to be reminded. There were two mail trains from Denver a day, one early in the day, the other in midafternoon, but most of the first class mail came in the morning. I didn't know whether to expect a reply or not, but I went through the letters every morning before I took the mail down to the office and put it on Father's desk.

A week later the letter came, in a gray envelope addressed in a firm, unfamiliar, feminine handwriting with blue ink. I thrust it into an inside pocket and couldn't wait to leave the office and start to school. Then I opened it, drew out the single page and read it quickly, just to know that it was a reply. Then I read it word for word. She thanked me for writing to her. She said she was homesick for the plains. She wanted me to tell her all about them. Please write again when I had time. There wasn't one sentimental word in it, but she signed it, "Love, Mabel."

That evening I wrote to her again. I told her how the February thaw was progressing, how the slew was filling up, that I had heard the coyotes howling a few nights before, and that a few horned larks were back already. And the next day, after I had mailed it, I kept watching and listening for things to tell her. After school I went down to Seal's slew—it really was at the pond stage, at that time of the year—to see what was happening at first hand. And the next day I went out onto the flats east of town and listened for a meadow lark. But it was too early for meadow larks, so I looked for signs of life at a big ant hill, and I found ants at work. I saw a ground squirrel out, looking lean and hungry. And in her next reply Mabel said she loved my letters, that they made her see and hear what was happening.

It was an early spring. I hadn't watched the birds, the grass, the wild flowers, the ants, even the clouds and the sunsets, so observantly since we left the homestead. And I had never before tried to put into words on paper what I saw. I wonder now why none of my teachers ever tried to rouse my interest in that world around me enough to get me to write about it as classwork. None of them did, perhaps because it was too close at hand, too familiar, too commonplace, even though none of them knew much about it. Instead, they assigned topics such as reviews of "classic" books, essays about what we hoped to do when we finished school, descriptions of scenes or characters in Shakespeare's *Midsummer Night's Dream*.

Through February and March I did my schoolwork with my left hand and gave most of my attention to the things I was writing about to Mabel. I wrote long, detailed letters full of the coming of spring to the High Plains. And she wrote warm, generous letters to me, usually with some amusing thing about her life in Denver, which she said was very dull.

Then one afternoon the first week in April the inevitable happened. A letter from Mabel came in the afternoon mail. When I went down the steps to the *News* office after school

I saw Mother, at the desk, glance over her shoulder, see it was me, then not even look up when I went in. I said hello and hung up my jacket, and I felt the tension. Father, at the back of the office, was wrapping out-of-town copies of the *News*—it was publication day; he glanced at me, drew a deep breath, and waited. Mother said, "Here's a letter that came in the afternoon mail." Her voice was icy. She held up the gray envelope with Mabel's handwriting, and with her return address on the back.

I took the letter and stood there a moment, not knowing what to do or say. "Well," Mother said, "aren't you going to open it?"

I tore it open. There was only one page. She said my letters had made her so homesick she was coming down to Flagler for a few days and didn't I want to meet her at the train? She would be on the afternoon train Friday. That would be tomorrow. I read it through and put it back into the envelope and thrust it into my pocket, undoubtedly blushing. I said, "It's from Mabel Seal."

"I saw her name on the envelope," Mother said coldly. "Her maiden name, just as though she had never been married and *divorced*." She made *divorce* a dirty word.

I knew I had to say it, get it said. "She is coming down from Denver tomorrow on the afternoon train. I'm going to meet her at the depot."

"You can't do that!"

"Why not?" It was Father speaking. He had come from the back of the office, a stubby little man almost an inch shorter than I was but a commanding figure just in the way he stood and looked at her, even in his ink-stained printer's apron, a smudge on his flushed cheek. "Why not?" he asked again.

Mother gasped. "Will Borland, are you in on this too?"

"I don't know what you mean, in on this. But there's no reason in the world he can't go down to the depot and meet

Mabel Seal, if he wants to. It's time you stopped treating him like a six-year-old."

Mother took off her nose-glasses and wiped her eyes with her handkerchief. Wanting to put an end to the scene, I took the letter from my pocket. "Here, read it yourself, if you think she's so awful!" I started to hand it to Mother but Father caught my arm.

"It's your letter," he said. "You don't have to show it to anyone." Then, to Mother, "He's my son too, and he's going to get a chance to grow up."

"This isn't the first letter you've had from her," Mother said, biting her lip to check herself.

"No. We've been writing to each other—"

"Behind my back!" It burst out of her. She turned to Father. "You don't care *how* you hurt me, either of you!" And she sprang to her feet, grabbed her coat from the hook, slammed the door behind her before she had even put the coat on.

We watched her run up the steps to the street. Then Father went back to the long table at the rear of the shop and went on wrapping papers, one by one. After a few minutes he said, "You can bundle them," and I got the ball of twine and gathered each pile of wrapped papers, which he had grouped by states, and tied them into bundles. Father finished the wrapping. I tied the last bundle, then took them to the post office.

When I returned, Father was at the basin washing up. He soaped his hands and arms deliberately with the gray bar of Lava soap, worked the lather into his skin and around his nails, then slowly rinsed it off. As he dried himself on the worn huck towel he said, "Mabel's a nice girl, far as I know. I always liked her."

"What's Mother got against her?" I asked.

"Well, for one thing, Mabel's another woman. Much as she likes Marjorie Miner, your mother got pretty touchy when you took Marjie out a few times. I guess she said more to me about it than she did to you."

"And," I said, "Mabel's been married."

"Oh, yes, that makes it ten times worse. It doesn't matter why she got the divorce. I've heard it was one of those intolerable situations and she showed good sense to get out of it, fast."

"What can I do about it? The way Mother feels, I mean?"

"Nothing. Nothing in the world. That's the way your Mother is. She loves you. She'd do anything in the world for you. *Except* let you run your own life. Or pick the woman you want to marry."

"I don't want to marry Mabel Seal! She's—she's just a good friend."

"And, as I said, another woman." Father hung up the towel, poured his wash water down the drain, and rolled down his sleeves. Then he sat down on the edge of his desk and rolled a fresh cigarette. "Remember how your mother and my mother never could get along?" he asked. "My mother—your Grandmother Borland—never did like Sarah. They were like two cats, clawing and spitting. That's one reason we moved away from Sterling and came to Colorado." He sighed. "I hope it won't be the same way with your mother and whoever you eventually marry. But don't be surprised if she rears up and goes on a rampage about any girl you get interested in."

He took a deep pull on his cigarette, let the smoke out slowly, and said, "Well, we'd just as well go on home. She'll be in bed with a sick headache, if I know the signs. We'll get ourselves something to eat. Bacon and eggs do for you?"

He put on his coat and hat and I turned off the lights at the back of the shop. We went up the stairs in the first dimness of April dusk. At the corner Father paused a moment, then turned toward the drug store. "Better get some headache powders. Save a trip back."

22

Only two people besides the station agent were at the depot when I got there, ten minutes before train time, a farmer and his wife from up north. I knew them only by sight, but they knew me. They were in the waiting room and she said they were meeting her brother, coming down from Denver. I couldn't sit down. I had to get back outside, walk, work off some of the tensions. I walked to the end of the brick platform and stood there looking south—and didn't see a thing. I was thinking about the scene at the office the previous afternoon, and what Father said after Mother left us. I thought of the silence and the darkness when we went home, Father and I, and how he went into the front bedroom and tried to talk to her and came out and closed the door and shook his head and said, "Let's get something to eat." And later, two hours later, he went in again and I heard voices and he came out and got a glass of water and one of the headache powders. Before he went back he said, "You'd just as well go on to bed, son."

I remembered this morning, when Father said, "Your mother's still sick. Don't bother with the chores at the office. I'll get over there after while and take care of things." Then, before I left the house for school, he said, "Better put on the clothes you want to wear to meet the train so you won't have to come home." And added, "Don't worry about your Mother. She'll be all right in another day or two."

So there I was, at the depot, in the clothes I had worn to school, fawn-colored corduroys, a black turtleneck jersey, the jacket from my gray herringbone suit, my "good suit." And wondering what to say, what to do, when she got off the train. Whether to kiss her, or shake hands, or just say hello. I felt as though I had known her for years, and actually I had never even walked across the street with her, just the two of us, never talked to her alone, never even sat in a class with her at school.

Mr. Groves arrived in his truck, bringing the outgoing mail sacks, waiting to take the incoming mail to the post office. He asked if I was going somewhere and I said, "No. I'm meeting a friend." And just then the train whistled for the crossing two miles west of town. There was a smudge of smoke and a faint *clack* on the rails, and a moment later another echoing shriek as the whistle was blown for a milepost. Then it was in plain sight, coming up the track, straight at me, it seemed. The brakes hissed and squealed, the bell clanged, the train slowed, and the big black locomotive crept past the depot. The station agent hauled the four-wheeled baggage truck toward the open door of the baggage car, and the train eased to a stop with a long, dying hiss of air. The conductor clanked his sheet-iron box step on the platform, and a pudgy man with a salesman's sample case came down the steps. Behind him was a tall, lean young man who waved to the farmer and his wife, the expected brother. And behind him came Mabel. The conductor reached up, swung her suitcase down, gave her his hand, and she came down the steps, saw me, exclaimed, "Hello! You *are* here!" and hugged me with one arm, looked up, and said, "I'm so glad!"

I had forgotten how small she was, only an inch or two over five feet. Her face was rounded, her eyes brown and crinkly at the corners when she laughed. She had a small, snubby nose, a rather wide mouth, a firm, round chin. She wore a simple little hat at a perky angle and she had a ruffly white blouse under her dark suit. I thought she was beautiful, and I couldn't think of a word to say after I said hello. She sensed it. "It seems forever," she said, looking around, "since I've been home." And I didn't know whether it was defiance or fear or excitement that made her eyes look the way they did.

The conductor shouted, "All aboooard," the locomotive chuffed, the bell clanged, the train began to move, and there we were, alone on the depot platform. Mabel looked south, toward the flats, then north, toward the town, and she drew a deep breath. Her lips set in a firm, straight line. Then she looked up at me and smiled and said, "Let's go!" I picked up her suitcase, she took my arm, and we went across the lot to the foot of Main Street.

As we started up Main Street she said, under her breath, "Talk to me," and she looked up at me, listening, as we walked.

I said the first thing I could think of. "There are ducks on the pond."

"Ducks? Already?"

"Yes."

"How many? What kind?"

"Four pairs of mallards and three pairs of canvasbacks."

"Any teal?"

"I haven't seen a teal yet."

"If it was October instead of April we could go duck hunting tomorrow."

The Lavington garage was just ahead of us. Several older men were loafing in the big open doorway. They were watching us.

"Teal," she said, "keep you on your toes. Canvasback or mallard is better eating, maybe, but any dub can shoot them."

"I'm one of those dubs," I said. "I seem to be too slow a wing-shot to get many teal."

She laughed. It was one of those laughs that starts as a

chuckle and becomes a soft, happy, rippling sound that makes you want to smile, just hearing it. "I'll bet you use a big old twelve-gauge. You'd be a lot faster with a sixteen."

We were in front of the garage. She turned her head and smiled at the men in the doorway and greeted one of them by name, a grizzled man old enough to be her grandfather. He gave her a broad, pleased smile, said, "Why, hello, Mabel!" and swept off his black broad-brimmed hat in respect. All the others at least touched their hat brims. I glanced at the garage office door, remembering for the first time that Mabel was, in a way, related to the Lavingtons. Her older brother, Clyde, was married to Leon's older sister. But there was no sign of Leon at the door or at his desk.

Mabel glanced up at me and her eyes crinkled at the corners as she said, "And that's the way it happened, just as simply as that!" She said it loud enough for the men to hear, and she gave me a quick little wink. I was baffled for an instant, then surprised even myself by saying, "It's wonderful that you found them at all!"

"It was luck," she said, "just a matter of luck. They really are quite rare. Did you ever see any?"

"I saw a pair of them once, out on the river. But they were awfully skittish. I never saw them again."

"They are very shy. What do you suppose they eat?"

"Red clover, when they can find it. But alfalfa too, if it is in bloom."

"That must be what makes their breath so sweet!"

She was almost laughing as she said it. But with the nonsense talk we had passed the pool hall and Cuckow's garage and the café. It was half past four and there were not many people on the street, but as we approached the post office several high school girls and two older women came out, heard us, and turned to stare. Mabel waved to the high school girls and they said, "Hello," and she greeted the women, "Hello, Nellie! Oh, Ida! How are you?" But she never paused or missed a step. They both said surprised hellos and obviously would have liked to stop and talk, but we went on, past the bank corner, across the side street, past the Congregational parsonage.

We were almost at the Seal house before Mabel stopped, caught her breath, and let it out in an audible sigh. She looked past a vacant lot, out across the flats all the way to the horizon. "Home," she said quietly. "It's still here, just as you said it was in your last letter." Then we went on, and she said, "What *were* we talking about, anyway?"

"Snarks," I said.

"Oh, you know your Lewis Carroll?"

"That's from Jack London," I said. "He called his boat the *Snark*, after some legendary animal, I think."

She didn't correct me or even mention *The Hunting of the Snark*, which I had never heard of. She said, "I'm *so* glad you were there to meet me."

We were almost at her father's house. "So am I. And I was wondering, if you aren't going to be busy tonight—"

"It's a date. Why don't you come over around seven-thirty or a quarter of eight?"

"I'll be here."

We were turning in at the gate. I went to the front door with her and she took the suitcase and said, "Thank you. See you tonight," and went inside.

I went back downtown feeling that the world had somehow taken on new dimensions, sensing it but not knowing quite how or in which way it was so different. The wind was softer, the sky was bluer, the sun seemed warmer. And something inside me was singing.

At the *News* office Father, who was distributing type from the paper's forms, said, "Hello. Meet that train?"

"Yes." I took off my jacket and hung it up.

"She was on it?"

"Yes."

286

Father went to the stone for another handful of type. He seemed full of something he wanted to say, something exciting. But he went back to the case and began distributing the type without saying it. Finally he said, "Going out tonight, I suppose."

"Yes." I put on my printer's apron and was ready to help distribute type. But Father said, "No need to get yourself all inked up. There's a couple of clean jobs I left for you to do." He pointed toward the back of the shop. "I printed two orders of billheads that you can make up into pads. And when you're through with that you can cut up some letterhead-size bond. We're about out. You can cut about ten reams of twenty-pound Hammermill."

He hesitated, and I thought again that there was something else he was about to say. But he turned back and went on distributing type and I went about the clean, easy jobs, thinking about Mabel. She had a sense of fun that was brand new to me. Like that nonsense talk. I wondered where she would want to go, what she would want to do, that evening.

Then Father said it was quitting time and we washed up. While he was drying his hands he said, "Why don't you go down to the café and have supper? I'll do whatever needs to be done at home." Then he added, "By tomorrow your mother probably will be feeling better." He went over and leaned against the edge of his desk and rolled a cigarette, relaxing as he so often did at the end of a day. He put away the papers and the bag of Bull Durham, lighted a match, got his smoke going, and looked at me with a little smile. "Can you keep something to yourself?" he asked.

"Sure I can."

He inhaled deeply, slowly let it out in a thin cloud, then said, "There are going to be some changes around here. Big changes."

I waited, knowing he had to come to it his own way.

"Before the year is out. Maybe by next fall."

I still waited.

"Dick Goodman was in town today. You've heard me talk about Dick. He worked out of Omaha when I was there. He's with the Western Newspaper Union in Denver now."

I vaguely remembered the name.

"Dick knows where I can pick up a linotype, a good one, for less than half what a new one would cost."

"Wonderful!" I said.

He didn't respond. He sat looking at his cigarette a long moment, smiling to himself, before he looked up at me and said, "Dick had a talk with Ed Gibson before he came to see me, and—well, Dick had the word I've been waiting for."

And I knew that, not the linotype, was the big, exciting thing. "Mr. Gibson is ready to sell you the *Progress!*"

He lifted a hand in caution. "Not a word, not even to your mother. I'll tell her, when the time comes. It won't be for a while yet, maybe till the end of the summer, but it's going to happen, just as sure as God made little green apples!" He looked around the office, his eyes glowing. "I started in here with a shirttail full of battered old type and two job presses, and one of these days soon I'm going to have the best damn print shop in this end of the state. And," he added softly, "the only paper in town."

He threw away his cigarette, put on his coat, set his hat at a jaunty angle. But before he went out the door he turned and asked, "Got enough money? For supper, I mean, and for tonight?"

"I've got enough."

"Well, I'll go along home. Lock up when you leave." And he went up the stairs with a spring in his step that I hadn't seen in a long time.

I went down to the café and ate supper at the counter, thinking about Father and the *News*. The *Progress*, now that I thought about it, had been losing business, or at best standing still, ever since the election that put the Democrats back in power in the state. Mr. Gibson was getting along in years.

And when he was ready to sell out he could tell someone like Dick Goodman and not have to come to Father and in effect say, "I'm licked, please buy me out." Dick Goodman would tell Father and the deal could be arranged without hurting Mr. Gibson's pride.

I ate and went back to the office and leafed through the Burlington *Record* and the Hugo *Range-Ledger,* and the Limon *Leader,* just going through the motions, hardly reading a word. A jumble of things was surging through my mind— Father and Ed Gibson, high school and Chautauqua, college and a linotype. They wouldn't unscramble, but the more I thought about them the less it mattered. When I looked at the clock it was twenty-five minutes of eight. I slicked down my hair with a wet comb, turned out the lights, locked the door, and left.

Mabel answered the door when I knocked. She was wearing a dark red corduroy skirt and a sweater that matched, a color that made her dark hair look black and her skin very pink. She said, "Come on in while I get a wrap," and I stepped into the front room. But before I could even sit down she came back with a brown tweed coat. I held it for her, and as we went out she said, "I borrowed Clyde's car."

We went around the house to where the Model T was parked in front of the stable. "You drive," Mabel said, and I opened the door, helped her in, then set the spark and throttle levers and went to the front and cranked it. We didn't own a car, but I had learned to drive while we lived in Brush. Harold Gray, whose father owned the Ford agency, showed me how so he and I could go places after he broke his wrist cranking a balky car. You didn't have to have a driver's license in those days, and there was no minimum age. So now I let the motor warm up a bit, then got behind the wheel and backed the car out to the street and asked, "Where shall we go?"

"Let's go out the Seibert road. And maybe stop at Kit Carson Hill. It's been years since I've been there."

I drove down the back street, past the church and the blacksmith shop, down to the grain elevator, then turned east on the gravel road that paralleled the railroad. It was a beautiful night, mild for mid-April, clear and calm. The car was a touring car with the top down, so the smell of the night came at us from all sides, mostly the faint smell of grass starting to grow again, though there still was only a hint of green on the hills in daylight.

Mabel's hair began to blow, and she tied a sillk scarf over it and looked like a gypsy girl. I said, "Now all you need is big gold hoops in your ears and you can tell fortunes."

"Want me to tell yours?"

"Sure, go ahead."

She took my right hand and held it in front of her in the darkness. She couldn't see a line in it, but she said, "After a troubled youth you will have a long, happy life." Then she said, "Why, you have a square, practical hand, almost like mine! Not long, slim fingers like poets are supposed to have."

"Who said I was a poet?"

"You write like one, sometimes. You could be an author, if you wanted to. You can do just about anything you want to, with those hands. And being a man," she added. "My hands are square and practical, but I have to fight even to do what I know *has* to be done. . . . But I'm not going to talk about me."

"I wish you would."

After a long moment she asked, "Why did you write to me?"

"Because—well, I saw a movie with Norma Talmadge, and she reminds me of you."

"Oh? Thank you!"

"And I remember you hunting ducks at the pond."

"And hated me because I'm a better wing-shot?"

"And I remembered the way you walk."

"How do I walk?"

"With your feet straight, not duck-footed. And from the

hips, not the knees like most girls do. Did you notice, we were in step all the way up from the depot?"

She laughed. "I learned to walk trying to keep up with three brothers. You never had a sister, did you?"

"No."

"Too bad. . . . Am I what you expected?"

"You're more fun to be with and talk to."

"Thanks for a *real* compliment. . . . Why do you think I answered you?"

"I don't know."

"I was lonely and I was homesick. And I remembered you, too. You always seemed to be nice." She chuckled. "There's a compliment for *you*. . . . I hoped you would tell me about home. Not the gossip. I knew enough about that. But about the wind and the sky and the birds and the coyotes and the grass. I needed to know they were still here. And you told me."

I didn't know what to say. I didn't know that was what I had been doing in my letters, but I couldn't very well say that.

A jack rabbit started to cross the road, was caught in the car's headlight beam, and loped down the road ahead of us. It looked like a female heavy with young, and she ran so slowly we began to gain on her. Finally I slowed down and let her get off the road. When she finally dodged to safety Mabel said, "That's another reason. I knew you wouldn't be cruel. To anything."

Self-conscious, I said, "All I really know about you is—"

"What people say," she said with a flick of bitterness.

"I was going to say the way you talk and the way you laugh and the way your nose wrinkles—"

"And the way I walk. Don't forget to mention that!"

"You're not at all like Norma Talmadge. You're just you, I guess."

And just then, directly in front of us on the eastern horizon, the rim of a moon two days past the full appeared, blood red. We were on the hill just west of the river, the whole valley in deep shadow in front of us. I pulled over to the right, parked, and turned off the lights. We sat in silence as the moon rose, first that fragment of the rim, then a slice like a banana, then a half moon; and, more swiftly than seemed possible, a moon so big it looked three times the size of a normal full moon. It seemed to leap into the sky and there it hung, only a hand's breadth above the horizon, still red but not blood red, more the color of a copper penny that has gone through fire.

Mabel whispered, "I'll bet you arranged it, just for me."

"Of course I did."

We sat and watched it rise another hand's span. Then it began to slow down. Such a moonrise seems to happen on a special schedule, twice as fast as usual. Physicists explain it in terms of light and refraction, but to me it is just a special High Plains moonrise. Finally Mabel said, "Let's go. I want to sit on Kit Carson Hill in the moonlight and see the whole world spread out in front of us."

We drove on down the slope, making an artificial moonset in the east as we dropped into the shadow of the valley, and then climbed the road that skirted the big hill. I parked the car and we climbed the hill on foot, up into the moonlight again, to the place where the stones were set in a rough square in the grass. Off to the west was the dim glow of Flagler with a few tiny sparkles. On a hilltop to the south, maybe two miles away, was the brief flicker of a moving light, probably a farmer going to the barn or the outhouse. To the north was only the deep shadow of the valley and its enclosing hills. It was, as she had said, the world spread out in front of us, with the tremendous dark bowl of sky over it.

We sat down in the grass, which was dry as at midday; dew on the hilltops is rare in that high country. In the western sky were only a few stars, the bright ones not yet overwhelmed by moonlight. Sirius, the dog star, and Orion, the hunter, and Castor and Pollux, the twins. High in the northern sky was Ursa Major, the big bear or dipper, upside down. And Polaris, the pole star, and below and to the left the big, irregular "W" of Cassiopeia. I pointed them out and Mabel said, "I won't remember, but tell me their names again."

We listened and far up the valley was the yelp of a coyote, then an answering yelp. Coyotes, like dogs, howl at the moon, and those two soon sounded like half a dozen with their warbling, ululating cries. I thought of kit foxes, wondered if I could tell her about George Sebastian. I started to, hesitated, and she said, "Go on. I want to hear it." I went on, and it was easier to tell in the quiet of the night. I even told her what he said about Nell Bainbridge. Mabel said nothing for some time after I had finished, just sat looking at the moonlit distance. Finally she said, "Men!" with acid in her voice. Then, softly, sadly, "Poor Nell."

"I shouldn't have told you," I said.

"Why not? You have to get something like that out of your system. You certainly need a sister!" And a moment later she said, "Let's go to Seibert and you can buy me a soda or a sundae."

We walked down the hill and drove on east to Seibert, the next little town. The street was deserted, only two places still open, the café and the drug store. The drug store had a fountain and the owner himself made ice cream sundaes for us. Then we drove back the way we had come.

"What are you going to do this summer?" Mabel asked. "I see by the paper that you are graduating. Class president, too."

I told her about the Chautauqua job and she said, "That sounds wonderful. You will get out and see what a big place the world is. But do you know something? This will still be a part of you. All this," and she gestured at the wide, moonlit horizon. "Like your blood, maybe."

Then we were at Kit Carson Hill again, and now the moonlight had reached down into the valley. It made the jumbled stones in the dry river bed glow like a scattering of giant marbles left over from a game. We crossed the concrete slab and I told her about the time the flash flood almost caught me there. And soon after that we were in the edge of town and I turned up the side street and drove slowly and quietly to their place and pulled into the driveway to the stable. The roofs glowed in the moonlight. The big cottonwood tree beside the driveway looked almost white, its dark twig tips like round lance heads with their fat, resiny buds.

Mabel said, "It's been a wonderful evening. I can't remember such a nice evening in a long, long time."

She opened the car door and I went around to help her but she didn't wait for my hand. We went to the front porch and she said, "I want to walk up to the pond tomorrow morning. Do you want to come along? About ten o'clock."

"Yes!" I started to put my arms around her, but she put her hands on my cheeks, drew my face down, and kissed me. Then she said, "Good night," turned and opened the door and was gone.

I went home, walking with giant strides, six feet six tall, feeling exalted, almost anointed. Life was all ahead, it was a big, big world, and I was going to live, be, explore, reveal. Life even had fun and laughter in it. I had been kissed by—by life.

Fritz heard me coming, recognized my step, came to meet me and licked my fingers. I hadn't changed at all, for him. He still knew me. I was somewhat disappointed at that; maybe that is what made me tiptoe into the house and go to my room more quietly than I ever had before. I undressed by moonlight, not wanting to break the spell. And I lay awake fully half an hour, remembering the moonrise, the look of the world from the hilltop, her voice, her laughter, her kiss. But no more than half an hour, I am sure. Even youth exalted and anointed doesn't lie long awake, no matter what the romancers say. I always had been, and still am, one of those who rarely stay awake five minutes after hitting the pillow. Half an hour would have been an eternity of sweet remembrance for me.

Mother was busy in the kitchen when I got up the next

morning. I heard her washing dishes as I dressed. Father must have gone to the office. I had no idea what time it was, maybe eight-thirty. At first I hesitated about going out to face her. Then I remembered yesterday and last night and I opened the door and went out into the kitchen. Mother turned and said, "Well, you finally did get up! I'd have got you up an hour ago, but your father said to let you sleep."

"I guess I was kind of tired."

She didn't even ask what time I got home. She did say, "It's almost nine o'clock," though the clock showed just eight-fifteen. To her, always, anything past the hour was "almost" the next one. She looked thin and pinched, and her dark eyes were full of questions. But all she asked was, "Shall I bake you some pancakes? I saved some batter."

I said yes and I washed up while the pancakes were cooking. My place was still set at the table, with butter and Karo syrup at hand. I sat down and ate, and still she asked no questions, not even where we went last night, the one she always asked when I had been out with a girl. She didn't even stay in the kitchen. She busied herself in the front bedroom. I finished eating and got my jacket and shouted a goodbye. She came to the living room door and there was that look in her eyes, half accusation, half deep inner hurt. I said, "I'm going over to the office," and I left.

Father asked no questions either and offered no explanation for Mother's silence. He said there wasn't anything special for me to do, that I could have the whole day off if I wanted it. I said I would probably be around part of the afternoon. But Father wasn't talking either. I seemed to be left in a kind of vacuum, all on my own. I waited around the office another hour, then at a quarter of ten I went up the street.

Mabel saw me coming and came out to meet me, and we went on up toward the new school, then down across lots to the pond. It was still a pond, well filled with spring melt. By late June it would be a slew, just a wet, boggy place that would dry up completely in July. But it was a pond that morning, with a fringe of bright new green around the edges where the grass was sprouting and with a green look to the water because the grass on the bottom was almost as green as lawn grass. The ducks were still there, the mallards and canvasbacks; and over at the far side were half a dozen newcomers, smaller ducks.

Mabel exclaimed, "Teal! My teal are here!" and we walked all the way around the pond for a closer look. The teal swam out toward the middle of the pond but didn't take wing, probably tired after their flight from somewhere down along the Arkansas river. We identified them as blue-wings, and there were three pairs.

We walked on and I found a sand lily in bloom in a little south-facing hollow and picked it for her. She put the little white star flower in a buttonhole of her blouse, and we went back up the slope. On the flats we saw a couple of ground squirrels and heard the horned larks and stopped to watch the big red harvester ants at one of their mounds. I told her about the man I met on the train, the entomologist, who told me things I never knew about those ants, and who said I should study the insects and the birds and the animals. She listened, then reached for my hand, looked at the lines in it, and said, "Books."

I didn't know what she was talking about, and we turned back soon after. We went back past the school and down the street, and she said, "I'm going back to Denver tomorrow, on the morning train, and I've got to spend this evening with the family."

"I'll go to the train with you."

"All right."

And the next morning I carried her suitcase to the depot and waited with her for the midmorning train. There wasn't much to say, somehow. We had said it all, everything that seemed to need saying, or maybe everything that could be said. And she wasn't looking at the plains, or even at the town. Once she said, "On a day like this, it probably is warm in Denver. Nice and warm." And I had the feeling that she was already gone.

We stood on the platform, the only people there, and she looked just as she did when she got off the train, the same perky little hat, the same ruffly white blouse under the dark suit. A girl I used to know but never even sat in the same class with. Then the train whistled down the tracks to the east and came rumbling up to the platform and rattled and wheezed to a stop. She looked up at me and put her arms around me and wrinkled her nose and crinkled the corners of her eyes and kissed me on the cheek. "Goodbye, Brother," she said, laughing. The conductor reached for her suitcase, helped her up the steps, and she went into the car ahead. The train began to move. I couldn't see whether she came to a window and waved.

A few days later a letter came, and in it she said almost exactly what she said before she left: "I can't remember when I had a nicer time than that night we watched the moonrise and the next morning when we saw my ducks." And she closed it with, "I know you will be very busy with graduation, but please don't forget all about me."

I am not sure even now what I had in mind when I wrote that first letter to her, but I think it's a safe bet that I didn't hope to acquire a volunteer sister. When she went back to Denver, and again when I got that "don't forget me" letter, I had that ache which starts down deep and works up into the throat and won't go away easily. That ache—and I can still remember it—was for something lost and gone forever, maybe boyhood innocence, maybe the mirage of imagined love. It certainly wasn't an ache of pleasure at being called Brother.

23

Mid-April till mid-May is magnificent on the High Plains, the very summary of spring. I had planned to spend all my free time outdoors, watching and making notes so I could write it all down in letters. But when I started to write such a letter the evening after I had the "don't forget me" letter from her, I went back after I had written a page or so and reread her letter. And I tore up what I had written and opened a text-book and studied advanced English.

I was busy with graduation; at least that's what I told myself. The senior class had sent away for class rings, and we had decided that instead of a formal class party we would have a Truant Day during the second week in May. We would just walk out, with the post-grads too if they wanted to come, and go somewhere and have a picnic and a final get-together. Of course we still had final examinations, but we didn't worry too much about them. There wasn't a senior who hadn't kept marks up, and for the last semester it was customary to go on classwork, not the exams, for the final mark. We were all going to be graduated. And unless my classwork had really taken a dive this past month or two I was going to head the class, which meant I would give the valedictory. But the day Miss Ward called me aside and said, "I think it would be a good idea for you to get some notes together for your speech at graduation," was not the ideal day to tell me. In fact, I said to her, "Miss Ward, I may not be here for graduation," and I turned and walked away before she recovered from the shock.

It had been one of those days, and it still wasn't over with. It began that morning when Mother opened my door and said, "Son, it's time for you to get up. It's almost eight o'clock."

I had sat up late the night before, trying again to write a letter and giving up again. I had a pile of notes, about flowers and birds and animals, even about grasshoppers and tumble-bugs, but when I tried to put them into a letter it sounded like a sixth-grade theme. Like a little boy writing a duty letter to his big sister, I told myself. I went to bed annoyed at her, mad at myself, and hating the world. When Mother called me and I got up and dressed and went out to the kitchen and saw that the clock showed only twenty minutes after seven I was all set to boil over. Father hadn't even gone to work, and she had told me it was almost eight o'clock.

She looked at me with that tight-lipped half smile she had had ever since the scene at the office over the letter. And I said, "I wish you would either learn to tell time or to tell the truth." I was as surly as a bear cub with a sore nose.

That was all that was needed to open the floodgate. "Why!" she exclaimed. "Why, what do you mean, talking like that to me? Saying I don't tell the truth!"

"You don't, about time. You—"

"I never told you a lie in your life! I tried to bring you up to be a credit to your father and me. I've tried! And now you think you can do just as you please. You sneak around behind my back, and then you say that I tell lies!"

"I haven't sneaked around behind anybody's back!"

"Oh, yes, you have."

"If you're talking about the letters, and the fact that I met a girl at the train—"

"Girl? A married woman. And divorced! And you, not even eighteen years old!"

"Mabel is a nice girl, and if I want to write to her I don't see that it's anybody else's business."

Just then Father came into the room. He had been out in the front yard filling a hole in the lawn that Fritz had dug, trying to dig out a ground squirrel. He came in and saw us spitting fire, both of us, and heard Mother say, "To think, that my own son would talk to me like that!"

"What's going on here?" Father asked sharply.

"Your son," Mother said, "called me a liar. And he just said it wasn't any of my business what he does."

He turned to me. "Well?"

"She said it was almost eight o'clock, and it was just a little after seven."

There was a hint of a smile in Father's eyes. "That," he said, "is just exaggeration. What else did you say?"

"I said I didn't think it was anybody's business who I write letters to."

"That," he said, "is debatable. You'd better apologize."

"Why? What for?"

"On general principles. Because you said things you shouldn't have said."

I hesitated. He said, "Let's not have any argument. Go on, apologize."

I said, "All right, I'm sorry."

Mother had begun to cry. Father looked at me and shook his head. He took her into his arms and said, "Don't take it so hard."

"You—you don't know how it hurts," she said, "when—when my own son talks to me like that."

Father was making gestures to me, signaling me to get out, go somewhere. I put on my jacket and left. I went over to the office, opened up, got the mail, went down to the café and had coffee and doughnuts. Father didn't arrive at the office till just before I had to leave for school. He took one look at me, shook his head, and shuffled through the letters in the morning mail. Then he said, "Won't you ever learn?"

"Learn what?"

"Learn not to *start* trouble."

"All I said was—"

"I don't care what you said, you shouldn't have said it."

"So you are going to give me a going-over too?"

"Any time I think you need it, yes. Just as long as you are at home you will hear from me if you start trouble. When you were a little kid your mother did the spanking. She thought it was her job. Now you're growing up and getting too big to spank."

"Thank you! At least you admit I am grown up!"

"*Growing* up, I said. Not grown. But it's time you began to *act* grown up. Don't you realize your mother is upset about a lot of things right now? You are, as I said, *growing* up. You are not her little boy any more. You are about to graduate from high school. You're going away for the summer, and after Chautauqua you'll be going to college. And on top of that, you've just been out with a girl who is older and a lot more experienced than you are."

"Less than two years older."

"All right! That's not the point. The least you can do is hold your temper and keep your mouth shut."

"Thank *you!*" I said, this time bitterly, and I stalked out of the office and went up the street to school. Simmering, full of resentment, a young rebel, 1918-style. And when I got to school Professor Ward called me into his office and said, "When are you seniors going to take this sneak day, or truant day, or whatever you call it?"

"Next week," I said, "or the week after."

"I want to know when."

"I'm not telling you when. It's a senior privilege to go when we feel like going."

"I need to know when." He had begun to flush, angry at my insubordination. "Do you know the date?"

"Yes."

"And you won't tell me?"

"No."

"Suppose I were to suspend the whole class."

"You don't have to suspend the whole class. Just expel me. Again," I added, completely rebellious. Actually, I had been thrown out twice that year, both times for pranks. The first time Little Doc and I locked two stray kittens in an equipment drawer in the science laboratory and threw the key out the window. The uproar lasted several hours, until the janitor was called and broke the lock. We admitted our guilt, were expelled and not allowed back in class until we went to Clarence Smith, head of the school board, and apologized. The second time was just before Christmas vacation, when I took a small bottle of carbon disulphide from the lab and left it uncorked back of a radiator in the auditorium. Within an hour the whole auditorium reeked with the odor of rotten eggs. It took three frigid days to air the place out, and I had to apologize to Mr. Smith again.

Professor Ward frowned at me now, then laughed. "I'll find out," he said.

"Not from me!" And I left his office with a great big chip on my shoulder, defying anybody to knock it off. Nobody tried.

I didn't go home for lunch. I went down to the café, and when the waitress asked, "Is this getting to be a habit, or are you really an orphan?" I said, "Who cares?"

When I went back to school a Marine in dress uniform was in the schoolyard, surrounded by half a dozen boys. I joined the group. The Marine was a recruiter, and two boys, farm boys in the junior class, had already signed up. The recruiter saw me join the group and handed me a couple of leaflets and an enlistment form. I took them and went on into the school building. I read them through before my first afternoon class began.

I paid practically no attention all through that class. When the next class started I took out the enlistment form and began filling it out, name, date of birth, parents' names, right down the list. I was really fed up, and I couldn't see that it mattered to anyone whether I enlisted in the Marines or what I did. I had been practically thrown out of my own home. Mother was fed up with me because I insisted I had a right to do things in my own grownup way. Father had given me a going-over, practically said I was all through around both the house and the office. Besides, he wouldn't need me at the office even if I stayed home. He was buying out the *Progress* and he was going to put in a linotype, which meant no more hand-set type. Anybody who could use a typewriter could run a linotype, so Mother probably would take that over. There wasn't any need for me around there, even if they wanted me. Which they obviously didn't. Good Lord, even my dog had walked out on me! Fritz seemed to have adopted Father, followed him around and spent most of his days at the office. When even your dog quits you, I told myself, you'd just as well get out.

I filled out the enlistment form. And when Miss Ward summoned me as I was leaving that class, and said what she did about getting notes together for what would be a valedictory speech, I was practically in the uniform of the United States Marine Corps, the Halls of Montezuma and the Shores of Tripoli behind me and all set for France and the Boche. I gave Miss Ward my answer and walked out. Out of the room, out of the school, out of the whole juvenile, schoolboy mess of triviality. I walked proudly across the schoolyard to the Marine Corps recruiter and handed him my enlistment form. He said, "Congratulations, son!"and he shook my hand. "You will be proud of this day all your life." Then he glanced down the form and said, "Oh," and scowled at me. "You're not eighteen?"

"I will be in a couple of weeks."

He sighed and leafed through his forms, chose one, clipped it to the one I had filled out, and gave them to me. "Get your father to sign this and give it to me down at the hotel this evening. Then," he added, "you'll be all set."

I glanced at it and walked away. It was a parental permit for a recruit under the age of eighteen to enlist.

I went down the street, anger and rebellion fighting pride and disappointment. The nearer I got to the *News* office, the more reluctant I was to face my father. I hesitated at the bank corner, killed time by going to the post office. Somebody had got the afternoon mail, probably Mother. I went back to the corner and tried to see if Mother was at the desk, if I had to face the two of them.

I was standing there, peering, like a six-year-old playing games, when a feminine voice behind me said, "Peek-a-boo!" Then the hearty laughter of Posey Briggs, Marjorie Miner's aunt, her mother's old-maid sister. I turned, undoubtedly flushing beet red, but Posey went on acros the street, laughing to herself. I went on down the stairs to the *News* office, too chagrined now to care whether I had to face one parent or both.

I was relieved to find Father alone. He looked up from the stone where he was making up the form for an order of letterheads, said hello, and went on with what he was doing. I hung up my coat and he said, "There's a letter for you there on the desk."

I looked for the familiar gray envelope and blue ink but couldn't find it. Then I saw a long fat envelope addressed on a typewriter, addressed to me. It was from the Standard Chautauqua Company, in Lincoln, Nebraska. I slit it open and found a letter and half a dozen enclosures. The letter welcomed me as "a member of the Standard Family" and told me when and where to report. It called attention to various enclosures. One was an itinerary for my particular tent, starting in western Nebraska, going through northern Colorado and over to the Western Slope, back to northern Nebraska, and finishing in central Iowa. One was a list of clothing I would need. One was a printed folder giving all the circuit's programs with the names of all the singers, lecturers and other entertainers. There was even a diagram of the tent, showing seats, stage, dressing rooms, and a list of materials the local committees were to provide.

I read the letter again, then took the whole sheaf over to Father. He wiped his hands on his apron and leafed through. "So," he finally said, "you'll have to leave here just two days after graduation to get there on time."

I hadn't taken that in.

Then I remembered the enlistment papers. I went to the coat rack, took them from my pocket. Father asked, "What have you got there?"

I handed them to him and he glanced at them and laid them down beside the chase. "I heard that fellow was in town. Wondered if you wouldn't run into him." He reached into the overhead rack for a slug, put it in the form he was making up, moving two lines of type a fraction of an inch farther apart. He nodded, said to himself, "That's better." I reached for the papers and he looked up, asked. "You want me to sign these?"

I didn't answer. I tore them in half and went over and dropped them into the waste basket. Father didn't seem to be watching, but when I went back to the stone he said, "Next fall, when you've fulfilled the contract you made with the Chautauqua company, you won't need any permit. If you'd rather enlist than go to college, nobody can stop you." Then, with only the slightest pause, "By the way, I told your mother about the *Progress*. Ed Gibson stopped in this morning and we had a talk. He wants to sell, and I'm going to buy him out. We haven't agreed on price, but we'll work things out. He'd rather wait till the end of the summer, and that's all right with me. I just want to consolidate the two papers before next fall's elections." He was silent for a moment. "As I started to say, your mother knows now. You don't have to keep it a secret from her any longer. But don't tell anyone else."

And I knew that enlistment, or Chautauqua, or whatever I did within reason was no longer the important thing. As Father had said that morning, I was growing up, and whether I was grown up or not—and my opinion didn't really count—I was at the point where his and Mother's primary attention could get back to themselves and to the newspaper that really was the center of their lives. I had a life of my own to live, a career to make, or whatever I was going to do with that life. They loved me and had cherished and protected and sheltered me, but they couldn't live that life for me. Whether they had talked it over or not—and they almost certainly had, one way or another—that's what Father was telling me, without saying it in so many words: that I was practically on my own.

It was impossible to say then, and I can't say now, just how it was done; but in the next few days I was made aware that while we were still a family, with the tight bonds that grow up around an only child, the bonds were being loosened for me. Instead of telling me which clothes to take and packing them for me, Mother asked which ones I wanted to take and suggested that I do the packing. Instead of saying I should see certain relatives in Nebraska, Father gave me the Lincoln address of his sister, Etta Buerstetta, and said he thought her son Ira, about my age, was at home now. He asked me if I had my Pullman reservations, and Mother didn't say, "You'd better get them for him, Will." Little things, even inconsequential matters, were handed to me for decision. And a new closeness seemed to have grown between Father and Mother, as though they were strengthening a bridge that would span the gap my going would leave.

Then everything was happening at once.

We went on our Truant Day, all eleven seniors and two post-graduates. We simply got up in assembly that morning and walked out, practically kidnapping Miss Ward on the way. We drove to the Breaks north of Limon, a freakish geological formation of rugged hills and steep gullies covered with pines and scrub oak. Legend said the Breaks had been a hideout for stage robbers and cattle rustlers in the old days, but I never found a shred of truth in it. We climbed the hills, slid down the gullies, and picnicked under the trees. Marjorie Miner and I sat under a pine tree and talked for an hour about You and Me and Life, all capitalized. We decided that Life was earnest but might be fun, and that we were going to shape it to our demands. Individually, not together. We didn't quite say it, but we agreed that it was good to be friends, just friends.

We took final exams, pretty much a formality. We got our final marks. I was at the head of the class, would be valedictorian. Professor Ward announced the names of scholarship winners in assembly. I got the one I wanted, to the University of Colorado.

We went to the baccalaureate service at the church. The Reverend Adna Moore was neither mealy-mouthed nor overly pious. He wasn't even very sententious. Even his own daughter said it was a good talk.

Graduation gifts came and were opened. Mostly from relatives and family friends, mostly silk socks and neckties, with two or three gift editions of memorable quotations and well-beloved poems. The day before graduation Father brought a small package home when he came to dinner, a package from Denver and addressed in blue ink and the familiar handwriting. I opened it and found a leather-bound selection of Emerson's essays. Inside was a card on which she had written, "I'm as proud as if I really were your sister. Love, M."

A good many years later, looking up something Emerson wrote, I came across that small leather-bound book in my library and leafed through it, wondering where it came from.

Then I found the card with its faded ink, and read it, and had to think twice before I remembered that "M" stood for Mabel.

At last there was the commencement program, too long, as high school commencements usually are. Too much talk. Too many speeches. I gave my valedictory, which lasted almost fifteen minutes, a good ten minutes longer than was necessary to say what I had to say. Dorothy Muckler, from the junior class, read a typical class prophecy. The scholarships were announced all over again. And finally there was the commencement address, by someone whose name I didn't hear and made no attempt to remember, too long, too orotund, too sententious, and too dull. And at last Professor Ward handed out the diplomas, which was the real purpose of the whole program. He called us up in alphabetical order and handed each of us a rolled parchment tied with a twined strand of purple and gold ribbon.

Alphabetical:

Borland.

Farquahar, Nina, gay, thin, tubercular.

Farr, Duncan, tall, lean, looking as his horseman father must have looked at eighteen.

Hartzler, Nancy, a farm girl, tall, self-conscious, one of the best brains in the class.

Jewell, Ruth, another farm girl, happy and dedicated.

Lewin, Fern, quiet, usually in the background.

Moore, Lora, gay, bright, auburn-haired daughter of the preacher.

Page, Iona, round-faced, pretty, vivacious.

Quinn, Hugh, youngest of the big Quinn family.

Robb, Pearl, stocky, serious son of a farmer.

Williams, Justin, wiry, almost puckish, but serious now, his commitment made to the medical profession.

Five young men in blue serge suits. Six girls in long white dresses. Flagler High School's third graduating class.

Then it was over. We said goodbyes to each other and to our teachers. Through with high school. Graduated. In a commencement, which the Reverend Mr. Moore had reminded us meant a beginning, not an end.

We walked home, Father and Mother and I, with little talk. Mother said my speech was very good. She was glad I had memorized it so I didn't have to keep looking at notes. Father said it was well organized. He wished the main speaker had organized his talk as well. And kept it as short.

Then we were at home, and Mother went to their bedroom and came back with a small gift-wrapped box. She handed it to me.

"What is it?"

"Open it and see."

"Who is it from?"

"Your father and me. Now go ahead and open it, see if you like it."

I opened it. Inside was a pocket watch, a thin gold Elgin, the first good watch I had ever owned. "Look on the back," Mother urged. I looked. There were my entwined initials and the year, 1918. I was awed, didn't know what to say. I said, "Thanks, I—I—well, I don't know how to thank you enough."

"We had to order it," Mother said. "From Denver. Almost two months ago."

I was staring at the watch, still there in my hand, but I made a quick calculation. Two months ago; that would have been the week before the big explosion over Mabel. I hugged Mother and kissed her, and for a moment she held me very tight. Then she let me go, stepped back, and she said, "You've got just two more days. Then you take the train for Lincoln. What do you want to do? Anything special?"

"Nothing very special," I said. "Tomorrow I'd just like to poke around. Maybe go out to the river, on my bike, and maybe out to the Indian caves."

"I'll make a couple of sandwiches for you. And you can

sleep late in the morning. Till—" She smothered a yawn. "My goodness, I guess I could use some sleep too. Till eight o'clock."

I tried again to thank them for the watch, but Father said, "You'd better go on to bed and be ready to get up in the morning."

The next day I went out to Kit Carson Hill and sat on the grass for a little while, thinking about the darkness and the stars, and her saying, "I won't remember their names, but tell me again." It seemed a long time ago, a long, long time. The first blossoms were just opening on the *Malvastrum coccineum*, cowboy's delight.

On the way back to town I stopped at the trail and went down to Crystal Springs to sit on the ledge and look out over the pond, remembering the first visit, when I saw the ducks and the killdeers and the falcon, and the big water snake. Only the killdeers were there this time. Maybe the snake was, but I didn't go to look. I went back to the road and to town.

At the edge of town I turned south, out the road to Verhoff's Dam. It was almost noon, but I went all the way to the dam before I stopped to eat. I went down close to the water, still high with spring melt, and sat on the grass and ate my sandwiches. And thought of the day Little Doc and Spider and I were there and watched the herons. Then I thought of the day Little Doc and I went there, that mild winter day of the funeral, and fired our farewell shots out over the water.

I finished my lunch and went back to the road and on down through the valley and up the steep slope beyond, and left my bike and climbed to the old Indian caves. We had always been going to dig one of them out, really dig it right down to rock, and see if we couldn't find a real Indian skeleton. I sat on the ledge above the caves and looked out across the flats, a view almost as broad as that from Kit Carson Hill. It was a big world. I sat there maybe half an hour, just feeling the plains in my blood and bones and sinew and marrow.

Then I went back to town. I rode all the way up Main Street to the school, left my bike there, and went down to the pond. It had begun to recede and had left a band of muddy grass and soggy sod maybe ten feet wide. The ducks had all gone several weeks ago, on north to nesting grounds where the water didn't shrink to nothing in July. I walked halfway around the pond, and I found a small white quartz arrowhead, a bird point, very small, perfect.

Then I went back to my bike and rode north a mile or so and came to a place with a scattering of big ant hills. I went over and squatted on my heels and watched the big red ants and remembered the scientific name the entomologist gave me for them: *Pognomyrmex occidentalis*. Strange, how acute the young memory can be. I even remembered that man's face and the tones of his voice.

Then I went back to town.

The next morning I put away the things I wouldn't need any more, the mementos from high school and the clippings about football games and track meets and debates I was in. And the letters. I tied them in a packet and put them with my report cards and other school papers. I told Mother I was putting all those things in a box with a lid on it and leaving it in the closet in my room, and if it was in the way she could move it or do whatever she wanted to do with it. "There isn't anything in it," I said, "that matters very much, I guess."

Then it was the last day, and I went over to the *News* office with Father in the morning. But he wouldn't let me do any work. He didn't do much work himself. He talked about what he planned to do with the office, how he was going to rearrange things after he bought out the *Progress*, what equipment he would sell and what he would keep. He asked my advice about where to put the stapler and the extra rack of type. And where to put the linotype so there would be good natural light. But I knew he was merely talking. He had everything all planned out in his own mind.

Clarence Smith stopped in, in midmorning, and took time to tell me about his first job away from home and ask about my summer itinerary. Before he left he said, "You know, I'm going to miss you. I never knew when you were going to walk into my office and say, 'I've got to apologize again.'" And he left laughing.

Father closed the office and locked up for the day when we went home for dinner. Mother had fried chicken and gravy and mashed potatoes and canned peas and cherry pie, a special dinner with every item a favorite of mine.

Fritz knew something was up. He kept coming to me, wanting to be patted, and every time I moved he looked around to see where I had gone. When we started down to the depot he insisted on going along. So there we were on the depot platform, Father, Mother, me and Fritz. And Ora Groves came down with the outgoing mail and asked me, with a sly smile, "Going somewhere, or just meeting a friend?" And wished me well.

Then the train whistled from two miles away, and I took one last look at the flats off to the south. Father asked, "Sure you've got your tickets, son?" Fritz whined. Mother said, "Don't forget to write. You can at least send us a post card once a week." Her mouth set in that firm, thin line that meant she either was mad as a wet hen or fighting back the tears.

The train screeched to a stop. Father asked the conductor, "Pullman?" and he said, "Third car back." I said, "Goodbye!" and grabbed my suitcase. Mother hugged me and kissed me and turned away.

Father put an arm around me and said, "Goodbye, son," his voice husky.

I ran down the platform toward the waiting Pullman conductor. Just before I got aboard I looked back and waved.

They were standing where I had left them, Mother with a white handkerchief in her hand, Father with his arm around her. He waved. Fritz barked. I went on up the steps. There was a faint call from up ahead, "All aboooard!" and the train began to move.

I stood in the vestibule for a last look, first to the north, at Flagler slipping past, then to the south, out across the old flats that had been the frontier and now were just the High Plains, where a new breed of men were plowing the grass and fencing the wind, or trying to, and making the memories of yesterday the legends of tomorrow.

Then the porter took my suitcase and led the way to my seat. The locomotive, far up there ahead, whistled a long, screaming blast for the crossing a mile east of town. Then we flashed past the tattered old cottonwood that was the only reminder of a store and post office called Bowserville. On toward Seibert, Stratton, Burlington, Goodland. East. Toward tomorrow, whatever and wherever it might be.

Borland

Country editor's boy